THE COMMONWEALTH GAMES IN

THE TWENTIETH CENTURY

-

THE WELSH PERSPECTIVE

by

Myrddin John

LLYFRAU
CAMBRIA

Published 2014 by Cambria Books, Carmarthenshire, Wales

THE WELSH TEAM

XVl COMMONWEALTH GAMES

KUALA LUMPUR 1998

TO MY WIFE SHEILA

AND DAUGHTER DELYTH

"the most important thing in the Olympic Games is not to win but to take part, just as the most important thing in life is not the triumph but the struggle. The essential thing is not to have conquered but to have fought well."

Pierre de Coubertin   *Ethelbert Talbot*

VALERIE E. DAVIES

WINNER OF THE FIRST COMMONWEALTH GAMES
MEDAL FOR WALES in 1930

On the nineteenth of July 1908, in his sermon at the St Paul's Cathedral, London, to celebrate the fourth Olympic Games the Right Reverend Ethelbert Talbot, Bishop of Central Pennsylvania, America stated –

"The important thing in these Olympic Games is not so much to have been victorious as to have taken part."

This statement had a profound effect on Pierre de Coubertin. In his lecture on Friday, July 24th 1908, Baron de Coubertin repeated this ideation, during a Government banquet, by augmenting to the words as seen on the previous page.**(Appendix 14) –**

"L'important dans ces Olympiades, c'est moins d'y gagner que d'y prendre part".

This axiom is often expressed on numerous occasions involved with Olympic events. I feel that it would be appropriate to employ these at other sporting events and especially those concerned with Commonwealth sport.

MJ

CONTENTS PAGE

MYRDDIN JOHN

THE AUTHOR – MYRDDIN JOHN, M.B.E.

by Dr Wayne Griffiths, M.B.E.

Having ambition to win and to succeed is the most notable feature that reflects the character of the author of this book, and has been the foundation on which he has risen to the top in a wide range of sporting achievements. Myrddin John has been a conscientious and enthusiastic sports administrator throughout his sporting career and is well known worldwide for his expert guidance and advice. He has a wide set of across-boundary skills that has greatly influenced the sporting community in Wales and far beyond his home in Blaenau, Ammanford.

I have had the privilege of working closely with Myrddin for over fifty years and during this time his desire to do his best for Wales has attracted recognition from across the world. His insistence of making Wales recognised by the rest of the world as a nation that competes in sport, independent from the rest of Britain has been the hallmark of his life's ambition.

Myrddin has the ability to break down the barriers that inhibits progress in sport and by using his skills and experience as a former athlete and coach he is able to recognise potentially successful young athletes and contribute to their success in a multidisciplinary manner. Myrddin holds degrees in Education from Trinity College, Carmarthen, and has spent over twenty years working to promote sport in the community before completing his career in administration as a Sports Director in Carmarthenshire. A dominant factor of his success in sport was his ability to communicate effectively with people of every age and background, his experience as a teacher, coach and manager enabled him to identify and nurture natural skills, to persevere with the most promising and encourage all under his direction to reach their full potential. Opportunities come to us all and we have the choice to accept or reject them. Myrddin embraced these opportunities and as a result has developed a range of skills in both sport and Welsh culture that has enabled him to contribute successfully to so many different domains.

His apprenticeship in sport started as a young athlete after scooping the Welsh title in his chosen sport of weightlifting when he was just eighteen years old and later with the Welsh Weightlifting Federation, where he was secretary for over fifty years. His extensive knowledge of sport at a local and international level has been rewarding for numerous sporting authorities where he has freely given of his knowledge and expertise. He is able to move quickly and easily between sporting disciplines and provide valuable advice which has led to his being highly respected by sporting authorities at home, the Commonwealth and the rest of the world.

He held the office of Chief Executive of the Commonwealth Games Council for Wales for twenty seven years, a Vice-President and now Life Vice President of the International Weightlifting Federation, an Executive Board Member of the European Weightlifting Federation, Chairman of the British Weightlifting Association, General Team Manager of the Welsh Team at the Commonwealth Games in Auckland and Edinburgh and a lecturer for the International Olympic Solidarity on numerous weightlifting related subjects. He was also a weightlifting coach and manager of the Welsh Commonwealth Weightlifting team on many occasions, a Member of the Sports Council for Wales and on two occasions has been responsible for organising for the success of the Queen's Commonwealth Relay in Wales.

Myrddin is an effective communicator in so many different settings in sport and is equally comfortable in training the novice as he is on public platforms, television and radio. He works with advantaged and disadvantaged athletes alike using the most appropriate modern methods. He is an insightful counsellor and a natural leader and works just as hard in mentoring young athletes as he is contributing to the many committees he presides over.

He has an un-paralleled ability to organize, and the secret of that is that he spends time in careful preparation; he is tenacious and perseveres to seek and demand the best of his athletes and his country. He has been recognised by a number of organizations who have benefited greatly from his contribution to sport and I will list only a few of the many honours he has received during his sporting career. In 1980 he won the Medal of Honour from the Sports Council for Wales, the MBE in 1983, the Honorary Medal of the British Weightlifting International Award in 1988 and the Commonwealth Games Council for Wales International Award in 2000. He won a Gold Medal in Asia for his contribution to weightlifting and the prestigious Gold Chain award by the International Weightlifting Federation for a life-long service to Weightlifting. In 2006 He was awarded the Chancellor's Medal by Glamorgan University for his sporting contribution. Myrddin is always dependable in times of need and he gives his time generously to support those in difficulty. He has a warm and sensitive personality but has a clear and uninterrupted view of what is needed for success and always demands the best and always gives his very best. His inclusive style of management and collaborative manner of working makes him a popular participant at all levels of sport administration.

Another feature of his success is his vision and ability to know who to nurture and encourage to contribute to that vision. He has the most infectious enthusiasm and will take advantage of any opportunity quickly yet ready to persevere in order to bring the plan to fruition. He is enterprising without losing sight of what has been planned and is a conscientious worker who accepts his responsibility serious. It is not difficult to understand why he was honoured by the Gorsedd of Bards with the White Robe and an MBE in the Queens Honours List when we realise his tireless efforts in the voluntary sector over many years.

Myrddin is a renaissance man and his loyalty to Wales continues to drive him forward.

Dr Wayne Griffiths, M.B.E.

Wales General Team Manager 2002

Past President Commonwealth Games Council for Wales

FOREWORD

by Randall Bevan, J.P. MSc.

I am honoured to have been asked to comment upon this erudite work by my friend of over seventy years who in compiling this data, has contributed greatly to, not only the standing of the Commonwealth Games, but also to the many athletes, able and disabled, who have thrilled us by their performances over many years and satisfied every generation's need for heroes.

The Amman Valley has inspired many of its residents to participate in and to compete at the highest level in multifarious sports. Myrddin John has continued this tradition having been a lifelong sportsman on the international and world stage as a competitor, judge and a distinguished general secretay of the Wales Commonwealth Games Council for many years. His devotion to his chosen sport of weightlifting is legend having been a Vice-President of the International Weightlifting Federation for four years. The IWF has nearly 200 member countries and today Myrddin is a Life Vice President, and I am aware that he has achieved the honour of being placed in the 'Hall of Fame' of this International body. There is no higher accolade in that sport and for our beloved country – Wales.

Myrddin's experience and authority in creating this anthology of achievement by able and disabled sports men and women is, I believe, unique being written by someone who 'was there' in that intimate atmosphere, living and breathing the excitement, cut and thrust, glory, courage, disappointment, drama, endeavour and the degree to which the human spirit is capable of reaching and even surpassing in those magic moments during competition. I cannot think of any other living representative of the Commonwealth Games Council with the depth and level of experience and knowledge than Myrddin.

The Commonwealth Games is regarded by some as the third largest of the international competitions after the Olympic and Asian Games, - also attended by Myrddin throughout his career. The story has been recorded in numerous editorials, biographies and by many state legislators. Its objectives and modus operandi are identical to other major Games – the pursuit of excellence, competitive ethics, international cooperation and fellowship. It has attracted participants from the farthest reaches of the globe since its inception in 1930, with athletes competing in Olympic, Commonwealth, Asian and other multifarious Games world wide.

This work is an excellent kaleidoscope of the 'Friendly' Games worldwide. As a former sports science student at the Loughborough University of Technology Ergonomics and Cybernetics Department, having had to peruse the relevant data for my research projects worldwide, it is apparent that this catalogue of results over many Games will provide essential research material upon the Games and 'peripherally' the implicit organisation, rules of the governing bodies, presentation of each sport together with the improved performances over the years with the inevitable challenges for those investigating the many facets of sports science in its contribution to performance enhancement. It is a record of twentieth century sport achievement at the highest level.

I therefore firmly believe that, from my experience in research and data compilation, this work will prove to be a standard reference for schools, colleges, universities and sports research projects that will benefit many generations to inspiration and enhanced performance in the multitude of sport cited. It will also be a 'ready reckoner' and testimony to success and achievements by able and disabled sports men and women who might well have passed into anonymity in the history of the Commonwealth Games but will now be justly commemorated in the columns listed in this work.

This comprehensive compilation of human achievement is yet another landmark in this remarkable Welshman's contribution to

Physical Education and sport that will be recognised by future generations who like Myrddin and me from those beautiful and ambitious Welsh Valleys, see sport as an entrée to so many wonderful adventures yet to come to enrich the lives of our young people.

Randall Bevan, J.P., M.Sc., Dip PE (Dist)., Cert Ed., F.B.I.M.

British Trampoline Champion 1961
Former British National Trampoline Coach

APPRECIATION

Following the production of my book – 'Chwareuon y Gymanwlad yn yr Ugeinfed Ganrif – Y Perspectif Cymreig', I have been requested by many friends to make an English translation of the book. It is my hope that having acquiesced to their wishes with some additions, these lovers of sport will feel that my book will justify some precious space on the shelves of their personal libraries.

I wish to thank the many people who impressed upon me, not only to commence writing this book, but to continue the work when the spirit was flagging under the weight of so many books, papers and reports.

I am especially thankful to those who have given me their support and have added significantly to my knowledge of sport, this as friends together with their expert contribution at a host of committee meetings.

My heartfelt thanks go to my dear friend Ieuan Owen of Caernarfon for creating the cover of this book which reflects his gift and profound knowledge in this type of work. I also pay tribute to Dr Wayne Griffiths, M.B.E. for his kind words about The Author and also to Randall Bevan, J.P., M.Sc. for writing the Foreword. I accepts their praise with the utmost humility. (I am thinking I would love to meet the person they are commenting on).

I am indebted to my son-in-law, the Reverend Paul Mainwaring, B.A. and my grandsons Aled Mainwaring, B.Sc., M.A. and Penri Mainwaring, M.A. for their help and their computer competence, especially when this creature was getting the better of me, and to my daughter Delyth Mainwaring, M.Sc. for proof reading the work on many occasions. I was delighted to share some of Wynne Oliver's memories when, as a schoolboy at Llanelli Grammar School, he represented Wales at the 1958 British Empire and Commonwealth Games.

I appreciate the advice I received from Chris Jones and am grateful to him and his company Llyfrau Cambria, for their erudite expertise which is reflected in the production of this book

During the research I made towards producing this book, it was necessary for me to read many articles by an indefinite number of people. I readily accept that any statement or facts which could be thought to be erroneous, should be laid at my door and mine only. Needless to say I have discovered some errors in my Welsh book which I have corrected in this work. Doubtless readers may come across one or maybe even two others.

Finally I thank my wife Sheila for her inspiring support, her immense help and her infinite patience.

MJ

BIBLIOGRAPHY

I used much of the knowledge I gleaned from the following bibliography which I have in my library, - not only to justify my work but also to pay tribute and respect to the detailed research made by those authors.

Here and there I came upon some small inconsistencies. When this occurred I used my personal experience and knowledge to rectify these few errors.

However, I would be most grateful to receive notice from any reader regarding any contrariety within the content of this book.

The Commonwealth Games Orca Book Publishers Cleve Dheensaw

Crossing the Finishing Line Bernama, Publishers National News Agency. SUKOM Committee Of Malaysia

Canada at the Vth British Empire and Commonwealth Games 1954 Published by the British Empire and Commonwealth Games Association of Canada

Official History 8th British Empire and Commonwealth Games. Kingston. Jamaica Published by Organising Committee. Sir Herbert MacDonald. K.B.E' assisted by Keith St. and G. Brown

Official History Of The 1Xth British Commonwealth Games. Edinburgh. Scotland Published by Organising Committee. William Carmichael and M. McIntyre Hood

X1 Commonwealth Games Official Pictorial Record Publishers Executive Sport Publications Ltd.

Brisbane '82 XII Commonwealth Games-Official Pre Commonwealth Games Souvenir Book Committee Joint Tourist Capital

Official History XII Commonwealth Games Brisbane 1982
Publishers O & B Holdings

The Games-Brisbane Telegraph Souvenir Magazine Queensland
Newspapers Pty Ltd.

1958 Brochure Committee   British Empire and Commonwealth
Games Wales 1958. Printed by Western Mail

The Compete Book of the Olympics Published by the Penguin
Group. David Wallechinsky

The Olympic Games   Publisher MacDonald & Jane's Ltd. Lord
Killanin and John Rodda

The Commonwealth Games Manchester 2002 Chris Murray

Crossing The Finishing Line 1998 Kuala Lumpur Published by
Bernama

The History of Welsh Athletics   John Collins. Alan & Brenda Currie.
Mike Walters and Clive Wiliams. Publishers Dragon Sports Books Ltd.
Llanelli

100 Greatest Olympians From-1896 Jim Tracky Publisher Savvas
Publishing

Let The Spirit Live On   Publisher Victoria Commonwealth Games
Society. Director Ben J. Pires

**_The Commonwealth Games Council for Scotland Golden Jubilee
1931-1981_**   Bill Grant. Printed by Graphic Arts Services

Following The Flame/Dilyn Y Fflam   Phil Cope. Funded by the
Legacy Trust UK

The Phenomenon of Welshness II   Siôn Jobbins. Published
by Carreg-Gwalch

PART 1

THE COMMONWEALTH

CHAPTER ONE

COMMONWEALTH GAMES FEDERATION

THE BEGINNING

It was an Englishman, the Reverend J. Astley Cooper (1858 – 1930) who was the initiator of the ideation of the British Empire Games when he wrote in the magazine, 'Greater Britain' in August 1891 of his dream to create this type of Games whose purpose would be -

'to draw closer the ties between the Nations of the Empire'.

In addition he wrote in the newspaper, The Times, in October 1892, that there was a need to create a British Empire Festival of Sport. The first of the modern Olympic Games was held in 1896 and possibly this had an influence on Astley Cooper, or perhaps Baron Pierre de Coubertin of France's passion to resuscitate and give impetus towards the restitution of the Olympic movement was given the necessary dynamism on learning of Cooper's ambition, - to exert himself even harder in his quest. Who knows?. Baron de Coubertin in his first lecture at the Sorbonne University, in Paris on the Twenty Fifth of November, 1892, emphasized that it was high time to rejuvenate the Olympic Games.

In June 1894 he organised an international conference at the Sorbonne in Paris where he invited leading personalities from the countries of the world in order to accentuate the importance of this conference. The purpose again was to form a strategic plan for the revival of the Olympic Games. Following some procrastination the

Conference delegates unanimously agreed that the Olympic Games be recreated. The Conference was a complete success.

It appears that the first Olympic Games was held in Olympia in 776 BC and that the sole event was a sprint. In the following Games the number of events was increased by including the 150 yards sprint, Long Jump, Throwing the Discus, Wrestling and Horse Chariot Racing. It is interesting to note that these events are founded on battle activities. The Games were prohibited by the Emperor Theodosius in 383 AD.

The first Modern Olympic Games were also held in Athens. The sports contested at these were, Athletics, Cycling, Fencing, Gymnastics, Rowing, , Shooting, Swimming, Tennis, Weightlifting and Wrestling. The next Olympic Games were held in Paris followed by St. Louis, USA in 1900 but all of these were organised so atrociously that the whole concept was endangered. London in 1908 did not fare well either with much political argument and disaccord regarding rule interpretations, which were under the control of Great Britain as the host nation. It took the Olympic Games in Stockholm, Sweden in 1912 to ameliorate matters and save the dream.

Although de Coubertin's wishes came to fruition in 1896, J. Astley Cooper's vision did not materialize until the year of his death in 1930, when the first British Empire Games were held. Eight Olympic Games were to pass before the first British Empire Games saw the light of day. Richard Coombes (18.03.1858 – 15.05.1935) was a strong supporter of Astley Cooper's ideas. Richard Coombes was born in Hampton Court, Middlesex but emigrated to Sydney, Australia in 1886 where he became President of the Australian Amateur Athletics Union from 1897 until 1934.

Coombes was critical of the leadership of Astley Cooper but admired and respected his initial idea of creating a British Empire Games. Norton H. Crowe in his final retirement address in 1924 stated -

"I would again bring before the Union the advisability of taking the initiative in an all British Empire Games to be held between the Olympic Games".

Norton N. Crowe was Secretary of the Amateur Athletics Union of Canada, a position he had occupied for 19 years and was a keen supporter of Richard Coombes.

During the Olympic Games in 1928 in Amsterdam. Mr Melville Marks 'Bobby' Robinson, organised a meeting to resurrect this aspiration. Bobby Robinson was a correspondent for The Spectator, in Hamilton, and was the manager of the Canadian Athletics Team at that time.

He argued energetically and eloquently and eventually succeeded to rekindle the flame and receive an agreement for the first British Empire Games to be held in Hamilton, Canada in 1930. Bobby Robinson was the owner of a farm and he was immensely interested in education as well as athletics. He was born on the 8th of April 1888 at Peterborough, Ontario and died on the 6th June 1974. He lived in Burlington, Ontario. He was a governor of Burlington High School and President from 1950 untl 1963. Bobby Robinson was honoured for his work in education by having a new school named after him, - the M.M. Robinson High School.

I had the great pleasure of meeting his daughter, Edna Robinson at her home in Hamilton. I spent a gratifying afternoon in her company listening to her memories of her father over a cup of coffee in her lounge. Edna was a delightful person who mirrored her father's interest in education. She showed a particularly lively interest when I mentioned my intention of writing this book on the Commonwealth Games. Later in her career Edna became Headmistress of one of the largest school's in Ontario which catered for over 2000 students. She died on Sunday, 13th, November 2005 at the age of 89.

Quite unintentially I had a photograph taken with Edna in her lounge. Hanging on the wall behind us was a photograph showing a country scene. I made comment that the landscape was similar to ours in Wales. She laughed and said it was from Wales, and was a presentation given to her father by a group of Welsh farmers, for his contribution to the farming industry.

Bobby Robinson was a special individual of many interests and I was privileged to have met his daughter.

In his letter to The Times Astley Cooper wrote –

"I have taken into consideration the fact that the future relationship of the various portions of the Empire rests chiefly in the hands of the young men of the Empire – of young Britain, young Australia, young South Africa, young Canada – an Imperial athletics contestant would be very attractive to most Britishers, whether settled in the United Kingdom or resident beyond the seas. I also believe that such a contest between selected representatives of the English-speaking races could command more attention and be more popular than any other contest which could be arranged."

THE BRITISH EMPIRE FESTIVAL 1911

Nothing tangible came of the vision of the Rev. Astley Cooper until the coronation of George Vth in 1911, when Australasia (Australia, New Zealand and Tasmania), Canada, Great Britain, Ireland, and South Africa, competed in a Festival of the Empire, in a sporting tournament to celebrate the coronation at the Crystal Palace, London on the 12th June. The occasion was used - *"to stimulate trade, Strengthen bonds that bind mother Country to her Sister States and Daughters."*

The sports that were contested and the champions were:

ATHLETICS

100 yards	Halbaus. Frank J.	Canada	10.4 secs.
220 yards	Halbaus. Frank J.	Canada	23.0 secs.
880 yards	Hill. J. M.	United Kingdom	1.58.6 secs.
1 mile	Tait. John Lyndsay	Canada	4.46.2 secs.

120 yards Hurdles

Powell. Kenneth United Kingdom   16 secs.

SWIMMING

100 yards Freestyle

Hardwick.Harold Hamptson, Australia

1 mile

George Hodgson, Canada.

BOXING

Heavyweight Hardwick. Harold Hamptson, Australia

WRESTLING

Middleweight   Bacon. S. V.   USA

It is noted that Harold Hardwick competed in two sports, - Swimming and Boxing.

The victorious country was Canada by one point. It was reported in The Times:-

"There is only one sentiment that animates us all, that of personal loyalty and affection quickened by a common impulse of imperial solidarity and sympathy."

Without doubt this was blatant imperial propaganda. In January 1930 Bobby Robinson travelled to London where he obtained an understanding that *Wales*, Scotland, Ireland and England could compete in Hamilton as individual countries. If this had not been done the Games would have been a rather insipid affair as far as the number of competing nations was concerned. Consequently we in *Wales* owe a debt of gratitude to Melville Marks Robinson, otherwise *Wales* would never have been permitted to compete in the British Empire Games as a country and perhaps the Games would not have continued.

It is interesting to note that not only was *Wales* competing as one of eleven countries in the first Empire Games but is one of only six nations that have competed in every Games since. It seems that England is prepared to recognise *Wales* as a country when it is advantageous to it.

When the Olympic Games were held in London in 1908, it was arranged for Hockey to be one of the competing sports for the first time, probably because Hockey was not played to a high standard in the world;

which would result in Great Britain winning a gold medal. As it was there was no interest so the competition went ahead with GBR England, **GBR Wales**, GBR Scotland and Ireland being the only countries although Germany competed with their entry being from one club. France also competed with entries only from 3 clubs but had to compete on their own and not against the other countries. As anticipated England won. However it was the only occasion that **Wales** could claim to have competed in an Olympic Games and also won a bronze medal. **(Index 2)**

I am convinced that the main reason was for Britain to win a gold medal rather than any sympathetic chimera towards any nationalistic illusion that Scotland and Wales might have.

Note: I have endeavoured to indicate names that have a Welsh connection in bold italics.

LONDSDALE CUP

Earl Lonsdale

Hugh Cecil Lowther, the Fifth Earl Lonsdale (25.01.1857-13.04.1944) presented a silver cup to acknowledge Canada's success in being the victorious country at the 1911 Festival of Empire. The cup was valuable being two and a half feet high and weighing 340 ounces.

Later in November 1934, the Earl consented to having the Cup which was based on a Queen Ann design by Richard Bayley in 1712, to be melted down and the silver used to make smaller cups. The main cup was subsequently given to the Federation. The remainder of the silver was used to create smaller copies to be presented, - one to the Earl of

Lonsdale and one each to the participating countres at the first Games who were: Australia, Bermuda, British Guyana, Canada, England, Newfoundland, New Zealand, Northern Ireland, Scotland, South Africa and Wales.

The following words are engraved on the Cup: -

"At the Festival of Empire in 1911 the Earl of Lonsdale presented Great Cup which was won by Canada by whom it was generously given to the British Empire Games Federation at the 1934 Games.

This Cup was melted down and made into a Principal Cup to be held by the Federation with copies for the Empire Games Associations in Great Britain, the Dominions and Colonies. "

PURPOSE OF THE GAMES

The purpose of the Games is identified in the following declaration:

"The Empire Games will be designed on the Olympic model, both in general construction and its stern definition of the amateur. But the Games will be different, free from both the excessive stimuluus and the babel of the international stadium.

They shall be merrier and less stern, and will subtitute the stimulous of a novel adventure for the pressure of international rivalry."

This dictum is also attributed to the authors of the Games in a pamphlet heralding the Games in Hamilton. Even in the intense competitive climate of modern sport, these fundamental principles are held as a central philosophy underpinning the Games. Only those athletes and officials who have participated in the Commonwealth Games fully appreciate and understand why these Games are known as

'The Friendly Games'.

TITLES OF THE GAMES

On Sunday, Seventh of August 1932, during the Tenth Olympic Games in Los Angeles, following the first British Empire Games, the British Empire Games Federation was formed. Colonel Evan Hunter was appointed as the Secretary. Colonel Hunter died in Flintshire, Wales where he owned property.

It was agreed that the British Empire Games would be held in between the Olympic Games and that they should be numbered with Hamilton 1930 being number One, thus obviating the frequent claim that the Festival of Empire 1911 was the first British Empire Games.

It is interesting to note that the names of the Games have from time to time changed to reflect the political feeling and relationship with Britain at the time in the twentieth century. On the twentieth of July 1952 the name was changed from the British Empire Games to the British Empire and Commonwealth Games.

On the seventh of August 1966 the name was again changed to British Commonwealth Games and then in 1974 to the Commonwealth Games.

CELEBRATION OF THE COMMONWEALTH AND OLYMPIC GAMES

COMMONWEALTH GAMES - **COM**

OLYMPIC GAMES - **OLY**

1896	Athens, Greece	**OLY**
1900	Paris, France	**OLY**
1904	St. Louis, USA	**OLY**
1908	London,Great Britain	**OLY**
1912	Stockholm, Sweden.	**OLY**
1916	**World War 1 ***	

* Berlin was alloted these Games but they were cancelled because of the war.

1920	Antwerp, Belgium	**OLY**
1924	Paris, France	**OLY**
1928	Amsterdam, Holland	**OLY**

British Empire Games

N⁰	Year	Place	Type
I	1930	Hamilton, Canada	**COM**
	1932	Los Angeles,USA	**OLY**
II	1934	London, England	**COM**
	1936	Berlin, Germany **	**OLY**
III	1938	Sydney, Australia	**COM**
	1940	**World War 2 ***	**OLY**
	1942	**World War 2**	**COM**
	1944	**World War 2 ******	**OLY**
	1946	**World War 2**	**COM**

	1948	London, Great Britain	**OLY**
IV	1950	Auckland, New Zealand	**COM**
	1952	Helsinki, Finland	**OLY**

** During the Games, South Africa was appointed to organise the next Games in 1934 but due to the problems associated with apartheid the Games were transferred to London.

*** Tokyo and Helsinki were appointed to organise these Olympic Games but they were cancelled because of World War 2.

**** London was appointed to organise these Games but they were cancelled because of World War 2.

British Empire and Commonwealth Games

V	1954	Vancouver, Canada	**COM**
	1956	Melbourne, Australia	**OLY**
VI	*1958*	*Cardiff, Wales*	**COM**
	1960	Rome, Italy	**OLY**
VII	1962	Perth, Australia	**COM**
	1964	Tokyo, Japan	**OLY**
VIII	1966	Kingston, Jamaica	**COM**
	1968	Mexico, Mexico	**OLY**

British Commonwealth Games

IX	1970	Edinburgh, Scotland	**COM**
	1972	Munich, Germany	**OLY**
X	1974	Christchurch, New Zealand	**COM**
	1976	Montreal, Canada	**OLY**

Commonwealth Games

XI	1978	Edmonton, Canada	**COM**
	1980	Moscow, Russia	**OLY**
XII	1982	Brisbane, Australia	**COM**
	1984	Los Angeles, USA	**OLY**
XIII	1986	Edinburgh,Scotland	**COM**
	1988	Seoul, Korea	**OLY**
XIV	1990	Auckland, New Zealand	**COM**
	1992	Barcelona, Spain	**OLY**
XV	1994	Victoria, Canada	**COM**
	1996	Atlanta, USA	**OLY**
XVI	1998	Kuala Lumpur, Malaysia	**COM**
	2000	Sydney, Australia	**OLY**

ORGANISING COMMITTEES OF THE GAMES

1930 **Chairman**   Robinson, K.B.E.   Melville. M.

       Director   Childs, CB., C.M.G. Wilfred

1934 **Chairman**   Leigh-Wood, Sir James

       Director   Evan, O.B.E. A. Hunter

1938 **Chairman**   Marks, Ernest Samuel

       Director   Eve. James S.W.

1950 **Chairman**   Moore, M.B.E. C. Rex

       Director   Cleal. Mrs C.L.

1954 **Chairman**   Smith. S.V.

       Director   Clerk. Blair M.

1958 *Chairman*   ***Llewellyn, Bt., C.B.. C.B.E., Sir Godfrey***

       Director   ***Newham, O.B.E. M.C.,T.D. Charles E.***

1962 **Chairman**   Howard, K.B.E. Sir Harry

       Director   Howson. John F.

1966 **Chairman**   MacDonald, K.B.E. Sir Herbert
       Director   Abrahams, C.B.E. A. George

1970 **Chairman**   Brechin, K.B.E., Sir Herbert

       Director   Carmichael, O.B.E. William

1974	**Chairman**	Scott. Ronald Stewart
	Director	Barrett. Allan W.
1978	**Chairman**	Van Vliet. Dr. M.I. (Maury)
	Director	McColl. D.N. (Don)
1982	**Chairman**	Williams, K.B.E. The Hon., Sir Edward
	Director	Whithead, Dan
1986	**Chairman**	Borthwick, C.B.E., D.L. Kenneth
	Director	Grosset, C.A. Blair
1990	**Chairman**	Richardson. Sir Earl
	Director	Aldridge. Tom
1994	**Chairman**	Heller. George (President)
	Director	Reed. Jim (Vice President)
1998	**Chairman**	Ali. General Tan Sri Hashim
	Director	Chin. Siew Foong

COUNTRIES THAT PARTICIPATED IN THE GAMES IN THE 20TH CENTURY

COUNTRY	GAMES	N°
Australia	1930.1934.1938.1950.1954.1958.1962.1966. 1970.1974.19781982.1986.1990.1994.1998	16
Canada	1930.1934.1938.1950.1954.1958.1962.1966. 1970.1974.1978.1982.1986.1990.1994.1998	16
England	1930.1934.1938.1950.1954.1958.1962.1966 1970.1974.1978.1982.1986.1990.1994.1998	16
New Zealand	1930.1934.1938.1950.1954.1958.1962.1966. 1970.1974.1978.1982.1986.1990.1994.1998	16
Scotland	1930.1934.1938.1950.1954.1958.1962.1966 1970.1974.1978.1982.1986.1990.1994.1998	16
Wales	*1930.1934.1938.1950.1954.1958.1962.1966.* *1970.1974.1978.1982.1986.1990.1994.1998*	*16*
Guyana	1930.1934.1938.1954.1958.1962.1966.1970. 1974.1978.1982.1990.1994.1998	14
Northern Ireland	1930.1934.1938.1954.1958.1962.1966.1970 1974.1978.1982.1986.1990.1998	14
Trinidad & Tobago	1934.1938.1954.1958.1962.1966.1970.1974. 1978.1982.1990.1994.1998	13
Bermuda	1930.1934.1938.1950.1958.1970.1974.1978. 1982.1990.1994.1998	12

Fiji	1938.1950.1954.1958.1962.1966.1970.1974. 1978.1982.1986.1998	**12**
India	1934.1938.1954.1958.1966.1970.1974.1978. 1982.1990.1994.1998	**12**
Jamaica	1934.1954.1958.1962.1966.1970.1974.1978. 1982.1990.1994.1998	**12**
Barbados	1954.1958.1962.1966.1970.1974.1978.1982. 1990.1994.1998	**11**
Ghana	1954.1958.1962.1966.1970.1974.1978.1982 1990.1994.1998	**11**
Gibraltar	1958.1962.1966.1970.1974.1978.1982.1986 1990.1994.1998	**11**
Isle of Man	1958.1962.1966.1970.1974.1978.1982.1986. 1990.1994.1998	**11**
Jersey	1958.1962.1966.1970.1974.1978.1982.1986. 1990.1994.1998	**11**
Kenya	1954.1958.1962.1966.1970.1974.1978.1982 1990.1994.1998	**11**
Singapore	1950.1958.1962.1966.1970.1974.1978.1982. 1986.1990.1998	**11**
Sri Lanka	1938.1950.1958.1962.1966.1970.1978.1982 1990.1994.1998	**11**
Bahamas	1954.1958.1962.1966.1970.1978.1982.1990. 1994.1998	**10**
Hong Kong	1934.1954.1958.1962.1970.1974.1978.1982. 1990.1994	**10**
Mauritius	1958.1962.1966.1970.1974.1978.1982.1990.	

	1994.1998	**10**
Nigeria	1950.1954.1958.1966.1970.1974.1982.1990. 1994.1998	**10**
Uganda	1954.1958.1962.1966.1970.1974.1982.1990 1994.1998	**10**
Zimbabwe	1934.1938.1950.1954.1958.1962.1982.1990 1994.1998	**10**
Papua New Guinea	1962.1966.1970.1974.1978.1982.1990.1994. 1998	**9**
Tanzania	1962.1966.1970.1974.1978.1982.1990.1994. 1998	**9**
Guernsey	1970.1974.1978.1982.1986.1990.1994.1998	**8**
Malawi	1970.1974.1978.1982.1986.1990.1994.1998	**8**
Malaysia	1966.1970.1974.1978.1982.1990.1994.1998	**8**
Malta	1958.1962.1970.1982.1986.1990.1994.1990	**8**
Pakistan	1954.1958.1962.1966.1970.1990.1994.1998	**8**
South Africa	1930.1934.1938.1950.1954.1958.1994.1998	**8**
St Vincent	1958.1966.1970.1974.1978.1990.1994.1998	**8**
Swaziland	1970.1974.1978.1982.1986.1990.1994.1998	**8**
Zambia	1954.1970.1974.1978.1982.1990.1994.1998	**8**
Sierra Leone	1958.1966.1970.1978.1990.1994.1998	**7**
Western Samoa	1974.1978.1982.1986.1990.1994.1998	**7**
Botswana	1974.1982.1986.1990.1994.1998	**6**
Gambia	1970.1978.1982.1990.1994.1998	**6**

Cayman Islands	1978.1982.1986.1990.1994.1998	6
Cook Islands	1974.1978.1986.1990.1994.1998	6
Lesotho	1974.1978.1986.1990.1994.1998	6
Antigua	1966.1970.1978.1994.1998	5
Belize	1962.1966.1970.1994.1998	5
Cyprus	1978.1982.1990.1994.1998	5
Dominica	1958.1962.1970.1994.1998	5
Falkland Islands	1982.1986.1990.1994.1998	5
Grenada	1970.1974.1978.1982.1998	5
St Lucia	1962.1970.1978.1994.1998	5
Tonga	1974.1982.1990.1994.1998	5
Bangladesh	1970.1990.1994.1998	4
Maldives	1986.1990.1994.1998	4
Norfolk Islands	1986.1990.1994.1998	4
Solomon Islands	1982.1990.1994.1998	4
St. Kitts	1978.1990.1994.1998	4
Vanuatu	1982.1986.1990.1994	4
Brunei Daresalam	1990.1994.1998	3
Malaya	1950.1958.1962	3
Seychelles	1990.1994.1998	3
Virgin Islands	1990.1994.1998	3

Montserrat	1994.1998	2
Namibia	1994.1998	2
Newfoundland	1930.1934	2
Sabah	1958.1962	2
Sarawak	1958.1962	2
South Arabia	1962.1966	2
St. Helena	1982.1998	2
Turks & Caicos Islands	1978.1998	2
Anguila	1998	1
Cameroon	1998	1
Kiribati	1998	1
Mozambique	1998	1
Nauru	1998	1
Tuvalu	1998	1

COUNTRIES WHO ORGANISED THE GAMES IN THE TWENTIETH CENTURY

CANADA	1930	1954	1978	1994
AUSTRALIA	1938	1962	1982	
NEW ZEALAND	1950	1974	1990	
SCOTLAND	1970	1986		
ENGLAND	1934			
JAMAICA	1966			
MALAYSIA	1998			
WALES	1958			

CHAPTER TWO

FEDERATION OFFICERS UP TO 2000

PATRONS

1930 – 1936   King George V

1936 – 1952   King George VI

1952 -   Queen Elizabeth Elizabeth II

PRESIDENTS

1932 – 1938   The Earl of Londsdale. K.G.,G.C.V.O.

1948 – 1955   The Earl of Gowrie.V.C., P.C., G.C. M.G., C.B.,D.S.O.

1955 - 2003   His Royal Highness, The Duke of Edinburgh. K.G.

LIFE VICE- PRESIDENTS

Duncan, O.B.E. K. Sandy   England

Phillips. Max B.   Australia

Heatley, C.B.E., D.L. Sir Peter   Scotland

Sales, C.B.E., J.P. Arnaldo De O. Hong Kong

VICE- PRESIDENTS

Oceania

1968 - 1970   Porritt, Bt., K.C. M.G., K.C.V.O.,

               C.B.E., F.R.C.S. Sir Arthur   New Zealand

Africa

1970 - 1974   Adefope. Major General

Henry Edmund Olufemi   Nigeria

America

1970 – 1974   Davies, C.D. Col. Jack W.   Canada

Asia

1970 – 1974   Razak. The Honourable

Tun Abdul   Malaysia

Europe

1970 – 1972   The Lord Beatty.   England

Caribbean

1970 – 1974   Henderson. K.

Oceania

1970 – 1974   Austad., C.B.E. Harold I.   New Zealand

Africa

1974 – 1978   Adefope. Major General

Henry Edmund Olufemi   Nigeria

America

1974 – 1978   Davies, C.E. Colonel Jack W. Canada

Asia

1974 – 1978   Sales, C.B.E., J.P. Analdo de O.

Hong Kong

Caribbean

1974 – 1978   Bridge, O.B.E. Roydel Anthony   Jamaica

Caribbean

1974 – 1978   Butler, K.C. M.G., J.P., D.L.C.
Sir Arlington G.   Bahamas

Europe

1974 – 1978   Carmichael. William   Scotland

Oceania

1974 – 1978   Young. H.J.

Africa

1978 – 1982   Adefope. Major General
Henry Edmund Olufemi   Africa

Asia

1978 – 1982   Sales, C.B.E.,J.P. Arnaldo de O.   Hong Kong

Caribbean

1978 – 1982   Bridge, O.B.E. Roydel Anthony   Jamaica

Europe

1978 – 1982   *Howell. Cyril Montague*   *Wales*

Oceania

1978 – 1982   Young. H. J.

Europe

1986 – 1990   Hunter, O.B.E. George A.   Scotland

Africa

1990 – 1994   Kabaga. Raphael A.   Tanzania

America

1990 - 1994   Dent. Ivor G.   Canada

Asia

1990 – 1994   Hamzah. The Hon. Tan Sri   Malaysia

Caribbean

1990 – 1994   Chapman, H.B.M.
Alexander B.   Trinidad & Tobago

Europe

1990 – 1994   Killey, M.B.E. Ron E.   Isle of Man

Oceania

1990 – 1994   Wightman. Brian J.   Tonga

America

1994 – 1998   Robertson. Bruce   Canada

Asia

1994 – 1998   Hamzah. The Hon. Tan Sri   Malaysia

Caribbean

| 1994 – 1998 | Chapman, H.B.M. Alexander B. | Trinidad & Tobago |

Europe

| *1994 – 1998* | *John, M.B.E. Myrddin* | *Wales* |

Oceania

| 1994 – 1998 | Tunstall, O.B.E. Arthur | Australia |

Africa

| 1998 – 2003 | Rogers. Edgar | Zimbabwe |

America

| 1998 – 2003 | Robertson. Bruce | Canada |

Asia

| 1998 – 2003 | Singh. Raja Randir | India |

Caribbean

| 1998 – 2003 | Chapman, H.B.M. Alexander B. | Trinidad & Tobago |

Europe

| 1998 – 1999 | McColgan, M.B.E. Richard | Northern Ireland |

Europe

| 1999 – 2003 | Emmerson. Ian | England |

Oceania

1998 – 2003   Tierney. John   Cook Islands

CHAIRMEN

1930 – 1938   Leigh-Wood, K.B.E.. C.B.

            Sir James   England

Sir James Leigh Wood. K.B.E., C.B., C.M.G

1948 – 1967   Porritt, Bt., K.C. M.G., C.B.E.,

        F.R.C.S. Lord Arthur   New Zealand

Lord Porritt

1968 – 1982   Ross. Sir Alexander   New Zealand

1986 - 1994	Heatley, C.B.E., D.L.	
	Sir Peter	Scotland
1994 – 1998	Sales, C.B.E., J.P. Arnaldo de O.	Hong Kong
1998 -	Fennell, O.J., C.D. The Hon. Michael	Jamaica

VICE-CHAIRMEN

1966 – 1968	Ross. Sir Alexander	New Zealand
1970 – 1982	Mbathi. Musembi	Kenya
1970 – 1982	Fennell, O.J., C.D. The Hon. Michael	Jamaica
1982 -	Mukora, M.P. The Hon. Charles	Kenya
1982 - 1999	Lee. Dato Alex	Malaysia

SECRETARIES

1932 – 1948   Hunter, O.B.E. Colonel Evan A.   England

E.A. Hunter. O.B.E.

1948 – 1982   Duncan, M.B.E. K. Sandy   England

1982 – 1999   Dixon. C.V.O. David M.   England

1999 -   Martin. C.B.E. Louise   Scotland

TREASURERS

1932 – 1952   Holt. E. J.   England

1952 – 1962   Leigh-Wood, K.B.E., C.B., C.M.G. Sir James   England

1962 – 1986   Phillips. Max B.   Australia

1986 -   Sealy, S.C.M. Austin L.   Barbados

LEGAL ADVISER

1982-   Rao. S. Sharad   Kenya

MEDICAL ADVISERS

1968 - 1982	Owen. Dr J.R.	England
1982 - 1986	Jones. Dr J. Howel	England
1986 -	Haigh, M.B., Ch.B., B.A. Dr Geoffrey	Canada

MEMBERS OF THE SPORTS COMMITTEE

1986 - 1990	*John, M.B.E. Myrddin*	*Wales*
1990 - 1994	*John, M.B.E. Myrddin*	*Wales*
1998 - 2003	Butt. Muhammed Latif	Pakistan
1998 - 2003	Cameron. Bruce	New Zealand
1998 - 2003	*John, M.B.E. Myrddin*	*Wales*
1998 - 2003	Kabaga. Raphael	Tanzania
1998 - 2003	Kent. Judy	Canada
1998 - 2003	McCook. Neville	Jamaica
1998 - 2003	Pitts, O.B.E., J.P. Edward	Belize

MEMBERS OF THE FINANCE COMMITTEE

1998 - 2003	Hemasiri. Fernando	Sri Lanca
1998 - 2003	Hooper. Michael	New Zealand
1998 - 2003	Hoskins. John	Bermuda
1998 - 2003	Oliver. Hugo	South Africa
1998 - 2003	Peterkin. Richard	St. Lucia
1998 - 2003	Wright, B.E.M. Gordon	Jersey

CHAPTER THREE

MEMBERS OF THE COMMONWEALTH GAMES FEDERATION IN 2000

Anguilla	Anguilla Amateur Athletic Association
Antigua & Barbuda	Antigua Olympic and Commonwealth Games Association
Australia	Australian Commonwealth Games Association
Bahamas	Bahamas Olympic Association
Bangladesh	Bangladesh Olympic Association
Barbados	Barbados Olympic Association
Belize	Belize Olympic and Commonwealth Games Association
Bermuda	Bermuda Olympic Association
Botswana	Botswana National Olympic Association
British Virgin Islands	British Virgin Islands Olympic Committee
Brunei Darussalam	Brunei Darussalam National Olympic Council
Cameroon	Cameroon National Olympic Committee
Canada	Commonwealth Games Association of Canada Inc.
Cayman Islands	Cayman Islands Olympic Committee
Cook Islands	Cook Islands Amateur Sports Association
Cyprus	Cyprus Commonwealth Games Association
Dominica	Dominica Amateur Athletic Association

England	Commonwealth Games Council for England
Falkland Islands	FIDF Rifle Association
Fiji	Fiji Comonwealth Games Association
Gambia	Gambia National Olympic Committee
Ghana	Ghana Olympic & Overseas Games Committee
Gibraltar	Commonwealth Games Association of Gibraltar
Grenada	Grenada Olympic Association
Guernsey	Guernsey Commonwealth Games Association
Guyana	Guyana Olympic Committee
India	India Olympic Association
Isle of Man	Commonwealth Games Association of Isle of Man
Jamaica	Jamaica Olympic Association
Jersey	Commonwealth Games Association of Jersey
Kenya	National Olympic Committee of Kenya
Kiribati	Kiribati Commonwealth Games Association
Lesotho	Lesotho Olympic Committee
Malawi	Olympic and Commonwealth Games Association of Malawi
Malaysia	Olympic Council of Malaysia
Maldives	Maldives Olympic Association
Malta	Malta Olympic Committee
Mauritius	Mauritius Olympic Committee

Montserrat	Montserrat Amateur Athletic Association
Mozambique	Mozambique National Olympic Committee
Namibia	Namibia National Olympic Committee
Nauru	Nauru Commonwealth Games Association
New Zealand	New Zealand Olympic Committee
Nigeria	Nigeria Olympic Committee
Niue	Niue Island Association & National Olympic Association
Norfolk Island	Norfolk Island Amateur Sports Council
Northern Ireland	Commonwealth Games Council for Northern Ireland
Pakistan	Pakistan Olympic Association
Papua New Guinea	Papua New Guinea Olympic Committee & Commonwealth Games Association
Samoa	Samoa Sports Federation
Scotland	Commonwealth Games Council for Scotland
Seychelles	Seychelles National Olympic Committee
Sierra Leone	Sierra Leone Olympic & Overseas Games Committee
Singapore	Singapore National Olympic Committee
Soloman Islands	National Olympic Committee of Soloman Islands
South Africa	South African Commonwealth Games Association
Sri Lanka	National Olympic Committee of Sri Lanka

St. Helena St.	National Amateur Sports Games Association of Helena
St Kitts & Nevis	St. Kitts & Nevis Olympic Association
St. Lucia	St. Lucia Olympic Committee
St. Vincent & the Grenadines	St.Vincent & the Grenadines Olympic Association
Swaziland	Swaziland Olympic & Commonwealth Games Association
Tanzania	Tanzania Olympic Committee
Tonga	Tonga Commonwealth Games Association
Trinidad & Tobago	Trinidad & Tobago Olympic Association
Turks & Caicos	Turks & Caicos Amateur Athletics Association
Tuvalu	Tuvalu Amateur Sports Association
Uganda	Uganda Olympic Committee
Vanuatu	Vanuatu Olympic Committee
Wales	***Commonwealth Games Council for Wales***
Zambia	National Olympic Committee of Zambia
Zimbabwe	Zimbabwe Commonwealth Games Association

72 member countries

CHAPTER FOUR

VENUES OF THE OPENING CEREMONIES AND THE CHAMPIONS

POSTER OF THE FIRST GAMES

OPENING CEREMONY VENUES OF THE GAMES

N°	Date
I	**16 – 23 August 1930**

Sports: Athletics. Lawn Bowls. Swimming. Boxing. Rowing. Wrestling

Venue: Civic Stadium, Hamilton, Canada

II	**4 – 11 August 1934**

Sports: Athletics. Cycling. Lawn Bowls. Swimming. Boxing. Wrestling

Venue: White City Stadium, London, England

III	**5 – 12 February 1938**

Sports: Athletics. Cycling. Lawn Bowls. Swimming. Boxing. Rowing. Wrestling

Venue: Cricket Ground, Sydney, Australia

IV   **4 – 11 February 1950**

Sports: Athletics. Cycling. Lawn Bowls. Weightlifting. Fencing.
Swimming. Boxing. Rowing. Wrestling

Venue: Eden Park, Auckland, New Zealand

V   **30   July - 7 August 1950**

Sports: Athletics. Cycling. Lawn Bowls. Weightlifting. Fencing.
Swimming. Boxing. Rowing. Wrestling

Venue: Empire Stadium, Vancouver, Canada

VI   **17 – 26 July 1958**

Sports: Athletics. Cycling. Lawn Bowls. Weightlifting. Fencing.
Swimming. Boxing. Rowing. Wrestling

Venue: *Arms Park, Cardiff, Wales*

VII   **21 November -1 December 1962**

Sports: Athletics. Cycling. Lawn Bowls. Weightlifting. Fencing.
Swimming. Boxing. Rowing. Wrestling

Venue: Perry Lake Stadium, Perth, Australia

VIII	**4 – 13 August 1966**

Sports: Athletics. Badminton. Cycling. Weightlifting. Fencing. Swimming. Boxing. Shooting. Wrestling

Venue: National Stadium, Kingston, Jamaica

IX	**16 – 25 July 1970**

Sports: Athletics. Badminton. Cycling. Lawn Bowls. Weightlifting. Fencing. Swimming. Boxing. Wrestling

Venue: Meadowbank Stadium, Edinburgh, Scotland

X	**24 January – 2 February 1974**

Sports: Athletics. Badminton. Cycling. Lawn Bowls. Weightlifting. Swimming. Boxing. Shooting. Wrestling

Venue: Queen Elizabeth II Park, Christchurch, New Zealand

XI	**3 – 12 August 1978**
Sports:	Athletics. Badminton. Cycling. Lawn Bowls. Weightlifting. Gymnastics. Swimming. Boxing. Shooting. Wrestling
Safle:	Commonwealth Stadium, Edmonton, Canada

XII	**30 September – 9 October 1982**
Sports:	Athletics. Badminton. Cycling. Lawn Bowls. Weightlifting. Swimming. Boxing. Archery. Shooting. Wrestling
Venue:	Queen Elizabeth II Stadium, Brisbane, Australia

XIII	**24 July – 2 August 1986**
Sports:	Athletics. Badminton. Cycling. Lawn Bowls. Weightlifting. Swimming. Boxing. Rowing. Shooting. Wrestling
Venue:	Meadowbank Stadium, Edinburgh, Scotland

XIV	**24 January – 3 February 1990**

Sports: Athletics. Badminton. Cycling. Lawn Bowls. Weightlifting. Gymnastics. Judo. Swimming. Boxing. Shooting

Venue: Mount Smart Stadium, Auckland, New Zealand

XV	**18 – 28 August 1994**

Sports: Athletics. Badminton. Cycling.Lawn Bowls. Weightlifting. Gymnastics. Swimming. Boxing. Shooting. Wrestling

Venue: Centennial Stadium, Victoria, Canada

XVI	**11 – 21 September 1998**

Sports: Athletics. Badminton. Cycling. Tenpin Bowling. Lawn Bowls. Weightlifting. Cricket. Hockey. Gymnastics. Swimming. Boxing. Netball. Rugby 7 A- Side. Shooting. Squash

Venue: National Stadium, Bukit Jalil, Kuala Lumpur, Malaysia

NUMBERS AT THE GAMES

Countries		Athletes	Officials	Total
1930	11	400	50	450
1934	16	500	50	550
1938	15	464	43	507
1950	12	590	73	633
1954	24	662	127	789
1958	35	1130	228	1358
1962	35	863	178	1041
1966	34	1050	266	1316
1970	42	1383	361	1744
1974	39	1276	372	1648
1978	46	1475	504	1979
1982	45	1583	571	2154
1986	26	1662	461	2123
1990	55	2073	789	2826
1994	63	2557	914	3471
1998	70	3638	1398	5036

SPORTS THAT PARTICIPATED AT THE GAMES

Archery

    1982   **(1)**

Athletics

    1930.1934.1938.1950.1954.1958.1962.1966
    1970.1974.1978.1982.1986.1990.1994.1998   **(16)**

Badminton

    1966.1970.1974.1978.1982.1986.1990.1994.1998   **(9)**

Boxing

    1930.1934.1938.1950.1954.1958.1962.1966.

    1970.1974.1978.1982.1986.1990.1994.1998   **(16)**

Cricket

    1998   **(1)**

Cycling

    1934.1938.1950.1954.1958.1962.1966.1970.

    1974.1978.1982.1986.1990.1994.1998   **(15)**

Fencing

  1950.1954.1958.1962.1966.1970   **(6)**

Gymnastics

  1978.1990.1994.1998   **(4)**

Hockey

  1994.1998   **(2)**

Judo

  1990   **(1)**

Lawn Bowls

  1930.1934.1938.1950.1954.1958.1962.1970.

  1974.1978.1982.1986.1990.1994.1998   **(15)**

Netball

  1998   **(1)**

Rowing

  1930.1938.1950.1954.1958.1962.1986.   **(7)**

Rugby Sevens

  1998   **(1)**

Shooting

1966.1974.1978.1982.1986.1990.1994.1998   **(8)**

Squash

1998   **(1)**

Swimming

1930.1934.1938.1950.1954.1958.1962.1966.

1970.1974.1978.1982.1986.1990.1994.1998   **(16)**

Tenpin Bowling

1998   **(1)**

Weightlifting

1950.1954.1958.1962.1966.1970.1974.1978.

1982.1986.1990.1994.1998   **(13)**

Wrestling

1930.1934.1938.1950.1954.1958.1962.1966.

1970.1974.1978.1982.1986.1994   **(14)**

NUMBER OF SPORTS IN GAMES 1930 - 1998

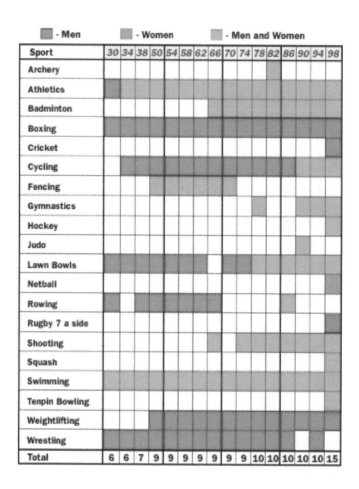

Women were included in eleven sports at the Kuala Lumpur Games compared with 1930 when women were included only in Swimming. There are only three sports that have been included in all these Games. They are Athletics, Swimming and Boxing. There has been a significant increase in the number of sports and consequently in the number of competitors and officials.

POSITION OF WALES AT THE GAMES 1930 - 1998

The highest position gained by Wales in the 20th Century on the medal list was 5th in 1986 as seen below. **(Index 3)**

Games	Rank
1930	7
1934	8
1938	6
1950	12
1954	13
1958	11
1962	13
1966	11
1970	11
1974	12
1978	9
1982	8
1986	5
1990	6
1994	9
1998	10

Care must be taken to ensure that the success of the Games does not destroy the spirit and aim of the Games as Astley Cooper had envisaged it to be. As we saw in the final Games of the Twentieth Century in 1998, the Games has seen considerable development with the number of sports and showing a phenomenal expansion in team sports as well as in the participation of women. Rightly or wrongly the result has been to show a significant high number of athletes and officials at the Games. This is a big challenge, especially for the poorer countries who wish to apply to host the Games.

As sports become more sophisticated the demands of athletes and the sports themselves require better facilities and more intricate planning etc. The number of athletes and their officials was only 450 in 1930, whereas in 1998 this number increased considerably. As well as this we now have to cater for a substantial increase in numbers of technical officials, administrators and helpers to satisfy the needs of modern sport, together with supplying the best in security for such large numbers.

The number increased from the initial 450 to 1,358 in 1958 at Cardiff, then to 3,471 in 1994 and to 5,036 in 1998. All this together with a corresponding increase in auxiliary personnel.   This large number demands a higher sophistication and expenditure. Perhaps it is an acceptable human trait to constantly strive to do better, but this immense demand on resources makes it more difficult, if not impossible, for smaller countries to respond. Without doubt the Federation must seriously address this problem and make any necessary changes within the Games structure and expectations in the near future.

THE COMMONWEALTH GAMES

1930   HAMILTON   Athletics. Boxing. Lawn Bowls. Rowing.
Swimming. Wrestling **(6)**

The first ever British Empire Games was organised in 1930, and it was a necessary paramountcy that they were successful.

Although there was a paucity of finance the Games proved to be a resounding success which ensured the continuance of the Games for the years to come.   J. Astley Cooper's dream had come to fruition and the tenacity of Richard Coombes had triumphed. The decision was made in February 1930 that the first Games would be held in Hamilton, Canada. These Games were to open in August 1930, and this was what came to pass.   This meant that the Games were organised in seven months, although one would be naïve to believe that some tentative plans had not already been made by Hamilton to   support their bid for these first Games.

400 competitors competed at the first Games from 11 countries. These were Australia, Bermuda, Canada, **Wales**, South Africa, British Guyana, Northern Ireland, England, New Zealand, Newfoundland, and Scotland.

The first champion of the Games was Gordon A. Smallacombe of Australia when he succeeded in winning the gold medal in the Triple Jump.

The first medal won by **Wales** was the bronze medal won by Valerie Davies in Swimming in the Freestyle race over 100 yards for women. She went on to win silver medals in the 100 yards Backstroke and the 400 yards Freestyle. She was the only member of the Welsh

Team and carried the Welsh flag at the Opening Ceremony. Swimming was the only competitive sport for women at these Games.

The competitors who received the honour of being named as carriers of the national flags in the Opening Ceremony of the first Games in 1930 were:

COUNTRY	COMPETITOR	SPORT
Australia	Henry Robert (Bobby) Pearce	Rowing
Bermuda	Don Freisenbruch	Swimming
Canada	Percy Williams	Athletics
Wales	*Valerie Davies*	*Swimming*
South Africa	Hendrick B. Hart	Athletics
British Guyana	J. F. Mathews	Rowing
Northern Ireland	* William (Bill) Britton	Athletics
England	Lord David Burghley	Athletics
New Zealand	W. John Savidan	Athletics
Newfoundland	Greg Power	Athletics
Scotland	Duncan McLeod Wright	Athletics

*The ship bringing the Irish Team to the Games encountered dense fog and arrived too late for the Opening Ceremony so P. Jack O'Reilly, a team member who resided in Canada carried the Irish flag on the day.

Poster Showing The Selected Flagbearers In Hamilton 1930

On the Rostrum 1. Percy Williams

Left

2. Hendrick B. Hart

3. Greg Power

4 Duncan McLeod Wright

5. *Valerie Davies*

6. Lord David Burghley

Right

7. W. John Savidlan

8. Don Freisenbruch

9. J. F Matthews

10. William Britton

11. Harry R.Pearce

The oath on behalf of the athletes, was read by the remarkable Canadian athlete Percy Williams, winner of the Gold medals in the 100 and 200 m. at the 1928 Olympic Games

The oath read was as follows:-

'We declare that we are loyal subjects of His Majesty the King Emperor, and will take part in the British Empire Games in the spirit of true sportsmanship, recognising the rules which govern them, desirous of participating in them for the honour of our Empire and for the glory of sport.'

The winners' medals should have been awarded at the end of the Games, but unfortunately due to the bad weather this was hastily rearranged and were presented at a special banquet that evening at the Royal Connaught Hotel. It was a fitting tribute that Bobby Robinson presided over this event for the medal presentations

1934   LONDON   Athletics. Boxing. Lawn Bowls. Rowing. Swimming. Wrestling (6)

At these Games, women competed in athletics for the first time. It was a sad occasion for Welsh athletics when England refused permission for **Reg H. Thomas** to represent Wales, although Wales had selected him to compete for his country in the 3 mile race. The reason given for this was that **Reg Thomas** had represented England at the 1930 Games athletic events, although Wales had not received an invitation in that sport. In the official programme of the Opening Ceremony on 4th August 1934 the following rule was printed:-

'Those who have already competed in the British Empire Games for one country cannot, in any circumstances, represent another country in the 1934 Empire Games.'

No official constitutional rules had been set up until August 1932, two years after the 1st Games. Consequently as Wales had not been invited to the athletic events, the only method available for **Reg Thomas** to compete, in 1930 was by representing England. **Reg Thomas** was born in Pembroke Dock, Wales on the 11th January 1907, where he resided until he joined the Royal Air Force as a young man. He competed in 9 Welsh National Athletic Championships and won 8 of these titles:-

	880 yards	**1 mile**
1929	1:58.6	4:27.0
1930	2:00.0	4:26.0
1931	2:01.6	4:31.8
1933		4:17.2
1936		4:21.4

Wales was given an invitation to compete in the Swimming events in 1930 but none was given to Welsh Athletics. Wales fought hard for **Reg Thomas** to be allowed to compete for Wales but to no avail, - this was even after the **Lord Aberdare**, a very influential figure in British sport tried to intervene. In all probability the main problem was that **Reg Thomas** was such an outstanding athlete who had already won a gold medal in the one mile race at Hamilton, 1930,- but for England. Sadly **Reg Thomas** was killed when as a pilot his bomber aeroplane crashed over Stroud, Gloucester on the 14th March 1946. He was 39 years old.

Without doubt England should have permitted **Reg Thomas** to represent his country in 1934. It is my opinion that there was no consistency in the rules at the time and that placing **Reg Thomas'** name (post humously) under Wales was a matter of principle and would have been an example of goodwill.

Canada's attitude to a somewhat similar occurrence was totally different to that of England and expressed more maturity and compassion. Phil Edwards had represented Canada at the Olympic Games in Amsterdam and Los Angeles, but was selected to represent British Guyana in the 1930 and 1934 Empire Games.

Philip Edwards was 4th in the 800m. in Amsterdam in the 1928 Olympic Games in 1:51.5, 3rd in 1936 in Berlin in 1:53.6 and 3rd at the Los Angeles Games in the 1,500m. in 3:52.8. Edwards was often called the 'Man of Bronze' in Canada, because of the number of times he won 3rd place at so many large international events.

Although we revel in the successes of **Reg Thomas**, officially these successes are claimed by England. Where is the fair play that England is alleged to be so famous for in these Games, that are known as the 'Friendly Games'?

Incidentally, in the 1990 Auckland Games, **Paul Edwards** of Wales won a Bronze medal in the Shot. When England applied to Wales to allow him to represent England at the the following Games in 1994, this was promptly given. How unlike the **Reg Thomas** issue.

The famous athlete Jack E. Lovelock of New Zealand was one of the stars of these Games and was victorious in the one mile race in 4:12.8. Lovelock went on to win the 1,500 m. at the Berlin Olympic Games in 1936. Gladys Lunn of England succeeded in winning the Women's 100 yards as well as throwing the Javelin. Noel Ryan of Australia did exceptsionally well in winning the gold medal in Swimming in the 440 yards Freestyle as well as the 1,500 yards, to mirror the same accomplishments he made in the 1930 Games. At these Games Wales was fortunate in having its own General Team Manager in **R. P. Green**.

The following messages indicate how important these Games are to the Royal Family and to Great Britain.

Below is the farewell message given by England at the termination of the Games:-

At the close of the British Empire Games we wish to express our warm thanks to all who have contributed to the remarkable success of the meeting.

Competitors and Officials have worked in complete loyalty and friendship to each other, and the purpose beyond the Games has, we believe, been fully achieved.

In bidding farewell to our friends from Overseas, as well as to those in the motherland, we wish each and every one great happiness.

We send herewith a copy of the gracious messages received from H. M. the King and H.R.H. the Prince of Wales as a memento of our Great Adventure.

Lonsdale: President

James Leigh-Wood: Chairman

London, August 11th, 1934.

A copy of the telegram sent to The King on the 4th August, 1934.

Nine hundred Athletes and Officials from England, Scotland, Wales, Northern Ireland, Canada, Australia, New Zealand, South Africa, Newfoundland, India, Bermuda, British Guiana, Hong Kong, Rhodesia and Trinidad, assembled in London to compete in the British Empire Games offer their humble duty to Your Majesty, with profound loyalty.

They are inspired by the belief that this meeting of Athletes engaged in friendly rivalry will Strengthen goodwill and understanding between the peoples of the Empire.

Lonsdale,   President.

James Leigh-Wood, Chairman.

A copy of the message received by telegram from The King from the Royal ship, Victoria and Albert, at Cowes on the 4th August 1934:-

Please express to the nine hundred athletes and officials assembled In London for the British Empire Games my sincere thanks for the loyal assurances contained in their message. I am glad to welcome representatives from so many parts of the Empire and I send my best wishes for the success of the competitions.

GEORGE R. I.

A copy of the letter from the Prince of Wales

St James's Palace. S.W.

4ʰ August. 1934

Dear Lord Lonsdale,

Though I much regret that I cannot be with you at the opening of the Empire Games today, I have had the opportunity of meeting the overseas athletes whom I was delighted to welcome at St. James's Palace on Wednesday.

Please convey to all my best wishes for a very successful meeting.

Yours sincerely.

Edward

1938   SYDNEY   Athletics. Boxing. Cycling.Lawn Bowls. Rowing.
Swimming. Wrestling **(9)**

Once more the Welsh Team travelled without a General Team
Manager with England having agreed to oversee the team. The voyage
was both long and tiresome with the athletes being forced to do limited
training on board the ship..

In these Games held at Sydney, *Jim Alford of Wales*, won the gold
medal for the mile race in athletics in 4:11.6. The Australian female
athlete, Decima Norman won five gold medals, - 100 yards & 220 yards.
Long Jump and two Relays. During these Games the 1942 Games were
allocated to Montreal, Canada but this was not to be, due to World War
I. Consequently the next Games was in 1950 in Auckland, New Zealand.

1942   NO GAMES BECAUSE OF WORLD WAR 2

1946   NO GAMES BECAUSE OF WORLD WAR 2

1950   AUCKLAND   Athletics. Cycling.Lawn Bowls. Fencing.
Weightlifting. Swimming. Rowing. Boxing. Wrestling **(9)**

This was the first Games that brought Marjorie Jackson, Australia to
the attention of the world. Marjorie won gold medals in the 100 yards
and 220 yards races as well as in the two relay races.

I had the pleasure of meeting Marjorie on several occasions. She
went on to win the two sprint races in 1954. In between these two
Games she succeeded in winning the two sprints at the Helsinki Olympic
Games. Another athlete to shine at the 1950 Games was the New
Zealander, Yvette Williams who was victorious in the Javelin and the
Long Jump and went on to win a gold medal at Helsinki in 1952

Tom Richards of Wales, won the Silver medal in the Marathon,
when coming second to Jack Holden of England.

In the Wrestling competitions, Robert Garrard won the Gold medal for the third consecutive Games in the lightweight class.

1954   VANCOUVER   Athletics. Boxing. Cycling. Fencing. Lawn Bowls. Rowing. Swimming. Weightlifting. Wrestling **(9)**

The whole world was looking on in anticipation of the battle between Roger Bannister of England and the Australian John Landy in the one mile athletics race.

At Oxford in May in May 1954 in Oxford, Roger Bannister succeeded in creating a world record of 3:59.4 for the mile. This was the first time for any athlete to break the 4 minute barrier for one mile. This record was not to remain for long before John Landy broke it in Turku, Finland with a time of 3:58.0. Therefore the scene was set for an epic battle with great expectancy. The world was not to be disappointed. Bannister won the race but with both athletes again breaking the 4 minute barrier.

The results of this never to be forgotten race was:-

1	Roger B. Bannister	England	3:58.8
2	John M. Landy	Australia	3:59.6
3	Richard K. Ferguson	Canada	4:04.6
4	Victor Milligan	Northern Ireland	4:05.0
5	Murray G. Halberg	New Zealand	4:07.2
6	I.H. Boyd	England	4:07.2
7	William D. Baillie	New Zealand	4:11.0

D.C. Lowe (England) failed to finish the race.

At these Games the winner of the Marathon race was Joseph McGhee of Scotland, but the race will be remembered by all for the bravery of the English runner, Jim Peters. Peters collapsed some ten times before failing to finish the race although he was around twenty minutes in front of McGee when he entered the stadium, way ahead of any competitor. This was one of the most disturbing scenes ever witnessed in sport. Peters pushed his body to its limit but all was in vain. It was a relief to know that on the following morning he was fully recovered from his ordeal.

Ten years later Jim Peters was invited to a ceremony at the Empire Stadium, Vancouver where, during a Football game he was given the privilege of completing his Marathon race of 1954 by running the final 220 yards of the course which he had failed to do at those Games.

It was during the Games at Vancouver, that Wales was invited to organise the 1958 Games at Cardiff.

1958   CARDIFF   Athletics. Boxing. Cycling. Fencing. Lawn Bowls. Rowing. Swimming. Weightlifting.Wrestling **(9)**

The 1958 British Empire and Commonwealth Games were organised in Cardiff the capital of Wales. The Opening Ceremony and Athletic events were held at the Cardiff Arms Park, the world famous rugby ground. The weightlifting events took place at the Memorial Hall, Barry with Rowing on the lake at Bala, North Wales.

At the Opening Ceremony, *Ken Jones* the renowned rugby player and athlete was given the privilege of carrying the Queen's baton into the Stadium containing her message to be read by the Duke of Edinburgh. The message was enclosed within the baton and carried by supporters of the Games from Buckingham Palace, London to its final destination, in the form of a huge relay, to be completed when *Ken Jones* handed the baton to the Duke of Edinburgh. The Duke read the message on behalf of the Queen to the crowds present, declaring the Games open.

THE QUEEN'S MESSAGE

To all athletes assembled at Cardiff for the Sixth British Empire and Commonwealth Games I send a warm welcome and my very best wishes.

I am delighted that so many Commonwealth countries have sent teams to Wales for these Games. The number is larger than ever and more than three times as great as for the first meeting at Hamilton 1930.

This is welcome proof of the increasing value which is being placed today on physical strength and skill as an essential factor in the development of the whole man; healthy in mind and body.

It also gives me the greatest personal pleasure to know that so many members of the Commonwealth family are meeting in friendly rivalry and competition.

I hope that many lasting friendships will grow from this great meeting of athletes and spectators and that you will all go home with a better understanding of the value of our Commonwealth of nations.

I am greatly looking forward to being with you at the end of next week.

Elizabeth R.

The star of the 1958 Games was Herb Elliott of Australia who won the 880 yards race and the one mile. Following these Games Herb Elliott ran a one mile race in 3:54.5 to break the world record by 02.7 secs. and then went on to run faster when breaking the world 1,500 m. record by 02.1 secs. which he recorded in Sweden. At the Olympic Games in Rome in 1960 Herb Elliott won the 1,500 m. 3:35.6. This time can be equated to 3:53.0 for a mile. This amazing time gives us an indication of what a remarkable athlete he was.

Another Australian who was a superb athlete at the Cardiff Games was Dave Power who won both the 6 mile and Marathon races. *John Merriman of Wales* did exceptionally well to place second in this 6 mile race. Tom Robinson of Bahamas was the winner of the 220 yards race and was a great favourite with the spectators not only for his ability on the track but also for his colourful personality and his beaming smile. Another popular athlete was Milkha Singh with his beautiful balanced running when winning the gold medal in the 440 yards race.

Howard Winstone won the gold medal for Wales in the bantamweight class in Boxing. This was the only gold medal won by Wales. Later in his boxing career Howard became a World Champion as a professional boxer. As well as Howard's gold medal at these Games, Wales also won three silver and seven bronze medals.

In the swimming events we were able to see exceptionally fine achievements by such world stars as Dawn Fraser, Lorraine Crapp, John Devitt, the brother and sister Jon and Ilsa Konrads of Australia, Judy Grinham and Anita Lonsbrough of England.

Peter Heatley of Scotland won gold in the Diving. In years to come Peter Heatley was appointed President of the Commonwealth Games Federation.

At the Closing Ceremony of these Games the following message from Queen Elizabeth ll was read:-

'I want to take this opportunity to speak to all Welsh people, not only in this Arena but wherever they may be. The British Empire and Commonwealth Games in the capital, together with all the activities of the Festival of Wales, have made this a memorable year for the Principality. I have therefore, decided to mark it further by an act which will, I hope, give as much pleasure to all Welshmen as it does to me. I intend to create my son Charles, Prince of Wales today. When he is grown up, I will present him to you at Caernarvon.' (Index 6)

1962 PERTH   Athletics. Cycling. Lawn Bowls. Fencing. Weightlifting. Swimming. Rowing. Boxing. Wrestling **(9)**

The star athlete at these Games was Peter Snell from New Zealand, - a powerful runner from New Zealand and a winner of gold medals at the 1960 Rome Olympic Games as well as at Tokyo in 1964.

Brian Phelps of England won two gold medals in the Diving events, and Anita Lonsborough also from England went one step further by winning three gold medals in Swimming. The Canadian swimmer, Richard William Duncan (Dick) Pound, became the champion in the 100 m. Freestyle. Dick Pound was to become famous for his efforts, as a member of the International Olympic Committee, in the fight against drug abuse. He also became the outspoken President of the World Anti-Doping Agency (WADA).

Ieuan Owen, was successful in winning a silver medal for Wales in Weightlifting at these Games. Ieuan went on to win a bronze medal in 1966, and silvers in 1970 and 1974. Thereby winning a medal in four Games but unfortunately being out of the medals in 1978. As well as Ieuan's silver medal in 1962, the remainder of the Welsh weightlifting team, *Peter Arthur,* silver and *Horace Johnson,* bronze were successful, thus becoming the only Welsh weightlifting team when all its team members brought medals back home.

1966   KINGSTON Athletics. Badminton. Cycling. Fencing. Weightlifting. Swimming. Boxing. Shooting. Wrestling **(9)**

Wales won 3 gold medals at Kingston. ***Lynn Davies,*** Athletics, ***Chung Kum Weng,*** Weightlifting, and ***Lord John Swansea,*** Shooting. Louis Martin won his second gold medal for England in weightlifting. Louis was born in Jamaica but lived in England and was a world champion, so he had wonderful support from the Jamaicans at the Games. Kipcho Keino from Kenya won his races with ease, the one mile in 3:55.3 and the three mile in 12:57.4.

Valerie Young emulated her 1962 successes by winning the Shot and the Discus throws. Betsy Sullivan was Jamaica's representative in the Springboard diving for women and is the youngest ever Commonwealth Games competitor. She was ten years old.

1970   EDINBURGH   Athletics. Badminton. Cycling. Lawn Bowls. Fencing. Weightlifting. Swimming. Boxing. Wrestling **(9)**

Two brothers from Scotland became the stars of these Games. Ian Stewart won the 5,000 m. in 13:22.8, and Laughlin (Lachie) Stewart the 10,000 m. in 28:11.8. Louis Martin won his third weightlifting gold medal for England. The winner of the gold medal in the Pole Vault was Michael Bull from Northern Ireland. He was the first athlete in the history of the Games to pole vault over 16 feet when he cleared 16' 8.75". Raelene Boyle, a very young athlete from Australia won the 100 and 200 m. together with the 4 x 100 m Relay . ***Welsh team captain Lynn Davies*** won his second gold medal in the long jump with 8.06 m.

17 year old Marilyn Neufville of Jamaica, set a world record when winning the women's 400 m. For the third successive Games, Pamela Kilburn of Australia followed her successes at Perth and Kingston when she lifted her third gold in the 100 m. Hurdles. Outstanding in the swimming pool was Michael Wendell of Australia, winning 4 gold medals and one silver.

These were the Games where the term 'Friendly Games' was coined as an unofficial name for the Games, and is used even to this day.

1974   CHRISTCHURCH Athletics. Badminton. Boxing. Cying. Fencing. Lawn Bowls. Swimming. Shooting. Weightlifting. Wrestling

The strong favourite for the 1,500 m. was New Zealander, John Walker, so it was a great disappointment to the home crowd when a relatively unknown Tanzanian athlete, Filbert Bayi won and at the same time set a new world record with 3:32.16 Two sprinters, Don Quarrie from Jamaica and Raelene Boyle of Australia, replicated their 1970 successes by winning their respective 100 m. and 200 m. races in 1974. Mary Peters from Northern Ireland won the women's Pentathlon while her fellow teammate Michael Bull won the men's Decathlon.

1978   EDMONTON   Athletics. Badminton. Boxing. Cycling. Gymnastics. Lawn Bowls. Shooting. Swimming. Weightlifting. Wrestling **(10)**

The gold medal for the 110 m Hurdles went to ***Berwyn Price of Wales***.   The shock winner of the Marathon was the Tanzanian, Gidemas Shahanga. Jerome Drayton of Canada was the expected winner as the Tasmanian was unknown. It is sad to know that Shahanga was killed in a road accident a year later This was the year that Englishman Daley Thompson, began his successful career in international athletics when he won the Decathlon.

Another athlete who gave notice of impending success was the boxer, Barry McGuigan, from Northern Ireland who won the gold medal in the Featherweight division. Gymnastics made its debut at these Games.

We must note here the achievement of Canadian cyclist Jocelyn Lovell who won three gold medals in the 1,000 m. Time Trial, 10 mile and in the over 10 mile Tandem.

Ieuan Owen of Wales had a long and successful career in Weightlifting, having competed in five Commonwealth Games, winning 3 Silver medals and 1 bronze but unfortunately he was beaten by Father Time in his fifth Games when he placed 7th in the 67.5 kg category. Ieuan was honoured to be the Welsh flag carrier at the 1966 Games in Kingston, Jamaica and at Christchurch in 1974 he was also further dignified by being selected as captain of the Welsh Team.

1982   BRISBANE Archery. Athletics. Badminton. Boxing. Cycling, Lawn Bowls. Shooting. Swimming. Weightlifting. Wrestling **(10)**

These Games were opened in the presence of Matilda. Matilda was the mascot chosen for the Games. It was a gigantic imitation kangaroo.

All the signage included replicas of Matilda which was a trend followed at many other Games. Archery became a Commonwealth Games sport. The highlight was a close competition involving Neroli Fairhall of New Zealand who had to score three Bulls with her final three arrows to win, which she did. The interesting point here was that Neroli was shooting from her wheelchair. Some people said that this gave her an advantage!

In the 200m Allan Wells of Scotland and Michael McFarlane of England finished in a dead heat in 20.43 seconds – the only time this had ever happened in the history of the Games. One world record was broken in swimming by Alex Bauman of Canada when he recorded 2:2.75 in the men's 200 m. Individual Medley.

1986   EDINBURGH   Athletics. Badminton. Boxing. Cycling. Lawn Bowls. Rowing. Shooting. Swimming. Weightlifting. Wrestling **(10)**

Left to Right- John Jones-Pritchard, Myrddin John, Sir Geraint Evans, Tommy Rees. The officials opening the 1986 Games Appeal.

Sir Geraint Evans, C.B.E. was Chairman of the National Appeal Committee to send the Welsh Team to the XIII Games in Edinburgh in 1986. Sir Geraint proved to be a popular and industrious chairman resulting in the appeal being extremely successful. We were also extremely grateful for the usual contribution from the Sports Council for Wales towards sending the Welsh Team to the Games. The financial support given by the Sports Council for Wales for most Games has always been greatly appreciated.

Myrddin John receiving a donation from Cllr. John Parry, on behalf of Anglesey County Council, in the company of Glyn Jones, the Director of Leisure for the county.

Mike Wright, President of the Commonwealth Games Council for Wales, receiving a donation from Cllr. Myrddin Evans, Chairman of Dyfed. <u>Rear left to right</u> – Cllr. D.G.E. Davies, C.B.E., Chairman Education Committee, Hugh Morse, County Treasurer, Myrddin John, M.B.E. Cllr. David T. Davies, O.B.E., M.M., D.L., Chairman Dyfed Appeal

Cllr. G. Alun Williams, presenting a donation to Myrddin John on behalf of Gwynedd County Council.

Chairmen of the Committees who made up the National Appeal Committee:

Industry	Gooding. O.B.E. A.J.
South Glamorgan	Williams. Bryn
Dyfed	Roberts. Cllr. Heulyn
West Glamorgan	Wignall. Derek
Mid Glamorgan	Rees. Cllr. G.
Gwent	Davies. Cllr. A. Jim
Gwynedd	Davies. Dr. Jim A.
Anglesey	Williams. Cllr. W.J.

Gary Taylor competed in the 1986 weightlifting events but failed to complete one of the disciplines. Following the Games, Gary won the very popular television competition for the World's Strongest Man.

1990 AUCKLAND Athletics. Badminton. Boxing. Cycling. Gymnastics. Judo. Lawn Bowls. Shooting. Swimming. Weightlifting. **(10)**

Of the 639 medals to be won at these Games, Australia won 162 to top the unofficial medals' table with England second with 129. Wales was [6th] with 25. 29 countries were featured in the table, so Wales could be well pleased with its results and that Wales had been so successful. In weightlifting David Morgan and Andrew Davies both won three gold medals each. It was most unfortunate that these successes were marred by two competitors being found guilty of using performance enhancing substances despite the every effort to prevent this type of thing from happening.

An internal inquiry was held by the governing body as well as the Sports Council for Wales, without any unfavourable result in the coaching and organisation of the governing body of the sport in Wales. It was the same result when the Commonwealth Federation examined the incident.**(Index 7)** Wales was successful in winning gold medals in athletics by Kay Morley and Colin Jackson, Louise Jones, Cycling, and Robert Morgan, Diving, plus the six in weightlifting, to make a Total of ten gold medals.

This was the first time for Judo to be featured in the Games and Helen Duston won a silver medal. Bronze medals were won by Lisa Griffiths, Moira Sutton, Phillippa Knowles and James Charles.

Noel Duston, Welsh Judo Coach, celebrates with his daughter Helen after she won the silver medal in the 48 kg class for women. This was the first Judo medal to be won by Wales at the Games.

For the second time Tessa Sanderson, England, won the Javelin and Linford Christie won another gold medal for England in the 100 m. Merlene Ottey of Jamaica won the Women's 100 m. in 11.02 secs. and the 200m. in 22.76 secs.

1994   **VICTORIA**   Athletics. Badminton. Boxing. Cycling. Gymnastics. Lawn Bowls. Rowing. Shooting. Swimming. Weightlifting. Wrestling **(11)**

The 1994 Welsh Team with Ian Grist, M.P., Welsh Under Secretary and Sir Geraint Evans.

It has now become a tradition for each Games to have its mascot. In Victoria the choice was a whale whose name was Klee Wyck. Klee Wyck had a large smile and apparently the translation of Klee Wyck was 'the one that smiles'. It measured 7ft 6ins in height and its wide happy smile welcomed all people to the Games.

The number of competitors grew to 2,557 from 64 countries. These were the Games when South Africa were welcomed back since the

1958 Cardiff Games. This was also the Games when the Commonwealth lost another country when Hong Kong became a part of China.

The Welsh Team at the Opening Ceremony, Edmonton

Australia's famous Cathy Freeman, won the 200 and 400 m. for women at these Games. Following these Games it was decided to introduce competitions for teams for the first time, and this is so to this day.

Colin Jackson won the gold medal in the 110 m. Hurdles with **Paul Gray** taking the bronze. **Colin Jackson** has given sterling service to Welsh achievement at Commonwealth Games but was never nominated for the captaincy nor as a flag bearer. It is a pity that this never happened as he epitomises all that is good in sport. Colin was a pleasant person who had dignity, was famous, a wonderful sense of humour and was a highly responsible person. It would have been an honour to have him as captain. It could be perhaps that Colin, due to his international commitments, was considered to be unavailable for the whole period of the Games and thus be unable to fulfil the duties of captaincy.

1998   **KUALA LUMPUR**   Athletics. Badminton. Boxing. Cricket. Cycling. Gymnastics. Hockey. Lawn Bowls. Netball. Rugby Sevens. Shooting. Swimming. Squash. Tenpin Bowling.Weightlifting. **(15)**

It was manifest that the Kuala Lumpur Games would be successful. The infinite and meticulous care taken with the initial bid procedures clearly indicated a desire for excellence. And it was a successful bid. This was the final Games of the millennium and the first by an Asian country; and in my opinion fully deserves the accolade of being the best ever Games, even by today's standard. 70 countries took part. Such was the excellence of every aspect of the Games that Kuala Lumpur gave a positive notice that it is capable of organising an Olympic Games and it would be no surprise if this should not happen one day. Up until these Games the maximum number of sports at any Games was 10, but on this occasion 15 sports were contested. The sports that had not previously been included in the Games programme were Tenpin Bowling, Cricket, Hockey, Netball, Rugby Sevens and Squash..

Welsh Gold medallists were, *Iwan Thomas* in Athletics in the 400m., *Kelly Morgan*, Badminton and *Desmond Davies* in Shooting. At these Games 670 medals were contested with Australia going home with 198 of these. Wales finished in tenth position with 15 medals. Twenty four countries won medals in the Kuala Lumpur Games.

It is gratifying to note that without exception the arrangements made by Wales, for all its athletes at all sixteen Games in the 20th Century, whatever the problems faced by each one, have been most ably discharged by the Commonwealth Games Councils of the time. Each one has contributed immensely and with pride to creating moments of historic sporting occasion.

COMMONWEALTH GAMES CHAMPIONS
1930 – 1998

ATHLETICS MEN

100 yards

1930	Williams. Percy	Canada	9.9 secs.
1934	Sweeney. Arthur W.	England	10.0 secs.
1938	Holmes. Cyril B.	England	9.7 secs.
1950	Treloar. John F.	Australia	9.7 secs.
1954	Agostini. Michael G	.Trinidad	9.6 secs.
1958	Gardner. Keith A.	Jamaica	9.4 secs.
1962	Antao. Seraphino	Kenya	9.5 secs.
1966	Jerome. Harry	Canada	9.4 secs.

100 m

1970	Quarrie. Donald. O.	Jamaica	10.2 secs.
1974	Quarrie. Donald. O.	Jamaica	10.4 secs.
1978	Quarrie. Donald. O.	Jamaica	10.03 secs.
1982	Wells. Allan	Scotland	10.02 secs.
1986	Johnson. Ben	Canada	10.07 secs.
1990	Christie. Linford	England	9.93 secs.
1994	Christie. Linford	England	9.91 secs.
1998	Boldon. Ato	Trinidad & Tobago	9.88 secs.

220 yards

1930	Englehart. Stanley E.	England	21.8 secs.
1934	Sweeney. Arthur W.	England	21.9 secs.
1938	Holmes. Cyril B.	England	21.2 secs.
1950	Treloar. John F.	Australia	21.5 secs.
1954	Jowett. Donald W.	New Zealand	21.5 secs.
1958	Robinson. Tom Augustus	Bahamas	21.0 secs.
1962	Antao. Seraphino	Kenya	21.1 secs.
1966	Allotey. Stanley F.	Ghana	20.7 secs.

200 m

1970	Quarrie. Donald. O.	Jamaica	20.5 secs.
1974	Quarrie. Donald. O.	Jamaica	20.7 secs.
1978	Wells. Allan	Scotland	20.12 secs.
1982	Wells. Allan	Scotland	20.43 secs.
1982	McFarlane.Michael	England	20.43 secs.
1986	Mahorn. Atlee	Canada	20.31 secs.
1990	Adam. Marcus	England	20.10 secs.
1994	Fredericks. Frankie	Namibia	19.97 secs.
1998	Golding. Julian	England	20.18 secs.

440 yards

1930	Wilson. Alex W.	Canada	48.8 secs.
1934	Rumpling. Godfrey L.	England	48.0 secs.
1938	Roberts. William	England	47.9 secs.
1950	Carr. Edwin W.	Australia	47.9 secs.
1954	Gosper. R.Kevin	Australia	47.2 secs.
1958	Singh. Milkha	India	46.6 secs.
1962	Kerr. George	Jamaica	46.7 secs.
1966	Mottley. W.	Trinidad	45.2 secs.

400 m

1970	Asati. Charles	Kenya	45.0 secs.
1974	Asati. Charles	Kenya	46.0 secs.
1978	Mitchell. Richard C.	Australia	46.34 secs.
1982	Cameron. Bert	Jamaica	45.89 secs.
1986	Black. Roger	England	45.57 secs.
1990	Clark. Darren	Australia	44.60 secs.
1994	Gitanga. Charles	Kenya	45.00 secs.
1998	*Thomas. Iwan*	*Wales*	*44.52 secs.*

880 yards

1930	Hampson. Thomas	England	1:52.4
1934	Edwards. Phil	British Guyana	1:54.2
1938	Boot. Vernon Pat	New Zealand	1:51.2
1950	Parlett. John	England	1:53.7
1954	Johnson. Derek I.	England	1:50.7
1958	Elliott. Herbert J.	Australia	1:49.3
1962	Snell. Peter G.	New Zealand	1:47.6
1966	Clough. Noel S.	Australia	1:46.9

800 m

1970	Ouko. Robert	Kenya	1:46.8
1974	Kipkurgat. John	Kenya	1:43.9
1978	Boit. Mike	Kenya	1:46.39
1982	Bourke. Peter	Australia	1:45.18
1986	Cram. Steve	England	1:43.22
1990	Tirop. Samuel	Kenya	1:45.98
1994	Konchella. Patrick	Kenya	1:45.18
1998	Kimutai. Japheth	Kenya	1:43.82

1 mile

1930	*Thomas. Reg H.*	England	4:14.0
1934	Lovelock. Jack E.	New Zealand	4:12.8
1938	*Alford. James W.*	*Wales*	*4:11.6*
1950	Parnell. William	Canada	4.11.0
1954	Bannister. Roger G.	England	3:58.8
1958	Elliott. Herbert J.	Australia	3:59.0
1962	Snell. Peter G.	New Zealand	4:04.6
1966	Keino. H. Kipchoge	Kenya	3:55.3

1,500 m

1970	Keino. H. Kipchoge	Kenya	3:36.6
1974	Bayi. Filbert	Tanzania	3:32.2
1978	Moorcroft. David	England	3:35.5
1982	Cram. Steve	England	3:42.37
1986	Cram. Steve	England	3:50.87
1990	Elliott. Peter	England	3:33.39
1994	Chesang. Reuben	Kenya	3:36.70
1998	Rotich. Laban	Kenya	3:39.48

3 mile

1930	Tomlin. Stanley A.	England	14:27.4
1934	Beavers. William J.	England	14:36.2
1938	Matthews. Cecil H.	New Zealand	13:59.6
1950	Eyre. Len	England	14:23.6
1954	Chataway. Christopher	England	13:35.2
1958	Halberg. Murray G.	New Zealand	13:15.0
1962	Halberg. Murray G.	New Zealand	13:34.2
1966	Keino. Kipchoge	Kenya	12:57.4

5,000 m

1970	Stewart. Ian	Scotland	13:22.8
1974	Jipcho. Ben W.	Kenya	13:14.4
1978	Rono. Henry	Kenya	13:23.04
1982	Moorcroft. David	England	13.33.00
1986	Ovett. Steve	England	13:24.11
1990	Lloyd. Andrew	Australia	13:24.86
1994	Denmark. Robert	England	13:23.00
1998	Komen. Daniel	Kenya	13:22.67

6 mile

1930	Savidon. John W.	New Zealand	30:49.6
1934	Penny. Arthur W.	England	31:00.6
1938	Matthews. Cecil H.	New Zealand	30:14.5
1950	Nelson. W. Harold	New Zealand	30:29.6
1954	Driver. Peter B.	England	29.09.4
1958	Power. W. David	Australia	28:47.8
1962	Kidd. Bruce	Canada	28:26.8
1966	Temu. Naftali	Kenya	28:14.6

10,000 m

1970	Stewart. J. Lachie	Scotland	28:11.8
1974	Tayler. Richard	New Zealand	27:46.4
1978	Foster. Brendan	England	28:13.65
1982	Shahanga. Gidamis	Tanzania	28:10.20
1986	Solly. Jonathan	England	27:57.42
1990	Martin. Eamonn	England	28:08.57
1994	Lameck. Agutu	Kenya	28:38.22
1998	Maina. Simon	Kenya	28:10.00

120 yards Hurdles

1930	Burghley. Lord	England	14.6 secs.
1934	Finlay. Donald Osborne	England	15.2 secs.
1938	Lavery. Tom P.	South Africa	14.0 secs.
1950	Gardner. Peter J.	Australia	14.3 secs.
1954	Gardner. Keith A.	Jamaica	14.2 secs.
1958	Gardner. Keith A.	Jamaica	14.0 secs.
1962	Raziq. Ghulam	Pakistan	14.1 secs.
1966	Hemery. David	England	14.1 secs.

110 m Hurdles

1970	Hemery. David	England	13.6 secs.
1974	Kimaiyo. Fatwell	Kenya	13.7 secs.
1978	*Price. Berwyn*	*Wales*	*13.70 secs.*
1982	McKoy. Mark	Canada	13.37 secs.
1986	McKoy. Mark	Canada	13.31 secs.
1990	*Jackson. Colin*	*Wales*	*13.08 secs.*
1994	*Jackson. Colin*	*Wales*	*13.08 secs.*
1998	Jarrett. Anthony	England	13.47 secs.

440 yards Hurdles

1930	Burghley. Lord	England	54.7 secs.
1934	Hunter. Alan	Scotland	55.2 secs.
1938	Loaring. John W.	Canada	52.9 secs.
1950	White. Duncan	Ceylon	52.5 secs.
1954	Lean. David F.	Australia	52.4 secs.
1958	Potgietor. Gerthardus	South Africa	4.7 secs.
1962	Roche. Ken J.	Australia	51.5 secs.
1966	Roche. Ken .J.	Australia	51.0 secs.

400 m Hurdles

1970	Sherwood. John	England	50.0 secs.
1974	Pascoe. Alan	England	48.8 secs.
1978	Kimaiyo. Daniel	Kenya	49.48 secs.
1982	Brown. Garry	Australia	49.37 secs.
1986	Beattie. Phil	Northern Ireland	49.60 secs.
1990	Akabusi. Kriss	England	48.89 secs.
1994	Matete. Samuel	Zambia	48.67 secs.
1998	Morgan. Dinsdale	Jamaica	48.28 secs.

Steeplechase 8 laps

1930	Bailey. George	England	9:52.0

2 miles Steeplechase

1934	Scarsbrook. Stanley	England	10:23.4

3,000 m Steeplechase

1962	Vincent. Trevor A.	Australia	8:43.4
1966	Welsh. R. Peter	New Zealand	8:29.6
1970	Manning. Anthony P	Australia	8:26.2
1974	Jipcho. Benjamin W.	Kenya	8:20.8
1978	Rono. Henry	Kenya	8:26.54
1982	Korir. Julius	Kenya	8:23.94
1986	Fell. Graeme	Canada	8:24.49
1990	Kariuki. Julius	Kenya	8:20.64
1994	Kipkoech. Johnstone	Kenya	8:14.72
1998	Kosgei. John	Kenya	8:15.34

Marathon

1930	Wright. Duncan McLeod	Scotland	2:43:43.0
1934	Webster. Harold	Canada	2:40:36.0

1938	Coleman. Johannes L.	South Africa	2:30:49.8
1950	Holden. Jack T.	England	2:32:57.0
1954	McGhee. Joseph	Scotland	2:39:36.0
1958	Power. W. David	Australia	2:22:45.6
1962	Kilby. Brian	England	2:21:17.0
1966	Alder. James N.C.	Scotland	2:22:07.8
1970	Hill. Ronald	England	2:09:28.0
1974	Thompson. Ian	England	2:09:12.0
1978	Shahanga. Gidamas	Tanzania	2:13:39.0
1982	Castella. Robert de	Australia	2:09:18.0
1986	Castella. Robert de	Australia	2:10.15.0
1990	Wakihursi. Douglas	Kenya	2:10:27.0
1994	Moneghetti. Stephen	Australia	2:11.49.0
1998	Moohabi. Thabiso	Lesotho	2:19:15.0

20 km Walking Road Race

| 1998 | A'Hern. Nicholas | Australia | 1:24:59 |

20 mile Walking Road Race (32.187 m)

| 1966 | Wallwork. Ron | England | 2:44.42.8 |
| 1970 | Freeman. Noel F. | Australia | 2:33.33.0 |

1974	Warhurst. John	England	2:35:23.0
1978	Flynn. Oliver	England	2:22:03.7
1982	***Barry. Steve***	***Wales***	***2:10:16.0***

30 km Walking Road Race

1986	Baker. Simon	Australia	2:07:47.0
1990	Leblanc. Guillaume	Canada	2:08:28.0
1994	A'Hern. Nicholas	Australia	2:07:53.0

50 km Walking Road Race

| 1998 | Saraanan. Gavindaswamy | Malaysia | 4:10:05 |

Long Jump

1930	Hutton. Leonard	Canada	7.20 m
1934	Richardson. Sam	Canada	7.17 m
1938	Brown. Harold	Canada	7.43 m
1950	Price. Neville	South Africa	7.31 m
1954	Wilmshurst. Kenneth	England	7.53 m
1958	Foreman. Paul	Jamaica	7.47 m
1962	Ahey. Michael	Ghana	8.05 m

1966	*Davies. Lynn*	*Wales*	*7.99 m*
1970	*Davies. Lynn*	*Wales*	*8.06 m*
1974	Lerwill. Alan	England	7.94 m
1978	Mitchell. Roy	England	8.06 m
1982	Honey. Gary	Australia	8.13 m
1986	Honey. Gary	Australia	8.08 m
1990	Alli. Yussuf	Nigeria	8.39 m
1994	Eregbu. Obinna	Nigeria	8.05 m
1998	Burge. Peter	Australia	8.22 m

Triple Jump

1930	Smallacombe. Gordon A.	Canada	4.75m
1934	Metcalfe. Jack P.	Australia	15.63m
1938	Metcalfe. Jack P.	Australia	15.49m
1950	Oliver. Brian T.	Australia	15.61m
1954	Wilmshurst. Kenneth S.	England	15.28m
1958	Tomlinson. Ian R.	Australia	15.74m
1962	Tomlinson. Ian R.	Australia	16.20m
1966	Igun. Samuel	Nigeria	16.40m
1970	May. Philip J.	Australia	16.72m
1974	Owusu. Joshua	Ghana	16.50m

1978	Connor. Keith	England	17.21m	
1982	Connor. Keith	England	17.81m	
1986	Herbert. John	England	17.27m	
1990	Hadjiandreou. Marius	Cyprus	16.95m	
1994	Golley. Julian	England	17.03m	
1998	Achike. Onochie	England	17.10m	

High Jump

1930	Viljoen. Johannes H.	South Africa	1.90m	
1934	Thacker. Edwin T.	South Africa	1.90m	
1938	Thacker. Edwin T.	South Africa	1.95m	
1950	Winter. John A.	Australia	1.98m	
1954	Ifeajuna. Emanuel A.	Nigeria	2.03m	
1958	Haisley. Ernest	Jamaica	2.05m	
1962	Hobson. Percy F.	Australia	2.10m	
1966	Pekham. Lawrence W.	Australia	2.08m	
1970	Pekham. Lawrence W.	Australia	2.14m	
1974	Windeyer. Gordon	Australia	2.16m	
1978	Ferragne. Claude	Canada	2.20m	
1982	Ottey. Milton	Canada		2.31m
1986	Ottey. Milton	Canada		2.30m

1990	Saunders. Clarence	Bermuda	2.36m
1994	Forsyth. Timothy	Australia	2.32m
1998	Grant. Dalton	England	2.31m

Pole Vault

1930	Pickard. Victor	Canada	3.73 m
1934	Apps. Sylvanus	Canada	3.81 m
1938	Du Plessis. Andries S.	South Africa	4.11 m
1950	Anderson. Tim D.	England	3.96 m
1954	Elliott. Geoffrey	England	4.26 m
1958	Elliott. Geoffrey	England	4.16 m
1962	Bickle. Trevor S.	Australia	4.49 m
1966	Bickle. Trevor S.	Australia	4.80 m
1970	Bull. Michael A.	Northern Ireland	5.10 m
1974	Baird. Donald	Australia	5.05 m
1978	Simpson. Bruce	Canada	5.10 m
1982	Boyd. Ray	Australia	5.20 m
1986	Ashurst. Andrew	England	5.30 m
1990	Arkell. Simon	Australia	5.35 m
1994	*Winter. Neil*	*Wales*	*5.40 m*
1998	Botha. Riaan	South Africa	5.60 m

Shot Put

1930	Hart. Hendrick B.	South Africa	14.58m
1934	Hart. Hendrick B.	South Africa	14.67m
1938	Fouche. Louis A.	South Africa	14.48m
1950	Tuicakau. Mataika	Fiji	14.63m
1954	Savidge. John A.	England	16.77m
1958	Rowe. Arthur	England	17.57m
1962	Lucking. Martin	England	18.08m
1966	Steen. David	Canada	18.79m
1970	Steen. David	Canada	19.21m
1974	Capes. Geoffrey	England	20.74m
1978	Capes. Geoffrey	England	19.77m
1982	Pauletto. Bruno	Canada	19.55m
1986	Cole. Billy	England	18.16m
1990	Williams. Simon	England	18.54m
1994	Simson. Matthew	England	19.49m
1998	Lambrechts. Burger	South Africa	20.01m

Discus

1930	Hart. Hendrick B.	South Africa	41.43m
1934	Hart. Hendrick B.	South Africa	41.53m
1938	Coy. Eric E.	Canada	44.76m
1950	Reed. Ian M.	Australia	47.74m
1954	Du Plessis. Stephanus J.	South Africa	51.70m
1958	Du Plessis. Stephanus J.	South Africa	55.94m
1962	Selvey. Warwick P.	Australia	56.48m
1966	Mills. Leslie R.	New Zealand	56.19m
1970	Puce. George	Canada	59.02m
1974	Tait. Robert D.	New Zealand	63.08m
1978	Chambul. Borys	Canada	59.70m
1982	Cooper. Bradley	Bahamas	64.04m
1986	Lazdins. Raymond	Canada	58.86m
1990	Olukaju. Adewale	Nigeria	62.62m
1994	Reiterer. Werner	Australia	62.76m
1998	Weir. Robert	England	64.42m

Hammer Throw

1930	Nokes. Malcolm C.	England	47.13m
1934	Nokes. Malcolm C.	England	48.25m
1938	Sutherland. George W.	Canada	48.71m
1950	Clark. Duncan M.	Scotland	49.94m
1954	Iqbal. Muhammad	Pakistan	55.37m
1958	Ellis. Michael J.	England	62.90m
1962	Payne. A. Howard	England	61.65m
1966	Payne. A. Howard	England	61.98m
1970	Payne. A. Howard	England	67.80m
1974	Chipchase. Ian	England	69.56m
1978	Farmer. Peter John	Australia	71.10m
1982	Weir. Robert	England	75.08m
1986	Smith. David	England	74.06m
1990	Carlin. Sean	Australia	75.66m
1994	Carlin. Sean	Australia	73.48m
1998	Rendell. Stuart	Australia	74.71m

Javelin

1930	Lay. Stanley A.	New Zealand	63.13m
1934	Dixon. Robert	Canada	60.02m
1938	Courtwright. James	Canada	62.80m
1950	Raininen. Leo J.	Canada	57.11m
1954	Achurch. James D.	Australia	68.52m
1958	Smith. Colin G.	England	71.29m
1962	Mitchell. Alfred	Australia	78.11m
1966	Fitzsimons. John	England	79.78m
1970	Travis. David H.	England	79.05m
1974	Clover. Charles	England	84.92m
1978	Olsen. Phil	Canada	84.00m
1982	O'Rourke. Michael	New Zealand	89.48m
1986	Ottley. David	England	80.62m
1990	Backley. Steve	England	86.02m
1994	Backley. Steve	England	82.74m
1998	Corbett. Marius	South Africa	88.75m

Decathlon

1966	Williams. Ray	New Zealand	7270pts.
1970	Smith. Geoffrey J.	Australia	7492pts.
1974	Bull. Michael A.	Northern Ireland	7417pts.
1978	Thompson. Daley	England	8464pts.
1982	Thompson. Daley	England	8410pts.
1986	Thompson. Daley	England	8663pts.
1990	Smith. Michael	Canada	8525pts.
1994	Smith. Michael	Canada	8326pts.
1998	Hames. Jagan	Australia	8490pts.

4 x 110 yards Relay

1930	Adams. Ralph E.	Canada	42.2 secs.
1930	Brown. James R.	Canada	42.2 secs.
1930	Fitzpatrick. Johnny R.	Canada	42.2 secs.
1930	Miller. Leigh	Canada	42.2 secs.
1934	Davis. Everard Inseal	England	42.2 secs.
1934	Rangeley. Walter	England	42.2 secs.
1934	Saunders. George T.	England	42.2 secs.
1934	Sweeney. Arthur W.	England	42.2 secs.

1938	Brown. James	Canada	41.6 secs.
1938	Haley. Patrick	Canada	41.6 secs.
1938	Loaring. John Wilfrid	Canada	41.6 secs.
1938	O'Connor. Gerrard	Canada	41.6 secs.
1950	De Gruchy. William	Australia	42.2 secs.
1950	Johnson. David	Australia	42.2 secs.
1950	Gordon. Alastair K.	Australia	42.2 secs.
1950	Treloar. John Francis	Australia	42.2 secs.
1954	McFarlane. James D.	Canada	41.3 secs.
1954	Nelson. Harold P.	Canada	41.3 secs.
1954	Springbett. Edward B.	Canada	41.3 secs.
1954	Stonehous. Don	Canada	41.3 secs.
1958	Breaker. AdrianFrancis	England	40.7 secs.
1958	Radford. Peter Frank	England	40.7 secs.
1958	Sandstrom. Eric	England	40.7 secs.
1958	Segal. David Hugh	England	40.7 secs.
1962	Carter. Leonard Walter	England	40.6 secs.
1962	Jones. David Henry	England	40.6 secs.
1962	Meakin. Alfred F.	England	40.6 secs.
1962	Radford. Peter Frank	England	40.6 secs.
1966	Addy. Ebenezer C.	Ghana	39.8 secs.

1966	Addy. James Aryee	Ghana	39.8 secs.
1966	Allotey. Stanley F.	Ghana	39.8 secs.
1966	Mends. Banner K.	Ghana	39.8 secs.

4 x 100 m Relay

1970	Stewart. Errol	Jamaica	39.4 secs.
1970	Miller. Lennox	Jamaica	39.4 secs.
1970	Lawson. Carl	Jamaica	39.4 secs.
1970	Quarrie. Donald O.	Jamaica	39.4 secs.
1974	Lewis. Gregory	Australia	39.3 secs.
1974	D'Arcy. Lawrence	Australia	39.3 secs.
1974	Ratcliffe. Andrew	Australia	39.3 secs.
1974	Haskell. Graham	Australia	39.3 secs.
1978	Jenkins. David	Scotland	39.24 secs.
1978	Wells. Allan	Scotland	39.24 secs.
1978	Sharp. Cameron	Scotland	39.24 secs.
1978	McMaster. Andrew	Scotland	39.24 secs.
1982	Adegbehinge. Lawrence	Nigeria	39.15 secs.
1982	Adeyanju. Iziaq	Nigeria	39.15 secs.
1982	Eseme. Ikpoto	Nigeria	39.15 secs.
1982	Oyeledun. Samson O.	Nigeria	39.15 secs.

1986	Johnson. Ben	Canada	39.15 secs.
1986	Mahorn. Atlee	Canada	39.15 secs.
1986	McKoy. Marcus	Canada	39.15 secs.
1986	Williams. Desai	Canada	39.15 secs.
1990	Adams. Marcus	England	39.15 secs.
1990	Callendar. Clarence	England	38.67 secs.
1990	Christie. Linford	England	38.67 secs.
1990	Jarrett. Anthony A.	England	38.67 secs.
1990	Regis. John Paul L.	England	38.67 secs.
1994	Bailey. Donovan	Canada	38.39 secs.
1994	Gilbert. Glenroy	Canada	38.39 secs.
1994	Chambers. Carlton	Canada	38.39 secs.
1994	Surin. Bruny	Canada	38.39 secs.
1998	Campbell. Darren A.	England	38.20 secs.
1998	Chambers. Dwain A.	England	38.20 secs.
1998	Devonish. Marlon	England	38.20 secs.
1998	Gardener. Jason John	England	38.20 secs.
1998	Golding. Julian A.	England	38.20 secs.

4 x 440 yards Relay Men

1930	Brangwin. Kenneth Colin	England	3:19.4
1930	Cecil. David	England	3:19.4
1930	Leigh-Wood. Roger	England	3:19.4
1930	Townend. Henry	England	3:19.4
1934	Baker. Geoffrey Noel	England	3:16.8
1934	Rampling. Godfrey Lionel	England	3:16.8
1934	Rathbone. Denis Lyle	England	3:16.8
1934	Stonely. Crew Hallet	England	3:16.8
1938	Dale. William	Canada	3:16.9
1938	Fritz. William Duncan	Canada	3:16.9
1938	Loaring. John Wilfrid	Canada	3:16.9
1938	Orr. Lee	Canada	3:16.9
1950	Carr. Edwin William	Australia	3:17.8
1950	Gedge. George V.	Australia	3:17.8
1950	Humphreys. James W.	Australia	3:17.8
1950	Price. Ross Edward	Australia	3:17.8
1954	Dick. Allan	England	3:11.2
1954	Fryer. Peter Goodwin	England	3:11.2
1954	Higgins. Francis Peter	England	3:11.2
1954	Johnson. Derek James N.	England	3:11.2

1958	Day. Gordon Raymond	South Africa	3.08.1
1958	Evans. Gerald Greig	South Africa	3.08.1
1958	Potgieter. Gerhardus C.	South Africa	3:08.1
1958	Spence. Malcolm Clive	South Africa	3:08.1
1962	Kerr. George Ezekiel	Jamaica	3:10.2
1962	Khan. Lawrence G.	Jamaica	3:10.2
1962	Spence. Malcolm A.E .	Jamaica	3:10.2
1962	Spence. Melville	Jamaica	3:10.2
1966	Bernard. Kent Bede	Trinidad & Tobago	3:02.8
1966	Mottey. Wendell Adrian	Trinidad & Tobago	3:02.8
1966	Roberts. Edwin Anthony	Trinidad & Tobago	3:02.8
1966	Yearwood. Lennox	Trinidad & Tobago	3:02.8

4 x 400 m Relay

1970	Nyamau. Hezakiah	Kenya	3:03.6
1970	Sang. Julius	Kenya	3:03.6
1970	Ouko. Robert	Kenya	3:03.6
1970	Asati. Charles	Kenya	3:03.6
1974	Asati. Charles	Kenya	3:04.4
1974	Mysyoki. Francis	Kenya	3:04.4

1974	Koskei. Bill	Kenya	3:04.4
1974	Sang. Julius	Kenya	3:04.4
1978	Njiri. Washinton	Kenya	3:03.5
1978	Kimaiyo. Daniel	Kenya	3:03.5
1878	Koskei. William	Kenya	3:03.5
1978	Ngetich. Joel	Kenya	3:03.5
1982	Bennett. Todd Anthony	England	3:05.45
1982	Brown. Philip Andrew	England	3:05.45
1982	Cook. Gary Peter	England	3:05.45
1982	Scutt. Steven	England	3:05.45
1986	Akabusi. Kris	England	3:07.19
1986	Bennett. Todd Anthony	England	3:07.19
1986	Black. Roger Anthony	England	3:07.19
1986	Brown. Philip	England	3:07.19
1990	Kitur. David	Kenya	3:02.48
1990	Kitur. Samson	Kenya	3:02.48
1990	Kipkemboi. Simeon	Kenya	3:02.48
1990	Mwanzia. Stephen	Kenya	3:02.48
1994	McKenzie. David	England	3:02.14
1994	Cramptson. Peter	England	3:02.14
1994	Patrick. Adrian	England	3:02.14

1994	Ladejo. Duaine	England	3:02.14
1998	MacDonald. Michael	Jamaica	2:59.03
1998	Roxbert. Martin	Jamaica	2:59.03
1998	Gregory. Haughton	Jamaica	2:59.03
1998	Clarke. Davian	Jamaica	2:59.03

ATHLETICS WOMEN

100 yards.

1934	Hiscock. Eileen	England	11.3 secs.
1938	Norman. Decima	Australia	11.1 secs.
1950	Jackson. Marjorie	Australia	10.8 secs.
1954	Jackson. Marjorie	Australia	10.7 secs.
1958	Matthews-Willard.Marlene	Australia	10.6 secs.
1962	Hyman. Dorothy	England	11.2 secs.
1966	Burge. Dianne	Australia	11.6 secs.

100 m

1970	Boyle. A. Raelene	Australia	11.2 secs.
1974	Boyle. A. Raelene	Australia	11.3 secs.
1978	Lanaman. Sonia	England	11.27 secs.

1982	Issajenko. Angella	Canada	11.00 secs.
1986	Oakes. Heather	England	11.20 secs.
1990	Ottey. Merlene	Jamaica	11.02 secs.
1994	Onyali. Mary	Nigeria	11.06 secs.
1998	Sturrup. Chandra	Bahamas	11.06 secs.

220 yards.

1934	Hiscock. Secondeen	England	25.0 secs.
1938	Norman. Decima	Australia	24.7 secs.
1950	Jackson. Marjorie	Australia	24.3 secs.
1954	Jackson. Marjorie	Australia	24.0 secs.
1958	Mathews-Willard. Marlene	Australia	23.6 secs.
1962	Hyman. Dorothy	England	23.8 secs.
1966	Burge. Dianne	Australia	23.8 secs.

200 m

1970	Boyle. Raelene A.	Australia	22.7 secs.
1974	Boyle. Raelene A.	Australia	22.5 secs.
1978	Boyd. Denise	Australia	22.82 secs.
1982	Ottey. Merlene	Jamaica	22.19 secs.
1986	Issajenko. Angella	Canada	22.91 secs.

1990	Ottey. Merlene	Jamaica	22.76 secs.
1994	Freeman. Catherine	Australia	22.25 secs.
1998	Peris-Kneebone. Nova	Australia	22.77 secs.

440 yards.

| 1966 | Pollock. Judy F. | Australia | 53.0 secs. |

400 m

1970	Neufville. Marilyn F.	Jamaica	51.0 secs.
1974	Saunders. Yvonne	Canada	51.7 secs.
1978	Hartley. Donna	England	51.69 secs.
1982	Boyle. Raelene A.	Australia	51.26 secs.
1986	Flintoff-King. Debbie	Australia	51.29 secs.
1990	Yusuf. Fatima	Nigeria	51.08 secs.
1994	Freeman. Catherine	Australia	50.38 secs.
1998	Richards. Sandie	Jamaica	50.17 secs.

880 yards.

1934	Lunn. Gladys	England	2:19.4
1938	Boot. Vernon	New Zealand	1:51.2
1962	Willis. Dixie	Australia	2:03.7

| 1966 | Hoffman. Abigail | Canada | 2:04.3 |

800 m

1970	Stirling. Rosemary O.	Scotland	2:06.2
1974	Rendina. Charlene	Australia	2:01.1
1978	Peckham. Judith	Australia	2:02.8
1982	*McDermott. Kirsty*	*Wales*	*2.01.31*
1986	*Wade. Kirsty*	*Wales*	*2:00.94*
1990	Edwards. Diane	England	2:00.25
1994	Turner. Inez	Jamaica	2:01.74
1998	Mutola. Maria	Mosambique	1:57.60

1,500 m

1970	Ridley. Rita	England	4:18.8
1974	Reiser. Glenda	Canada	4:07.8
1978	Stewart. Mary	England	4:06.3
1982	Boxer. Christina	England	4:08.28
1986	*Wade. Kirsty*	*Wales*	*4:10.91*
1990	Chalmers. Angela	Canada	4:08.41
1994	Holmes. Kelly	England	4:08.86
1998	Maranga. Jackline	Kenya	4:05.27

3,000 m

1982	Audain. Anne	New Zealand	8:45.53
1986	Williams. Lynn	Canada	8:54.29
1990	Chalmers. Angela	Canada	8:38.38
1994	Chalmers. Angela	Canada	8:32.17

10,000 m

1990	McColgan. Liz	Scotland	32:23.56
1994	Murray. Yvonne	Scotland	31:56.97
1998	Wanjiru. Esther	Kenya	33:40.13

80 yards Hurdles

1934	Clark. Marjorie	South Africa	11.8 secs.
1938	Burke. Barbara	South Africa	11.7 secs.
1950	Strickland. S. Barbara	Australia	11.6 secs.
1954	Maskell. Edna	Northern Rhodesia	10.9 secs.
1958	Thrower. Norma C.	Australia	10.7 secs.
1962	Kilborn. Pamela	Australia	10.9 secs.
1966	Kilborn. Pamela	Australia	10.9 secs.

100 m Hurdles

1970	Kilborn. Pamela	Australia	13.2 secs.
1974	Vernon. Judy	England	13.5 secs.
1978	Boothe. Lorna	England	12.98 secs.
1982	Strong. Shirley	England	12.78 secs.
1986	Gunnell. Sally	England	13.29 secs.
1990	*Morley. Kay*	*Wales*	*12.91 secs.*
1994	Freeman. Michelle	Jamaica	13.12 secs.
1998	Russell. Gillian	Jamaica	12.70 secs.

400 m Hurdles

1982	Flintoff-King. Debbie	Australia	55.89 secs.
1986	Flintoff-King. Debbie	Australia	54.94 secs.
1990	Gunnell. Sally	England	55.38 secs.
1994	Gunnell. Sally	England	54.51 secs.
1998	Blackett. Andrea	Barbados	53.91 secs.

Marathon

1986	Martin. Lisa	Australia	2:26:07
1990	Martin. Lisa	Australia	2:55:28
1994	Rouillard. Carole	Canada	2:30:41
1998	Turland. Heather	Australia	2:41:24

10 km Road Walk

1990	Maxby. Kerry	Australia	45:03 secs.
1994	Maxby-Junna. Kerry	Australia	44:25 secs.
1998	Saville. Jane	Australia	43:57 secs.

Long Jump

1934	Bartholomew. Phyllis	England	5.46 m
1938	Norman. Decima	Australia	5.80 m
1950	Williams. Yvette W.	New Zealand	5.90 m
1954	Williams. Yvette W.	New Zealand	6.08 m
1958	Hoskins. Sheila H.	England	6.02 m
1962	Kilborn. Pamela	Australia	6.26 m
1966	Rand. Mary	England	6.36 m
1970	Sherwood. Sheila	England	6.73 m
1974	Oshikoya. Modupe	Nigeria	6.46 m
1978	Reeve. Susan	England	6.59 m
1982	Ferguson. Shun	Bahamas	6.91 m
1986	Oladapo. Joyce	England	6.43 m
1990	Fleming. Jane	Australia	6.78 m
1994	Boegman. Nicole	Australia	6.82 m
1998	Wise. Joanne	England	6.63 m

Triple Jump

1998	Hansen. Ashia	England	14.32m

High Jump

1934	Clark. Marjorie	South Africa	1.60 m
1938	Odam. Dorothy B.	England	1.60 m
1950	Odam-Tylor. Dorothy	England	1.60 m
1954	Hopkins. Thelma E.	Northern Ireland	1.67 m
1958	Mason. Michelle M.	Australia	1.70 m
1962	Woodhouse. Robyn	Australia	1.72 m
1966	Mason. Michelle	Australia	1.72 m
1970	Brill. Debbie A.	Canada	1.78 m
1974	Lawton. Barbara	England	1.84 m
1978	Gibbs. Katrina Mavis	Australia	1.93 m
1982	Brill. Debbie A.	Canada	1.88 m
1986	Stanton. Christine	Australia	1.92 m
1990	Murray. Tania	New Zealand	1.88 m
1994	Inverarity. Allison	Australia	1.94 m
1994	Weavers. Charmaine	South Africa	1.94 m
1998	Sorbeck. Hestrie	South Africa	1.91 m

Pole Vault

1998	George. Emma	Australia	4.20 m

Shot Put

1954	Williams. Yvette W.	New Zealand	13.95m
1958	Sloper. Valerie I.	New Zealand	15.54m
1962	Sloper – Young. Valerie I.	New Zealand	15.22m
1966	Sloper – Young. Valerie I.	New Zealand	16.50m
1970	Peters. Mary E.	Norther Ireland	16.13m
1974	Haist. Jane	Canada	16.12m
1978	Mulhall. Gael	Australia	17.10m
1982	Oakes. Judith	England	17.92m
1986	Martin. Gail	Australia	19.00m
1990	Augee. Myrtle S. M.	England	18.48m
1994	Oakes. Judith	England	18.16m
1998	Oakes. Judith	England	18.83m

Discus

1954	Williams. Yvette W.	New Zealand	32.18m
1958	Allday. Susan	England	45.91m
1962	Sloper – Young. Valerie I.	New Zealand	50.20m

1966	Sloper – Young. Valerie I.	New Zealand	49.78m
1970	Payne. C.Rosemary	Scotland	54.46m
1974	Hait. Jane	Canada	55.52m
1978	Ionesco. Carmen	Canada	62.16m
1982	Ritchie. Margaret	Scotland	62.98m
1986	Martin. Gail	Australia	56.42m
1990	Visaniari. Lisa-Marie	Australia	56.38m
1994	Contain. Daniela	Australia	63.72m
1998	Famuina. Beatrice	New Zealand	65.92m

Hammer

1998	Sosimenko. Deborah	Australia	66.56m

Javelin

1934	Lunn. Gladys	England	32.18m
1938	Higgins. Robina	Canada	38.28m
1950	McGibbon-Weekes. Charlotte	Australia	38.84m
1954	Swanpoel. Magdalena	South Africa	43.83m
1958	Pazera. Anna	Australia	57.40m
1962	Platt. Susan	England	50.25m
1966	Parker. Margaret	Australia	51.38m

1970	Rivers. Petra	Australia	52.00m
1974	Rivers. Petra	Australia	55.48m
1978	Sanderson. Tessa	England	61.34m
1982	Howland. Suzanne	Australia	64.46m
1986	Sanderson. Tessa	England	69.80m
1990	Sanderson. Tessa	England	65.72m
1994	McPaul. Louise	Australia	63.76m
1998	McPaul. Louise	Australia	66.96m

Pentathlon

1970	Peters. Mary E.	Northern Ireland	5148pts.
1974	Peters. Mary E.	Northern Ireland	4455pts.
1978	Jones – Konihowski. Diane	Canada	4768pts.

Heptathlon

1982	Nunn. Glynis	Australia	6282pts.
1986	Simpson. Judy	England	6282pts.
1990	Flemming. Jane	Australia	6695pts.
1994	Lewis. Debbie	England	6325pts.
1998	Lewis. Denise	England	6513pts.

440 yards Mixed Relay (220 110 110)

1934	Halstead. Eleanor	England	49.4 secs.
1934	Hiscock. Eileen Mary	England	49.4 secs.
1934	Maguire. Elsie Evelyn	England	49.4 secs.
1938	Coleman. Jean	Australia	49.1 secs.
1938	Norman. Decima	Australia	49.1 secs.
1938	Wearne. Alice Eileen	Australia	49.1 secs.
1950	Johnston. Verna	Australia	47.9 secs.
1950	Nelson. Marjorie	Australia	47.9 secs.
1950	Strickland. Shirley Barbara	Australia	47.9 secs.

4 x 110 m Relay

1954	Cripps. Winsome	Australia	46.8 secs.
1954	Fogarty. Nancy N.	Australia	46.8 secs.
1954	Nelson. Marjorie	Australia	46.8 secs.
1954	Wallace. Gwendoline	Australia	46.8 secs.
1958	Hyman. Dorothy	England	45.3 secs.
1958	Paul. June Florence	England	45.3 secs.
1958	Weston. Violet	England	45.3 secs.
1958	Young. Heather Jay	England	45.3 secs.
1962	Beasley. Genys Anne	Australia	46.6 secs.
1962	Bennett. Joyce Elaine	Australia	46.6 secs.

1962	Cox. Paula Joyce	Australia	46.6 secs.
1962	Cuthbert. Elizabeth	Australia	46.6 secs.
1966	Bennett. Joyce Elaine	Australia	45.0 secs.
1966	Burge. Dianne Marie	Australia	45.0 secs.
1966	Lamy. Jennifer Frances	Australia	45.0 secs.
1966	Ryan. Pamela	Australia	45.0 secs.

4 x 100 m Relay

1970	Lamy. Jennifer Frances	Australia	44.1 secs.
1970	Kilborn. Pamela	Australia	44.1 secs.
1970	Hoffman. Marion	Australia	44.1 secs.
1970	Boyle. Raelene A.	Australia	44.1 secs.
1974	Lamy. Jennifer Frances	Australia	43.5 secs.
1974	Robertson. Denise	Australia	43.5 secs.
1974	Boak. Robin	Australia	43.5 secs.
1974	Boyle. Raelene A.	Australia	43.5 secs.
1978	Goddard. Beverly	England	43.70 secs.
1978	Smallwood. Kathryn	England	43.70 secs.
1978	Colyear. Sharon	England	43.70 secs.
1978	Lanaman. Sonia May	England	43.70 secs.
1982	Callender. Beverley L	England	43.15 secs.

1982	Cook. Kathryn Jane	England	43.15 secs.
1982	Hoyte. Wendy Patricia	England	43.15 secs.
1982	Lanaman. Sonia May	England	43.15 secs.
1986	Baptiste. Joan Jeanetta	England	43.39 secs.
1986	Cook. Kathryn Jane	England	43.39 secs.
1986	Oakes. Heather Regina	England	43.39 secs.
1986	Thomas. Paula	England	43.39 secs.
1990	Dunstan. Monique	Australia	43.87 secs.
1990	Freeman. Catherine	Australia	43.87 secs.
1990	Johnson. Kerry	Australia	43.87 secs.
1990	Sambell. Kathy	Australia	43.87 secs.
1994	Idehev. Faith	Australia	42.99 secs.
1994	Onysli. Mary	Australia	42.99 secs.
1994	Opara-Thompson. Christy	Australia	42.99 secs.
1994	Tombiri. Mary	Australia	42.99 secs.
1998	Van-Heer. Tania	Augustrala	43.39 secs.
1998	Hewitt. Lauren	Australia	43.39 secs.
1998	Cripps. Sharon	Australia	43.39 secs.
1998	Peris-Kneebone. N.	Australia	43.39 secs.

660 yards Mixed Relay (2 x 220. 2 x 110)

1934	Dearnley. Audrey	Canada	1:14.4
1934	Meagher. Eileen Aletha	Canada	1:14.4
1934	Palmer. Lilian Emily	Canada	1:14.4
1934	White-Lewington. Betty	Canada	1:14.4
1938	Coleman. Jean	Australia	1:15.2
1938	Norman. Decima	Australia	1:15.2
1938	Peake. Thelma	Australia	1:15.2
1938	Woodland. Joan	Australia	1:15.2
1950	Johnstone. Verna	Australia	1:13.4
1950	Nelson. Marjorie	Australia	1:13.4
1950	Shanley. Ann Patricia	Australia	1:13.4
1950	Strickland. Shirley Barbara	Australia	1:13.4

4 x 400 m Relay

1974	Elder. Verona Marolin	England	3:29.2
1974	Kennedy. Ruth	England	3:29.2
1974	Pettett. Susan	England	3:29.2
1974	Roscoe. Janette Veronica	England	3:29.2
1978	Elder. Veronica Marolin	England	3:27.19
1978	Hartley. Donna Marie L.	England	3:27.19

1978	Hoyte-Smith. Joslyn Y.	England	3:27.19
1978	Kennedy. Ruth	England	3:27.19
1982	Crooks. Charmaine A.	Canada	3:37.70
1982	Issajenko. Angela	Canada	3:37.70
1982	Kinsbeck. Mary	Canada	3:37.70
1982	Richardson. Cheryl	Canada	3:37.70
1986	Crooks. Charmaine A.	Canada	3:28.92
1986	Kingsbeck. Mary	Canada	3:28.92
1986	Payne-Wiggins. Manta	Canada	3:28.92
1986	Richardson. Jillian Cheryl	Canada	3:28.92
1990	Gunnell. Sally Jane	England	3:28.08
1990	Keogh. Linda	England	3:28.08
1990	Piggford. Angela Mary	England	3:28.08
1990	Stoute. Jennifer Elaine	England	3:28.08
1994	Gunnell. Sally Jane	England	3:27.06
1994	Joseph. Tracy Carol	England	3:27.06
1994	Keogh. Linda	England	3:27.06
1994	Smith. Phyllis	England	3:27.06
1998	Andrews. Susan	Australia	3:27.28
1998	Lewis. Tamsyn	Australia	3:27.28
1998	Naylor. Lee	Australia	3:27.28

1998   Van-Heer. Tania   Australia   3:27.28

BADMINTON

Singles Men

1966	Tan. Aik Mong	Malaysia
1970	Paulson. James E.	Canada
1974	Gunalan. Punch	Malaysia
1978	Padukone. Prakash	India
1982	Madi. Syed	India
1986	Baddeley. Stephen	England
1990	Sidek. Rashid	Malaysia
1994	Sidek. Rashid	Malaysia
1998	Choong. Han Wang	Malaysia

Singles Women

1966	Bairstow. Angela	England
1970	Beck. Margaret	England
1974	Gilkes(nee Perrin). Gillian	England
1978	Ng. Sylvia	Malaysia
1982	Troke. Helen	England
1986	Troke. Helen	England
1990	Smith. Fiona	England

| 1994 | Campbell. Lisa | Australia |
| *1998* | *Morgan. Kelly* | *Wales* |

Pairs Men

1970	Ng. Boon Bee	Malaysia
1970	Panchacharam.	Malaysia
1974	Talbot. Derek	England
1974	Stuart. Elliott	England
1978	Stevens. Raymond	England
1978	Tredgett. Michael	England
1982	Sidek. Razif	Malaysia
1982	Beng. Teong Ong	Malaysia
1986	Gilliand. William (Billy)Allan	Scotland
1986	Travers. Daniel (Dan)	Scotland
1990	Sidek. Razif	Malaysia
1990	Sidek. Jalaria	Malaysia
1994	Soon. Kit Cheah	Malaysia
1994	Beng. Kiang Soo	Malaysia
1998	Lee. Wan Wah	Malaysia
1998	Choong. Tan Fook	Malaysia

Pairs Women

1970	Boxall. Margaret	England
1970	Whetnall. Susan	England
1974	Beck. Margaret	England
1974	Gilkes(nee Perrin). Gillian	England
1978	Perry. Nora	England
1978	Statt. Anne	England
1982	Blackhouse. Claire	Canada
1982	Falardeau. Johanne	Canada
1986	Clark. Gillian	England
1986	Gowers. Gillian	England
1994	Muggeridge. Jo	England
1994	Wright. Joanne	England
1998	Kellog. Donna	England
1998	Goode. Joanne	England

Mixed Pairs

1966	Mills. Roger	England
1966	Bairstow. Angela	England
1970	Talbot. Derek	England
1970	Boxall. Margaret	England

1974	Talbot. Derek	England
1974	Gilks. Gillian M.	England
1978	Tredgett. Michael	England
1978	Perry. Nora	England
1982	Dew. Martin	England
1982	Chapman. Karen	England
1986	Scandolera. Mike	Australia
1986	Tucker. Audrey	Australia
1990	Chan. Chi Choi	Hong Kong
1990	Chan. Amy	Hong Kong
1994	Hunt. Chris	England
1994	Clark. Gillian	England
1998	Archer. Simon	England
1998	Goode. Joanne	England

Men's Team

1998	Ong. Ewe Hock	Malaysia
1998	Yong. Hock Kin	Malaysia
1998	Cheah. Soon Kit	Malaysia
1998	Yap. Kim Hock	Malaysia
1998	Lee. Wan Wah	Malaysia
1998	Choong. Tan Fook	Malaysia

Women's Team

1998	Mann. Julia	England
1998	Hallam. Tracey	England
1998	Pantane. Rebecca	England
1998	Kellog. Donna	England
1998	Goode. Joanne	England
1998	Davies. Joanne	England

Mixed Team

1986	Baddersley. Stephen	England
1986	Good. Andrew	England
1986	Clarke. Gillian	England
1986	Elliott. Fiona	England
1986	Gowers. Gillian	England
1986	Outterside. R.	England
1986	Tier. N.	England
1986	Troke. Helen	England
1986	Yates. Nick	England
1994	Archer. Simon	England
1994	Bradbury. Julie	England
1994	Clark. Gillian	England
1994	Hunt. Chris	England

1994	Knowles. Peter	England
1994	Lane. Suzanne Louis	England
1994	Muggeridge. Jo	England
1994	Nielsen. Anders	England
1994	Ponting. Nick	England
1994	Wright. Joanne	England

CYCLING

184 km Road Race Individual Massed Start Men

| 1998 | Sweet. Jay | Australia | 4:31:56.00 |

92 km Road Race Individual Massed Start Women

| 1998 | Bessette. Lyne | Canada | 2:24:59.00 |

Time Trial Road Race Women

| 1998 | Wilson. Anna | Australia | 37:34.00 |

Time Trial Road Race Men

| 1998 | Wohlberg. Eric | Canada | 53:15.00 |

Team Time Trial Road Race Women

1994	Nolan. Louise	Australia	1:04:03.20
1994	Reardon. Catherine Susan	Australia	1:04:03.20
1994	Victor. Rachel Marianne	Australia	1:04.03.20
1994	Watt. Kathryn Anne	Australia	1:04:03.20

20 km Scratch Men

| 1998 | Rogers. Michael | Australia | 25:18.340 |

1,000 m Time Trial Men

1934	Gray. Edgar	Australia	1:16.4
1938	Porter. Robert	Australia	1:15.2
1950	Mockridge. Russell	Australia	1:13.4
1954	Ploog. Richard	Australia	1:12.5
1954	Swift. Alfred	South Africa	1:12.5
1958	Tong. Neville	England	1:12.1
1962	Bartels. Peter	Australia	1:12.9
1966	Gibbon. Roger	Trinidad & Tobago	1:09.6
1970	Kent. Harry D.	New Zealand	1:08.69
1974	Paris. Dick	Australia	1:11.85
1978	Lovell. Jocelyn	Canada	1:06.00

1982	Adair. Craig	New Zealand	1:06.95
1986	Vinnicombe. Martin	Australia	1:06.230
1990	Vinnicombe. Martin	Australia	1:05.572
1994	Kelly. Shane	Australia	1:05.386
1998	Kelly. Shane	Australia	1:04.018

4,000 m Individual Pursuit Men

1950	Cartwright. Cyril	England	5:16.3
1954	Sheil. Norman L.	England	5:03.5
1958	Sheil. Norman L.	England	5:10.2
1962	Langshaw. Maxwell	Australia	5:08.8
1966	Porter. Hugh	England	4:56.6
1970	Hallam. Ian	England	5:01.4
1974	Hallam. Ian	England	5:05.46
1978	Richards. Michael	New Zealand	4:49.74
1982	Turtur. Michael	Australia	4:50.99
1986	Woods. Dean	Australia	4:27.767
1990	Anderson. Gary John	New Zealand	4:44.610
1994	McGee. Bradley John	Australia	4:31.371

4,000 m Team Pursuit Men

1974	Bennet. Michael	England	4:10.5
1974	Evans. Richard	England	4:10.5
1974	Hallam. Ian	England	4:10.5
1974	Moore. William	England	4:10.5
1978	Fitzgerald. Colin John	Australia	4:29.43
1978	Nichols. Kevin John	Australia	4:29.43
1978	Sutton. Gary John	Australia	4:29.43
1978	Sutton. Shane John	Australia	4:29.43
1982	Grenda. Michael Ronald	Australia	4:26.09
1982	Nichols. Kevin John	Australia	4:26.09
1982	Turtur, Michael Colin	Australia	4:26.09
1982	West. Gary Martin	Australia	4:26.09
1986	Clarke. Glenn	Australia	4:26.94
1986	Dutton. Brett Allan	Australia	4:26.94
1986	McCarney. Wayne	Australia	4:26.94
1986	Turtur. Michael Colin	Australia	4:26.94
1986	Woods. Dean Anthony	Australia	4:26.94
1990	Anderson. Gary John	New Zealand	4:22.760
1990	Connell. Craig	New Zealand	4:22.760
1990	Donnelly. Nigel	New Zealand	4:22.760

1990	McLeay. Glen	New Zealand	4:22.760
1990	Williams. Stuart	New Zealand	4:22.760
1994	Aitken. Brett	Australia	4:10.485
1994	McGee. Bradley John	Australia	4:10.485
1998	Lancaster. Brett	Australia	4:13.405
1998	Lyons. Timothy	Australia	4:13.405
1998	McGee. Bradley John	Australia	4:13.405
1998	Roberts. Luke	Australia	4:13.405
1998	Rogers. Michael	Australia	4:13.405

100 km Road Race Men

1938	Binneman. Hendrick	South Africa	2:53:29.6
1950	Sutherland. Hector	Australia	3:13.06.4
1954	Thompson. Eric G.	England	2:44:08.1

120 mile Road Race Men

1958	Booty. Ray	New Zealand	5:16:33.7
1962	Mason. Wesley	England	5:20:26.2
1966	Buckley. Peter	Isle of Man	5:07:52.5

164 km Road Race Men

| 1970 | Biddle. Bruce W. | New Zealand | 4:38:06.0 |

183 km Road Race Men

| 1974 | Sefton. K. Clyde | Australia | 5:07:16.7 |

188 km Road Race Men

| 1978 | Anderson. Philip Grant | Australia | 4:22:34.41 |

184 km Road Race Men

1982	Elliott. Malcolm	England	4:34:40.06
1986	Curran. Paul	England	4:08.50.00
1990	Miller. Graeme John	New Zealand	4:34:00.19
1994	Rendell. Max	New Zealand	4:46:07.91

Sprint Tandem Men

1970	Johnson. Gordon	Australia	11.5 secs.
1970	Jonker. Ron	Australia	11.5 secs.
1974	Crutchlow. Ernest	England	10.71 secs.
1974	Cooke. Geoffrey	England	10.71 secs.
1978	Lovell. Jocelyn	Canada	15.32 secs.
1978	Singleton. Gordon	Canada	15.32 secs.

3,000 m Individual Pursuit Women

1990	Harris. Madonna	New Zealand	3:54.670
1994	Watt. Kathryn Anne	Australia	3:48.522
1998	Ulmer. Sarah	New Zealand	3:41.667

1,000 m Sprint Men

1934	Higgins. Ernest W.	England	
1938	Gray. Edgar L.	Australia	
1950	Mockridge. Russell	Australia	
1954	Peacock. Cyril F.	England	
1958	Ploog. Richard	Australia	
1962	Harrison. Thomas	Australia	
1966	Gibbon. Roger	Trinidad & Tobago	
1970	Nicholson. John M.	Australia	
1974	Nicholson. John M.	Australia	
1978	Tucker. Kenrick Gregory	Australia	
1982	Tucker. Kenrick Gregory	Australia	
1986	Neiwand. Gary Malcolm	Australia	
1990	Neiwand. Gary Malcolm	Australia	
1994	Neiwand. Gary Malolm	Australia	10.587
1998	Hill. Darryn	Australia	10.258

1,000 m Sprint Women

1990	*Jones. Louise*	*Wales*	
1994	Dubnicoff. Tanya	Canada	12.129
1998	Dubnicoff. Tanya	Canada	11.490

24 km Points Race Women

| 1998 | Burns. Alayna | Australia | 34 pts. |

25 km Points Race Women

| 1994 | McGregor. Yvonne | England | 35 pts. |

10 mile Scratch Race Men

1934	McLeod. Robert	Canada	24:26.2
1938	Maxfield. William Wallace	England	24:44.0
1950	Heseltine. William	Australia	23:23.4
1954	Cooks. Lindsay J.	Australia	21:59.5
1958	Browne. Ian	Australia	21:40.2
1962	Adams. Douglas	Australia	22.14.8
1966	Alsop. Ian	England	21:46.3
1970	Lovell. Jocelyn	Canada	20:46.7
1974	Heffernan. Stephen	England	20:51.25
1978	Lovell. Jocelyn	Canada	20.05.81
1982	Nicholls. Kevin	Australia	19:56.56
1986	McCarney. Wayne	Australia	19:40.61
1990	Anderson. Gary John	New Zealand	19:44.20
1994	O'Grady. Stuart Peter	Australia	18:50.52

40 km Points Race Men

| 1998 | Tomson. Glen | New Zealand | 35 pts. |

50 km Points Race Men

| 1990 | Burns. Robert | Australia | 81 pts. |
| 1994 | Aitken. Brett | Australia | 38 pts. |

72 km Road Race Women

| 1990 | Watt. Kathryn Anne | Australia | 1:55:11.60 |
| 1994 | Watt. Kathryn Anne | Australia | 2:48:04.73 |

TENPIN BOWLING

Singles Women

| 1998 | Honeychurch. Cara | Australia | 6406 pts. |

Singles Men

| 1998 | Ang. Kenny | Malaysia | 6046 pts. |

Pairs Women

| 1998 | Honeychurch. Cara | Australia | 3678 pts. |
| 1998 | Nable. Maxine | Australia | 3678 pts. |

Pairs Men

1998	Ang. Kenny	Malaysia	3552 pts.
1998	Heng. Ben	Malaysia	3552 pts.

Mixed Pairs

1998	Ryan. Francis	Australia	3605 pts.
1998	Honeychurch. Cara	Australia	3605 pts.

LAWN BOWLS

Singles Women

| 1998 | Hartwell. Lesley | South Africa | |

Pairs Women

1986	Johnston. Margaret	Northern Ireland
1986	Elliott. Freda	Northern Ireland
1990	Howat. Judy	New Zealand
1990	Watson. P. Maria	Scotland
1994	Gourlay. Sarah	Scotland

Triples Women

1982	Bates. Anna	Zimbabwe
1982	Kennedy. Florence	Zimbabwe
1982	Mills. Margaret	Zimbabwe

Fours Women

1986	*Evans. Linda*	*Wales*
1986	*Jones. Rita*	*Wales*
1986	*Parker. Linda*	*Wales*
1986	*Rickets. Joan*	*Wales*
1990	Stevens. Marion	Australia
1990	Shaw. Daphne	Australia
1090	Rutherford. Dorothy	Australia
1990	Roche. Dorothy	Australia
1994	Becher. Hester	South Africa
1994	Grondein. Colleen	South Africa
1994	Pretorius. Anna	South Africa
1994	Trigwell. Lorna	South Africa
1998	Becher. Hester	South Africa
1998	Trigwell. Loma	South Africa
1998	Victor. Loraine	South Africa
1998	Steyn. Trish	South Africa

Singles Men

1930	Colquhoun. Robert	England
1934	Sprot. Robert	Scotland

1938	Harvey. Horace	South Africa
1950	Pirret. James	New Zealand
1954	Hodges. Ralph F.	Southern Rhodesia
1958	Danilowitz. Phineas	South Africa
1962	Bryant. David J.	England
1970	Bryant. David J.	England
1974	Bryant. David J.	England
1978	Bryant. David J.	England
1982	Wood. William	Scotland
1986	Dickinson. Ian	New Zealand
1990	Parrella. Ron	Australia
1994	Corsie. Richard	Scotland
1998	Garden. Roy	Zimbabwe

Pairs Men

1930	Hills. Tommy C.	England
1930	Wright. George W.	England
1934	Hills. Tommy C.	England
1934	Wright. George W.	England
1938	Macey. Lance L.	New Zealand
1938	Denison. William Walter	New Zealand

1950	Henry. Robert	New Zealand
1950	Exelby. Exelby P.	New Zealand
1954	Romsbotham. William J.	Northern Ireland
1954	Watson. Percy	Northern Ireland
1958	Morris. John M.	New Zealand
1958	Pilkington. Richard E.	New Zealand
1962	Robson. Hugh H.J.	New Zealand
1962	MacDonald. Robert L. M.	New Zealand
1970	King. Norman	England
1970	Line. Peter A.	England
1974	Christie. John	Scotland
1974	McIntosh. Alex	Scotland
1978	Liddell. Eric	Hong Kong
1978	Delgado. Clement	Hong Kong
1982	Watson. John	Scotland
1982	Gourlay. David	Scotland
1986	Adrian. George	Scotland
1986	Knox. Grant	Scotland
1990	Morris. Trevor	Australia
1990	Schuback. Ian	Australia
1994	Johnston. Rex Winfred	Australia

1994	Curtis. Cameron	Australia
1998	Duprez. Brett	Australia
1998	Jacobson. Mark	Australia

Fours Men

1930	Edney. J.	England
1930	Frich. J.	England
1930	Gudgeon. E.F.	England
1930	Hough. P.	England
1934	Biggin. F.	England
1934	Gudgeon. E.F.	England
1934	Slater. R.	England
1934	Tomlinson. P.D.	England
1938	Whittaker. William	New Zealand
1938	Robertson. H.Alec	New Zealand
1938	Jury. A. Ernie	New Zealand
1938	Bremmer. William	New Zealand
1950	Atkinson. H.	South Africa
1950	Blumberg. A.	South Africa
1950	Currer. H.	South Africa
1950	Walker. N.S.	South Africa

1954	Anderson. John W.H.	South Africa
1954	Mitchell. Frank N.	South Africa
1954	Randall. Wilfred A.	South Africa
1954	Wilson. George L.	South Africa
1958	Bettles. George H.	England
1958	King. Norman	England
1958	Phillips. Walter F.	England
1958	Scadgell. George H.	England
1962	Bryant. David J.	England
1962	Drysdale. Sidney	England
1962	Fleming. George T.	England
1962	Watson. John L.	England
1970	Delgado. Clement C.	Hong Kong
1970	Kitchell. Abdul R.	Hong Kong
1970	Da Silva. Roberto E.	Hong Kong
1970	Souza. George A.	Hong Kong
1974	Clark. Kerry	New Zealand
1974	Baldwin. Dave	New Zealand
1974	Somerville. John	New Zealand
1974	Jolly. Gordon	New Zealand
1978	Chok. K.F.R.	Hong Kong

1978	Da Silva. Roberto E.	Hong Kong
1978	Hassan. Majid	Hong Kong
1978	Dallah. O.K.	Hong Kong
1982	Dubbins. John	Australia
1982	Poole. Keith Frank	Australia
1982	Sharpe. Herbert	Australia
1982	Sherman. Donald Percy	Australia
1986	*Morgan. James*	*Wales*
1986	*Thomas. Havard*	*Wales*
1986	*Thomas. William*	*Wales*
1986	*Weale. Robert*	*Wales*
1990	Adrian. George	Scotland
1990	Bruce. Ian	Scotland
1990	Love. Denis	Scotland
1990	Wood. William	Scotland
1994	Burkett. Neil Anthony	South Africa
1994	Lofthouse. Alan	South Africa
1994	Piketh. Donald	South Africa
1994	Rayfield. Robert	South Africa
1998	McHugh. Martin	Northern Ireland
1998	McClure. Ian	Northern Ireland

1998	Booth. Neil	Northern Ireland
1998	McCloy. Gary	Northern Ireland

FENCING

Individual Foil Men

1950	Paul. Rene Roy R.	England
1954	Paul. Rene Roy R.	England
1958	Paul. Rene Roy R.	England
1962	Lekie. Alexander	Scotland
1966	Jay. Allan	England
1970	Breckin. Michael J.	England

Individual Foil Women

1950	Glen-Haig. Mary A.	England
1954	Glen-Haig. Mary A.	England
1958	Sheen. Gillian	England
1962	Coleman. Melody	New Zealand
1966	Wardell-Yerburgh. Janet	England
1970	Wardell-Yerburgh. Janet	England

Foil Team Men

1950	Anderson. R.J.	England
1950	Paul. Rene Roy R.C.	England
1950	Pilbrow. Arthur G.	England
1954	Cooperman. Arnold	England
1954	Jay. Allan Louis N.	England
1954	Paul. Rene Roy R.C.	England
1958	Cooke. H.	England
1958	Paul. Raymond R.R.V.	England
1958	Paul. Rene Roy R.C.	England
1962	Cooperman. Arnold	England
1962	Jay. Louis N.	England
1962	Paul. Rene Roy R.C.	England
1966	Hoskyns. Henry W.T.	England
1966	Jay. Allan Louis N.	England
1970	Brechin. M.J.	England
1970	Paul. Barry R.	England
1970	Paul. Grahame A.	England

Foil Team Women

1966	Parker. Shirley A.	England
1966	Pearce. Joyce L.	England
1966	Wardell-Yerburgh. Janet C.	England
1970	Green. S.	England
1970	Henley. C.	England
1970	Wardell-Yerburgh. Janet C.	England

Épée Individual Men

1950	Beaumont. Charles-Louis de	England
1954	Lund. Ivan Bernard	Australia
1958	Hoskyns. William	England
1962	Lund. Ivan B.	Australia
1966	Hoskyns. William	England
1970	Hoskyns. William	England

Épée Team Men

1950	Jay. Allan Louis N.	Australia
1950	Lund. Ivan Bernard	Australia
1954	De Beaumont, C.L.	England
1954	Jay. Allan Louis N.	England

1954	Paul. Rene Roy R.C.	England
1958	Hoskyns. Henry William F.	England
1958	Howard. M.J.P.	England
1958	Jay. Louis N.	England
1962	Howard. M.J.P.	England
1962	Jacobs. Peter	England
1962	Pelling. John A.	England
1966	Hoskyns. Henry William	England
1966	Jacobs. Peter	England
1966	Pelling. John A.	England
1970	Hoskyns. Henry W.F.	England
1970	Jacobs. Peter	England
1970	Johnson. W.R.	England

Sabre Individual Men

1950	Pillbrow. Arthur G.	England
1954	Amberg. Michael J.	England
1958	Hoskyns. Henry William F.	England
1962	Cooperman. Arnold	England
1966	Cooperman. Arnold	England
1970	Leckie. Alexander	Scotland

Sabre Team Men

1950	Anderson. R.J.	England
1950	Pilbrow. Arthur G.	England
1954	Asselin. Roland G.A.R.	Canada
1954	Krasa. Leslie	Canada
1954	Schwende. Carl	Canada
1958	Amberg. Michael J.	England
1958	Cooperman. Arnold	England
1958	Hoskyns. Henry William F.	England
1958	Verebes. Eugen M.	England
1962	Amberg. Michael	England
1962	Birks. G.T.	England
1962	Cooperman. Arnold	England
1966	Cooperman. Arnold	England
1966	Oldcorn. Richard	England
1966	Rayden. William J.	England
1970	Acfield. D.L.	England
1970	Cohen. R.A.	England
1970	Craig. R.	England

WEIGHTLIFTING

52 kg Snatch

| 1990 | Raghavan. Chandekharan | India | 105 kg |

52 kg Jerk

| 1990 | Raghavan. Chandekharan | India | 127.5 kg |

52 kg Total

1970	Vasil. George	Australia	639.75 lbs.
1974	McKenzie. Precious	England	215 kg
1978	Karunkaran. Ekambaram	India	205 kg
1982	Voukelatos. Nick	Australia	207.5 kg
1986	Hayman. Greg	Australia	212.5 kg
1990	Raghavan. Chandekharan	India	232.5 kg

56 kg Snatch

| 1990 | Punnuswamy. Rangaswamy | India | 110 kg |
| 1998 | Yagci. Mehmet | Australia | 107.5 kg |

56 kg Jerk

1990	Punnuswamy. Rangfaswamy	India	137.5 kg
1998	Wilson. Dharmaraj	India	140 kg

56 kg Total

1950	Hung. Tho Fook	Malaysia	655 lbs.
1954	Megennis. Maurice	England	620 lbs.
1958	Gaffley. Reg	South Africa	660 lbs.
1962	Kim. Chua Pung	Singapore	710 lbs.
1966	McKenzie. Precious	England	705 lbs.
1970	McKenzie. Precious	England	738 lbs.
1974	Adams. Mike	Australia	225.5 kg
1978	McKenzie. Precious	New Zealand	220 kg
1982	Laws. Geoffrey	England	235 kg
1986	Voukelatos. Nick	Australia	245 kg
1990	Punnuswamy. Rangaswamy	India	247.5 kg
1998	Pandian. K. Arwmugan	India	245 kg

60 kg Snatch

| 1990 | Stephen. Marcus | Nauru | 112.5 kg |

62 kg Snatch

| 1998 | Stephen. Marcus | Nauru | 125 kg |

60 kg Jerk

| 1990 | Sharma. Parvesh Chandler | India | 145 kg |

62 kg Jerk

| 1998 | Stephen. Marcus | Nauru | 167.5 kg |

60 kg Total

1950	Tong. Kog Eng	Malaysia	685 lbs.
1954	Wilkes. Rodney	Trinidad	690 lbs.
1958	Tan. Ser Cher	Singapôr	685 lbs
1962	Newton. George	England	720 lbs.
1966	*Chung. Kum Weng*	*Wales*	*743.5 lbs.*
1970	Perrins. George	England	754.75 lbs.
1974	Vasiliades. George	Australia	239.5 kg
1978	Mercier. Michel Alex	Canada	237.5 kg

1982	Willey. Dean	England	267.5 kg
1986	***Williams. Raymond***	***Wales***	***252.5 kg***
1990	Sharma. Parvesh Chandler	India	257.5 kg

62 kg Total

| 1998 | Stephen. Marcus | Nauru | 292.5 kg |

67.5 kg Snatch

| 1990 | Sharma. Parvesh Chandler | India | 130 kg |

69 kg Snatch

| 1998 | Groulx. Sebastien | Canada | 130 kg |

69 kg Jerk

| 1998 | Hidayat. Muhamad | Malaysia | 167.5 kg |

67.5 kg Total

1950	Halliday. Jim	England	760 lbs.
1954	Barberis. Vern	Australia	765 lbs.
1958	Tan. Howe Liang	Singapore	790 lbs.
1962	Goring. Carlton	England	775 lbs.

1966	Gittins. Harold	Trinidad	809.75 lbs
1970	Newton. George	England	821 lbs.
1974	Newton. George	England	260 kg
1978	Stellios. Basilios	Australia	272.5 kg
1982	*Morgan. David*	*Wales*	*295 kg*
1986	Willey. Dean	England	315 kg
1990	Sharma. Paramjit	India	295 kg
1998	Groulx. Sebastien	Canada	297.5 kg

75 kg Snatch

| 1990 | Mondal. Kamadhar | India | 135 kg |

77 kg Snatch

| 1998 | Rai. Satheesha | India | 147.5 kg |

75 kg Jerk

| 1990 | Laycock. Ron | Australia | 177.5 kg |

77 kg Jerk

| 1998 | Brown. Damian | India | 187.5 kg |

75 kg Total

1950	Gratton. Gerry A.	Canada	785 kg
1954	Halliday. Jim	England	800 lbs.
1958	Blenman. Blair	Barbados	795 lbs.
1962	Tan. How Liang	Singapore	860 lbs.
1966	St. Jean. Pierre	Canada	892.5 lbs.
1970	Pery. Russell Neville	Australia	909 lbs.
1974	Ebert. Anthony J.	New Zealand	275 kg
1978	Castiglione. Salvatore	Australia	300 kg
1982	Pinsent. Stephen	England	312.5 kg
1986	Stellios. Bill	Australia	302.5 kg
1990	Laycock. Ron	Australia	319 kg

77 kg Total

1998	Brown. Damian	Australia	327.5 kg

82.5 kg Snatch

1990	*Morgan. David*	*Wales*	*155 kg*

82.5 kg Jerk

1990	*Morgan. David*	*Wales*	*192.5 kg*

85 kg Snatch

1998	Ward. Stephen	England	157.5 kg

85 kg Jerk

1998	Griffin. Leon	England	192.5 kg

82.5 kg Total

1950	Varaleau. Jack	Canada	815 lbs.
1954	Gratton. Gerry A.	Canada	890 lbs.
1958	Caira. Phillip	Scotland	875 lbs.
1962	Caira. Philip	Scotland	900 lbs.
1966	Vakakis. George	Australia	925.5 lbs
1970	Ciancio. Nick	Australia	986.5 lbs.
1974	Ford. Tony	England	302.5 kg
1978	Kabbas. Robert	Australia	322.5 kg
1982	Burrowes. Newton	England	325 kg
1986	*Morgan. David*	*Wales*	*350 kg*
1990	*Morgan. David*	*Wales*	*347.5 kg*

85 kg Total

1998	Griffin. Leon	England	347.5 kg

90 kg Snatch

| 1990 | Dawkins. Duncan | England | 162.5 kg |

94 kg Snatch

| 1998 | Kounev. Kiri | Australia | 165 kg |

90 kg Jerk

| 1990 | Dawkins. Duncan | England | 195 kg |

94 kg Jerk

| 1998 | Kounev. Kiri | Australia | 205 kg |

90 kg Total

1954	Daly. Keevil	Canada	880 lbs.
1958	Santos. Manny	Australia	890 lbs.
1962	Martin. Louis	England	1035 lbs.
1966	Martin. Louis	England	1019.25 lbs.
1970	Martin. Louis	England	1008.25 lbs.
1974	Ciancio. Nick	Australia	332.5 kg
1978	Langford. Gary Leroy	England	335 kg

1982	Kabbas. Robert	Australia	337.5 kg
1986	Boxall. Keith	England	350 kg
1990	Dawkins. Duncan	England	357.5 kg

94 kg Total

1998	Kounev. Kiri	Australia	370 kg

100 kg Snatch

1990	Saxton. Andrew	England	165 kg

105 kg Snatch

1998	Sandor. Akos	Canada	167.5 kg

105 + kg Snatch

1998	Liddel. Darren	New Zealand	165 kg

100 kg Jerk

1990	Saxton. Andrew	England	197.5 kg

105 kg Jerk

1998	Sandor. Akos	Canada	192.5 kg

105 + kg Jerk

1998	Liddel. Darren	New Zealand	202.5 kg

100 kg Total

1978	*Burns. John*	*Wales*	*340 kg*
1982	Orok. Oliver	Nigeria	350 kg
1986	Garon. Denis	Canada	360 kg
1990	Saxton. Andrew	England	362.5 kg

105 kg Total

1998	Sandor. Akos	Canada	360 kg

105 + kg Total

1998	Liddel. Darren	New Zealand	367.5 kg

110 kg Snatch

1990	Thomas. Mark	England	160 kg

110 kg Jerk

1990	Thomas. Mark	England	197.5 kg

110 kg Total

1950	Cleghorn. R. Harold	New Zealand	900 lbs
1954	Hepburn. Doug	Canada	1040 lbs.
1958	MacDonald. Ken	Australia	1005 lbs.
1962	Shannos. Arthur	Australia	1025 lbs.
1966	Oliver. Don	New Zealand	1096.25 lbs.
1970	Prior. Russell	Canada	1079.75 lbs.
1974	Prior. Russell	Canada	352.5 kg
1978	Prior. Russell	Canada	347.5 kg
1982	*Burns. John*	*Wales*	*347.5 kg*
1986	Roy. Kevin	Canada	375 kg
1990	Thomas. Mark	England	357.5 kg

110 kg+ Snatch

| *1990* | *Davies. Andrew* | *Wales* | *180 kg* |

110 kg+ Jerk

| *1990* | *Davies. Andrew* | *Wales* | *222.5 kg* |

110 kg+ Total

| 1970 | Rigby. Ray | Australia | 1102.5 lbs. |

1974	May. Graham	New Zealand	342.5 kg
1978	Cardinal. Jean-Marc	Canada	365 kg
1982	Lukin. Dean	Australia	377.5 kg
1986	Lukin. Dean	Australia	392.5 kg
1990	*Davies. Andrew*	*Wales*	*402.5 kg*

105 kg+ Total

1998	Liddel. Darren	New Zealand	367.5 kg

CRICKET

1998	Pollock. Shaun	South Africa
1998	Bacher. Adam	South Africa
1998	Gibbs. Herschelle	South Africa
1998	Kallis. Jacques	South Africa
1998	Dawson. Alan	South Africa
1998	Benkenstein. Dale	South Africa
1998	Crookes. Derek	South Africa
1998	Boje. Nicky	South Africa
1998	Elworthy. Steve	South Africa
1998	Ntini. Makhaya	South Africa

1998	Adams. Paul	South Africa	
1998	Williams. Henri	South Africa	
1998	Boucher. Mark	South Africa	
1998	Rindel. Mike	South Africa	
1998	Hudson. Andrew	South Africa	

GYMNASTICS

Artistic Team Competition Women

1978	Goermann. Monica	Canada	113.250 pts.
1978	Hawco. Sherry Louise	Canada	113.250 pts.
1978	Kelsall. Karen Barbara	Canada	113.250 pts.
1978	Schlegel. Elfi	Canada	113.250 pts.
1990	Lowing. Larissa	Canada	116.784 pts.
1990	Morin. Janet	Canada	116.784 pts.
1990	Strong. Lori	Canada	116.784 pts.
1990	Umeh. Stella	Canada	116.784 pts.
1994	Brady. Jacqueline	England	114.225 pts.
1994	Reeder. Annika	England	114.225 pts.
1994	Lusack. Zita	England	114.225 pts.
1994	Szymko. Karin	England	114.225 pts.

1998	McIntosh. Trudy	Australia	111.408 pts.
1998	McLaughlin. Zeena	Australia	111.408 pts.
1998	Slater. Allana	Australia	111.408 pts.
1998	Skinner. Lisa	Australia	111.408 pts.

Individual All round Women

1978	Schlegel. Elfi	Canada	38.25 pts.
1990	Strong. Lori	Canada	38.912 pts.
1994	Umeh. Stella	Canada	38.400 pts.
1998	McLaughlin. Zeena	Australia	37.917 pts.

Individual All round Rhythmic Women

| 1990 | Fuzesi. Mary | Canada | 37.650 pts. |
| 1994 | Takahashi. Kasumi | Australia | 36.850 pts. |

Rhythmic Rope Women

| 1990 | Walker. Angela | New Zealand | 9.300 pts. |

Rhythmic Ball Women

| 1990 | Gimotea. Madonna | Canada | 9.450 pts. |
| 1994 | Takahashi. Kasumi | Australia | 9.200 pts. |

Rhythmic Hoops Women

| 1990 | Fuzesi. Mary | Canada | 9.400 pts. |
| 1994 | Takahashi. Kasumi | Australia | 9.300 pts. |

Rhythmic Ribbon Women

| 1990 | Fuzesi. Mary | Canada | 9.400 pts. |
| 1994 | Takahashi. Kasumi | Australia | 9.200 pts. |

Rhythmic Clubs Women

| 1994 | Takahashi. Kasumi | Australia | 9.400 pts. |

Rhythmic Team Women

1994	Martens. Camille	Canada	106.900 pts.
1994	McLennan. Gretchen	Canada	106.900 pts.
1994	Richards. Lindsay	Canada	106.900 pts.

Uneven Parallel Women

1990	Allen. Monique Marie	Australia	9.875 pts.
1994	Stoyel. Rebecca	Australia	9.25 pts.
1998	Skinner. Lia	Australia	9.612 pts.

Floor Exercises Women

1990	Strong. Lori	Canada	9.887 pts.
1994	Reeder. Annika	England	9.750 pts.
1998	Reeder. Annika	England	9.675 pts.

Beam Women

1990	Strong. Lori	Canada	9.850 pts.
1994	Willis. Salli	Australia	9.075 pts.
1998	McIntosh. Trudy	Australia	9.550 pts.

Vault Women

1990	Jenkins. Nicola	New Zealand	9.712 pts.
1994	Umeh. Stella	Canada	9.556 pts.
1998	Mason. Lisa	England	9.231 pts.

Individual All round Men

1978	Delesalle. Philip	Canada	56.40 pts.
1990	Hibbert. Curtis	Canada	57.950 pts.
1994	Thomas. Neil	England	55.950 pts.
1998	Kravtsov. Andrei	Australia	54.675 pts.

Floor Exercise Men

1990	Thomas. Neil	England	9.750 pts.
1994	Thomas. Neil	England	9.662 pts.
1998	Kravtsov. Andrei	Australia	9.325 pts.

Pommeled Horse

1990	Dowrick. Brennan James	Australia	9.825 pts.
1994	Dowrick. Brennan James	Australia	9.425 pts.
1998	Kravtsov. Andrei	Australia	9.487 pts.

Rings Men

1990	Hibbert. Curtis	Canada	9.775 pts.
1994	McDermott. Lee	England	9.475 pts.
1998	Mamine. Pavel	Australia	9.337 pts.

Parallel Bars Men

1990	Hibbert. Curtis	Canada	9.800 pts.
1994	Hogan. Peter Ross	Australia	9.400 pts.
1998	Kravtsov. Andrei	Australia	9.637 pts.

Horizontal Bar Men

1990	Hibbert. Curtis	Canada	9.850 pts.
1994	Nolet. Alan	Canada	9.512 pts.
1998	Jeltkov. Alexander	England	9.425 pts.

Vault Men

1990	May. James	England	9.625 pts.
1994	Hudson. Bret	Australia	9.375 pts.
1998	Hutcheon. Simon	South Africa	9.537 pts.

Team Competition Men

1978	Choquette. Jean	Canada	165.55 pts.
1978	Delesalle. Philip L.	Canada	165.55 pts.
1978	Rothwell. Nigel	Canada	165.55 pts.
1978	Walstrom. Owen Carl	Canada	165.55 pts.
1990	Bobkin. Lorne	Canada	171.800 pts.
1990	Hibbert. Curtis	Canada	171.800 pts.
1990	Latendrese. Claude	Canada	171.800 pts.
1990	Nolet. Alan	Canada	171.800pts.
1994	Burley. Kristan	Canada	164.700 pts
1994	Ikeda. Richard	Canada	164.700 pts.

1994	Nolet. Alan	Canada	164.700 pts.
1994	Romagnoli. Travis	Canada	164.700 pts.
1998	Atherton. Andrew	England	162.275 pts.
1998	Heap. Craig	England	162.275 pts.
1998	Brewer. Ross	England	162.275 pts.
1998	Smethurst. John	England	162.275 pts.

HOCKEY WOMEN

1998	Allen. Katie	Australia
1998	Andrews. M.	Australia
1998	Annan. Alyson	Australia
1998	Dobson. Louise	Australia
1998	Haslam. Juliet	Australia
1998	Hawkes. Rechelle	Australia
1998	Imison. Rachel	Australia
1998	Langham. Bianca	Australia
1998	Mott. Claire	Australia
1998	Mott. Nikki	Australia
1998	Peek. Allison	Australia
1998	Powell. Katrina	Australia
1998	Powell. Lisa	Australia

1998	Sowry. Justine	Australia
1998	Starre. Kate	Australia
1998	Towers. Kristen	Australia

JUDO

Extra Featherweight Class Men

| 1990 | Finney. Carl | England |

Extra Featherweight Class Women

| 1990 | Briggs. Karen | England |

Half Featherweight Class Men

| 1990 | Cooper. Brent | New Zealand |

Half Featherweight Class Women

| 1990 | Rendle. Sharon | England |

Featherweight Class   Men

| 1990 | Stone. R. | England |

Featherweight Class Women

1990   Cusack. Loretta   Scotland

Half Middleweight Class Men

1990   Southby. David   England

Half Middleweight Class   Women

1990   Bell. Diane   England

Middleweight Class Men

1990   White. Densign   England

Middleweight Class Women

1990   Mills. Sharon   England

Half Heavyweight Class Men

1990   Stevens. Raymond   England

Half Heayweight Class   Women

1990   Morris. Jane   England

Heavyweight Class Men

1990	Gordon. Elvis	England

Heavyweight Class Women

1990	Lee. Sharon	England

Open Weight Men

1990	Gordon. Elvis	England

Open Weight Women

1990	Lee. Sharon	England

SWIMMING

50 m Freestyle Men

1990	Baildon. Andrew	Australia	22.76 secs.
1994	Foster. Mark	England	23.12 secs.
1998	Foster. Mark	England	22.58 secs.

100 yards Freestyle Men

1930	Bourne. Munro	Canada	56.0 secs.

| 1934 | Burleigh. George | Canada | 55.0 secs. |

110 yards Freestyle Men

1938	Pirie. Robert	Canada	59.6 secs.
1950	Salmon. Peter	Canada	60.4 secs.
1954	Hendricks. Jon	Australia	56.6 secs.
1958	Devitt. John	Australia	57.0 secs.
1962	Pound. Richard	Canada	55.9 secs.
1966	Wenden. Michael. V.	Australia	54.0 secs.

100 m Freestyle Men

1970	Wenden. Michael V.	Australia	53.06 secs.
1974	Wenden. Michael V.	Australia	52.73 secs.
1978	Morgan. Mark Lincoln	Australia	52.70 secs.
1982	Brooks. Neil	Australia	51.14 secs.
1986	Fasala. Greg	Australia	50.95 secs.
1990	Baildon. Andrew	Australia	48.80 secs.
1994	Clarke. Stephen	Canada	50.21 secs.
1998	Klim. Michael	Australia	1:02.43 secs.

110 yards Breaststroke Men

| 1962 | O'Brien. Ian | Australia | 1:11.4 |
| 1966 | O'Brien. Ian | Australia | 1:08.2 |

100 m Breaststroke Men

1970	Mahoney. William	Canada	1:09.0
1974	Leigh. David	England	1:06.52
1978	Smith. Graham W.	Canada	1:03.81
1982	Moorhouse. Adrian	England	1:02.93
1986	Davis. Victor	Canada	1:03.01
1990	Moorhouse. Adrian	England	1:01.49
1994	Rogers. Philip	Australia	1:02.62
1998	Cowley. Simon Peter	Australia	1:02.00

110 yards Butterfly Stroke Men

| 1962 | Berry. Kevin | Australia | 59.6secs. |
| 1966 | Jacks. Ronald B. | Canada | 60.3 secs. |

100 m Butterfly Stroke Men

1970	MacDonald. A. Byron	Canada	58.44 secs.
1974	Rogers. Neil	Australia	56.58 secs.
1978	Thompson. Dan David	Canada	55.04 secs.
1982	Thompson. Dan David	Canada	54.71 secs.
1986	Jameson. Andrew	England	54.07 secs.
1990	Baildon. Andrew	Australia	53.98 secs.
1994	Miller. Scott	Australia	54.39 secs.
1998	Huegill. Geoffrey A.	Australia	52.81 secs.

100 yards Backstroke Men

| 1930 | Tippett. John W. | England | 1:05.4 |
| 1934 | Francis. Willie | Scotland | 1:05.2 |

110 yards Backstroke Men

1938	Oliver. Percy	Australia	1:07.9
1950	Wild. Jackie C.	South Africa	1:07.7
1954	*Brockway. John*	*Wales*	*1:06.5*
1958	Monckton. John J.	Australia	1:01.7
1962	Sykes. Graham	England	1:04.5
1966	Reynolds. Peter	Australia	1:02.4

100m Backstroke Men

1970	Kennedy. William R.	Canada	1:01.65
1974	Tonelli. Mark	Australia	59.65 secs.
1978	Patching. Glenn Scott	Australia	57.90 secs.
1982	West. Michael	Canada	57.12 secs.
1986	Tewksbury. Mark	Canada	56.45 secs.
1990	Tewksbury. Mark	Canada	56.07 secs.
1994	Harris. Martin	England	55.77 secs.
1998.	Versfeld. Mark	Canada	55.52 secs.

200 yards Breaststroke Men

| 1930 | Aubin. Jack | Canada | 2:35.4 |
| 1934 | Hamilton. Norman | Scotland | 2:41.6 |

220 yards Breaststroke Men

1938	Davies. John Goldup	England	2:51.9
1950	Hawkins. David	Australia	2:54.1
1954	Doms. John	New Zealand	2:57.6
1958	Gathercole. Terry	Australia	2:41.6
1962	O'Brien. Ian	Australia	2:38.2
1966	O'Brien. Ian	Australia	2:29.3

200 m Breaststroke Men

1970	Mahoney. William	Canada	2:30.29
1974	Wilkie. David	Scotland	2:24.42
1978	Smith. Graham W.	Canada	2:20.86
1982	Davis. Victor	Canada	2:16.25
1986	Moorhouse. Adrian	England	2:16.35
1990	Cleveland. A. Jon	Canada	2:14.96
1994	Gillingham. Nick	England	2:12.54
1998	Cowley. Simon Peter	Australia	1:08.71

200 m Butterfly Stroke Men

1978	Nagy. George Michael	Canada	2:01.99
1998	Hickman. James	Australia	1:57.11

200 m Freestyle Men

1970	Wenden. Michael V.	Australia	1:56.69
1974	Badger. Stephen	Australia	1:56.72
1978	McKeon. Ronald John	Australia	1:52.06
1982	Astbury. Andrew	England	1:51.52

1986	Gleria. Robert	Australia	1:50:57
1990	Roberts. Martin	Australia	1:49.58
1994	Perkins. Kieran	Australia	1:49.31
1998	Thorpe. Ian James	Australia	1:46.70

220 yards Backstroke Men

| 1962 | Carroll. Julian | Australia | 2:20.9 |
| 1966 | Reynolds. Peter | Australia | 2:12.0 |

200 m Backstroke Men

1970	*Richards. Mike J.*	*Wales*	*2:14.53*
1974	Cooper. Bradford	Australia	2:06.31
1978	Hurring. Gary Norman	New Zealand	2:04.37
1982	Henning. Cameron	Canada	2:02.55
1986	Goss. Sandy	Canada	2:02.55
1990	Anderson. Gary	Canada	2:01.69
1994	Ruckwood. Adam	England	2:00.79
1998	Versfeld. Mark	Canada	1:59.67

200 m Individual Medley Men

| 1970 | Smith. W. George | Canada | 2:13.72 |

1974	Wilkie. David A.	Scotland	2:10.11
1978	Smith. Graham W.	Canada	2:05.25
1982	Baumann. Alex	Canada	2:02.25
1986	Baumann. Alex	Canada	2:01.80
1990	Anderson. Gary	Canada	2:02.94
1994	Dunn. Matthew S.	Australia	2:00.28
1998	Dunn. Matthew S.	Australia	2:00.26

400 yards Freestyle Men

| 1930 | Ryan. Noel P. | Australia | 4:39.8 |

440 yards Freestyle Men

1934	Ryan. Noel P.	Australia	5:03.0
1938	Pirie. Robert	Canada	4:54.6
1950	Garrick. D.Agnew	Australia	4:49.4
1954	Chapman. Gary	Australia	4:39.8
1958	Konrads. John	Australia	4:25.9
1962	Rose. Murray	Australia	4:20.0
1966	Windle. Robert	Australia	4:15.0

400 m Freestyle Men

| 1970 | White. Graham | Australia | 4:08.48 |

1974	Kulasalu. John	Australia	4:01.44
1978	McKeon. Ronald John	Australia	3:54.43
1982	Astbury. Andrew	England	3:53.29
1986	Armstrong. Duncan	Australia	3:52.25
1990	Brown. Ian	Australia	3:49.91
1994	Perkins. Kieron	Australia	3:45.77
1998	Thorpe. Ian James	Australia	3:44.35

440 yards Individual Medley Men

| 1962 | Alexander. Alexander | Australia | 5:15.3 |
| 1966 | Reynolds. Peter | Australia | 4:50.8 |

400 m Individual Medley Men

1970	Smith. George W.	Canada	4:48.87
1974	Treffers. Mark	New Zealand	4:35.90
1978	Smith. Graham W.	Canada	4:27.34
1982	Boumann. Alex	Canada	4:23.53
1986	Baumann. Alex	Canada	4:18.29
1990	Bruce. Robert	Australia	4:20.26
1994	Dunn. Matthew	Australia	4:17.01
1998	Steed. Trent Joseph	Australia	4:1989

1,500 yards Freestyle Men

1930	Ryan. Noel P.	Australia	18:55.4
1934	Ryan. Noel P.	Australia	18:25.4

1,650 yards Freestyle Men

1938	Leivers. Robert H.	England	19:46.4
1950	Johnston. Graham M.	South Africa	19:55.7
1954	Johnston. Graham M.	South Africa	19:01.4
1958	Konrads. Jon	Australia	17:45.5
1962	Rose. Murray	Australia	17:18.1
1966	Jackson. Ron	Australia	17:25.9

1,500 m Freestyle Men

1970	Windeatt. Graham	Australia	16:23.82
1974	Holland. Stephen	Australia	15:34.73
1978	Metzker. Maxwell R.	Australia	15:31.92
1982	Metzker. Maxwell R	Australia	15:23.94
1986	Plummer. Jason	Australia	15:12.62
1990	Housman. Glen	Australia	14:55.25
1994	Perkins. Kieron	Australia	14:41.66
1998	Hackett. Grant	Australia	14:50.92

3 x 110 yards Relay Medley Men

1938	Davies. John	England	9:19.0
1938	Dove. Frederick	England	9:19.0
1938	Taylor. Michael	England	9:19.0

4 x 100 m Freestyle Relay Men

1978	Sawchuk. Bill Mathew	Canada	3:27.94
1978	Smith. Graham W.	Canada	3:27.94
1978	MacDonald. Gary W.	Canada	3:27.94
1978	Szmidt. Peter Charles	Canada	3:27.94
1998	Klim. Michael	Australia	3:17.83
1998	Callus. Ashley John	Australia	3:17.83
1998	Thorpe. Ian James	Australia	3:17.83
1998	Fydler. Christopher J.	Australia	3:17.83

4 x 100 m Medley Men

1978	Tapp. Jay Greville	Canada	3:52.93
1978	Smith. Graham W.	Canada	3:52.93
1978	Thompson. Dan David	Canada	3:52.93

1978	Sawchuk. Bill Matthew	Canada	3:52.93
1998	Watson. Josh	Australia	3:38.52
1998	Cowley. Simon Peter	Australia	3:38.52
1998	Huegill. Godfrey A.	Australia	3:38.52
1998	Klim. Michael	Australia	3:38.52

4 x 220 yards Medley Relay   Men

1938	Frederick. Dove	England	9:19.0
1938	French-Williams. Mostyn	England	9:19.0
1938	Leivers. Robert	England	9:19.0
1938	Wainwright. Norman	England	9:19.0

4 x 200 m Freestyle Relay Men

1978	Morgan. Mark Lincoln	Australia	7:50.13
1978	McKeon. Ronald John	Australia	7:50.13
1978	Metzker. Maxwell Raymond	Australia	7:50.13
1978	Brewer. Graeme	Australia	7:50.13
1998	Thorpe. Ian J.	Australia	7:11.86
1998	Kowalski. Daniel S.	Australia	7:11.86
1998	Dunne. Matthew Stephen	Australia	7:11.86
1998	Klim. Michael	Australia	7:11.86

50 m Freestyle Women

| 1990 | Curry-Kenny. Lisa | Australia | 25.80 secs. |
| 1998 | Rolph. Sue | England | 25.82 secs. |

100 m Breaststroke Women

| 1978 | Corsiglia. Robin Marie | Canada | 1:13.56 |
| 1998 | Denman. Helen | Australia | 1:08.71 |

220 yards Breaststroke Women

1938	Storey. Doris	England	3:06.30
1938	Lacey. Evelyn de	Australia	1:10.10
1978	Klimpel. Carol	Canada	57.78 secs.

100 m Freestyle Women

| 1998 | Rolph. Sue | England | 55.17 secs. |

100 m Butterfly Stroke Women

1978	Quirk. Wendy Patricia	Canada	1:01.92
1990	Curry-Kenny. Lisa	Australia	1:00.66
1998	Thomas. Petria Ann	Australia	59.42 secs

110 yards Backstroke Women

1938	Norton. Pat	Australia	1:19.50

100 m Backstroke Women

1978	Forster. Debra Lynn	Australia	1:03.97
1998	Rooney. Giaan	Australia	1:02.43

4 x 110 yards Freestyle Relay Women

1938	Baggaley. Mary	Canada	4:48.30
1938	Dewar. Phyllis	Canada	4:48.30
1938	Lyon. Dorothy	Canada	4:48.30
1938	Oxenbury. Noel	Canada	4:48.30

3 x 110 yards Medley Relay Women

1938	Hinton. Margery	England	3:57.70

| 1938 | Framptson. Lorna | England | 3:57.70 |
| 1938 | Storey. Doris | England | 3:57.70 |

4 x 100 m Medley Relay Women

1990	Curry-Kenny. Lisa	Australia	4:10.87
1990	Hooiveld. Lara	Australia	4:10.87
1990	Livingston. Nicole	Australia	4:10.87
1990	Wirdum. Karen Van	Australia	4:10.87

200 m Breaststroke Women

| 1978 | Borsholt. Lisa Ann | Canada | 2:37.70 |
| 1998 | Riley. Samantha L.P. | Australia | 2:27.30 |

200 m Butterfly Stroke Women

| 1978 | Ford. Michelle Jan | Australia | 2:11.29 |
| 1998 | O'Neil. Susan | Australia | 2:06.60 |

200 m Freestyle Women

| 1970 | Mo. Karen | Australia | 2:09.78 |
| 1974 | Gray. Sonya | Australia | 2:04.27 |

1978	Perrot. Rebecca	New Zealand	2:00.63
1982	Croft. June	England	1:59.74
1986	Baumer. Susan	Australia	2:00.61
1990	Lewis. Hayley	Australia	2:00.86
1994	O'Neil. Susan	Australia	2:00.86
1998	O'Neil. Susan	Australia	2:00.24

200 m Backstroke Women

| 1978 | Gibson. Cheryl Anne | Canada | 2:16.57 |
| 1998 | Sexton. Katy | England | 2:13.18 |

200 m Individual Medley Women

| 1978 | Davies. Sharron | England | 2:18.37 |
| 1998 | Limpert. Marianne | Canada | 2:15.05 |

440 yards Freestyle Women

| 1938 | Green. Dorothy | Australia | 5:39.7 |

400 m Freestyle Women

| 1978 | Wickham. Tracey Lee | Australia | 4:08.45 |
| 1998 | O'Neil. Susan | Australia | 4:12.38 |

400 m Individual Medley Women

| 1978 | Davies. Sharron | England | 4:52.44 |

4 x 400 m Individual Medley Relay Women

| 1998 | Malar. Joanne | Canada | 4:43.74 |

800 m Freestyle Women

| 1978 | Wickham. Tracey Lee | Australia | |
| 1998 | Harris. Rachel Amanda | Australia | 8:42.43 |

4 x 100 m Medley Relay Women

1978	Boivin. Helene	Canada	4:15.26
1978	Stuart. Marian	Canada	4:15.26
1978	Quirk. Wendy Patricia	Canada	4:15.26
1978	Klimpel. Carol	Canada	4:15.26

4 x 100 m Freestyle Women

| 1978 | Amunedrud. Gail Ann | Canada | 3:50.28 |
| 1978 | Klimpel. Carol | Canada | 3:50.28 |

1978	Sloan. Sue	Canada	3:50.28
1978	Quik. Wendy Patricia	Canada	3:50.28
1990	Curry-Kenny. Lisa	Australia	3:50.28
1998	Creedy. Rebecca	Australia	3:42.61
1998	Ryan. Sharah	Australia	3:42.61
1998	Munez. Lori M.	Australia	3:42.61
1998	O'Neil. Susan	Australia	3:42.61

4 x 200 m Freestyle Women

1998	Greville. Julia	Australia	8:03.73
1998	O'Neil. Susan	Australia	8:03.73
1998	Windsor. Anna M.	Australia	8:03.73
1998	Munez. Lori M.	Australia	8:03.73

Diving 3 m Springboard Men

| 1938 | Masters. Ron | Australia | 126.36 |
| 1978 | Snode. Christopher | England | 643.83 |

Diving 10 m Platform Men

| 1938 | Tomalin. Doug | England | 108.74 |
| 1978 | Snode. Christopher | England | 538.96 |

Diving 3 m Springboard Women

| 1938 | Donnett. Irene | Australia | 91.18 |
| 1978 | Nutter. Janet Ruth | Canada | 477.33 |

Diving 10 m Platform Women

| 1938 | Hook. Lurline | Australia | 36.47 |
| 1978 | Cuthbert. Linda Joanne | Canada | 397.44 |

BOXING

Light Flyweight Class

1970	Odwari. James	Uganda
1974	Muchoki. Stephen	Kenya
1978	Muchoki. Stephen	Kenya
1982	Wachire. Abraham	Kenya
1986	Olson. Scott	Canada
1990	Juko. Justin	Uganda
1994	Ramadhani. Haman	Kenya

48 kg Class

| 1998 | Biki. Sapok | Malaysia |

Flyweight Class

1930	Smith. Jacob N.	South Africa
1934	Palmer. Patrick	England
1938	Joubert. Johannes	South Africa
1950	Riley. Hugh	Scotland
1954	Currie. Richard	Scotland
1958	Brown. Jackie	Scotland
1962	Mallon. Robert	Scotland
1966	Shittu. Sulley	Ghana
1970	Needham. David	England
1974	Larmour. David B.	Northern Ireland
1978	Urungu. Michael	Kenya
1982	Mutua. Michael	Kenya
1986	Lyon. John	England
1990	McCullough. Wayne	Northern Ireland
1994	Shepherd. Paul	Scotland

51 kg Class

| 1978 | Irunegu. Michael | Kenya |
| 1998 | Sunee. Richard | Mauritius. |

Bantamweight Class

1930	Mizler. Hyman	England
1934	Ryan. Freddy	England
1938	Butler. William Henry	England
1950	Rensburg. Johannes Van	South Africa
1954	Smillie. John W.	Scotland
1958	*Winstone. Howard*	*Wales*
1962	Dynevor. Geoffrey	Australia
1966	Ndukwu. Edward	Nigeria
1970	Shittu. Sulley	Ghana
1974	Cowdell. Patrick	England
1978	McGuigan. Finbar (Barry)	Northern Ireland
1982	Orewa. Joe	Nigeria
1986	Murphy. Sean	England
1990	Mohammed. Sabo	Nigeria
1994	Peden. Robert	Australia
1998	Yomba. Michael	Tanzania

Featherweight Class

1930	Meacham. F.R.	England
1934	Cotteral. Charles	South Africa
1938	Henricus. Ansdale William	Sri Lanca
1950	Gilliland. Henry	Scotland
1954	Leisching. Leonard	South Africa
1958	Taylor. Wally	Australia
1962	McDermott. John	Scotland
1966	Waruinge. Philip	Kenya
1970	Waruinge. Philip	Kenya
1974	Ndukwu. Edward	Nigeria
1978	Nelson. Azuma	Ghana
1982	Konyegwachie. Peter	Nigeria
1986	Downey. Bill	Canada
1990	Irwin. John	England
1994	Patton. Casey	Canada
1998	Arthur. Alex	Scotland

Lightweight Class

Year	Name	Country
1930	Rolland. James	Scotland
1934	Cook. Leslie	Australia
1938	Groves. Harry George T.	England
1950	Latham. Ronald	England
1954	Staden. Piet Van	Southern Rhodesia
1958	McTaggart. Richard	Scotland
1962	Blay. Eddie	Ghana
1966	Andeh. Anthony	Nigeria
1970	Adeyemi. Abayoni	Nigeria
1974	Kalule. Ahub	Uganda
1978	Hamil. Gerard	Northern Ireland
1982	Khalili. Hussein	Kenya
1986	Dar. Asif	Canada
1990	Nyakana. Godfrey	Uganda
1994	Strange. Michael	Canada
1998	Narh. Raymond	Ghana

Light Welterweight Class

1954	Bergin. Mickey	Canada
1958	Loubscher. Henry J.	South Africa
1962	Quartey. Clement	Ghana
1966	McCourt. James	Northern Ireland
1970	Muruli. Muhamad	Uganda
1974	Nwakpa. Obisia	Nigeria
1978	Braithwaite. Winfield	Guyana
1982	Ossai. Christopher	Nigeria
1986	Grant. Howard	Canada
1990	Kane. Charles	Scotland
1994	Richardson. Peter	England
1998	Strange. Michael	Canada

Welterweight Class

1930	Hall. Leonard A.	South Africa
1934	McCleave. David	England
1938	Smith. William	Australia
1950	Ratcliffe. Terence	England
1954	Gargano. Nicholas	England

1958	Greyling. Joseph A.	South Africa
1962	Coe. Wallace	New Zealand
1966	Blay. Eddy	Ghana
1970	Ankudey. Emma F.	Ghana
1974	Muruli. Muhamed	Uganda
1978	McCallum. Midrai	Jamaica
1982	Pyatt. Christopher	England
1986	Dyer. Darren	England
1990	Defiagbon. David	Nigeria
1994	Sinclair. Neil	Northern Ireland
1998	Molitor. Jeremy	Canada

Light Middleweight Class

1954	Greaves. Wilfred	Canada
1958	Webster. A.Grant	South Africa
1962	Mann. Harold	Canada
1966	Rowe. Mark	England
1970	Imrie. Thomas	Scotland
1974	Mwale. Lotti	Zambia
1978	Perlette. Kelly	Canada
1982	O'Sullivan. Shawn	Canada

1986	Sherry. Dan	Canada
1990	Woodhall. Richard	England
1994	Webb. James	Northern Ireland
1998	Bessey. Chris	England

Middleweight Class

1930	Malin. Frederick	Scotland
1934	Shawyer. Alfred	England
1938	*Reardon. Denis Patrick*	*Wales*
1950	Schalkwyk. Theunis Van	South Africa
1954	Kolff. Johannes Van Der	South Africa
1958	Milligan. Terry	Northern Ireland
1962	Colquhoun. Cephos	Jamaica
1966	Darkey. Joe	Ghana
1970	Conteh. John	England
1974	Lucas. Frankie	St. Vincent
1978	McElwaine. Philip	Australia
1982	Price. Jimmy	England
1986	Douglas. Rod	England
1990	Johnson. Chris	Canada
1994	Donaldson. Rowan	Canada
1998	Pearce. John	England

Lightheavyweight Class

1930	Goyder. Joe W.	England
1934	Brennan. George J.	England
1938	Wilmarans. Nicholaas	South Africa
1950	Scott. Donald	England
1954	Vuuren. Piet Van	South Africa
1958	Madigan. Anthony M.	Australia
1962	Madigan. Anthony M.	Australia
1966	Tighe. Roger	England
1970	Ayinla. Fatai	Nigeria
1974	Knight. William	England
1978	Fortin. Roger	Canada
1982	Sani. Fine	Fiji
1986	Moran. Jim	England
1990	Akhasamba. Joseph	Kenya
1994	Brown. Dale	Canada
1998	Fry. Courtney	England

Heavyweight Class

1930	Stuart. Victor A.	England
1934	Floyd. Pat	England
1938	Osborne. Thomas	Canada

1950	Creagh. Frank	New Zealand
1954	Harper. Brian	England
1958	Becher. Daniel W.	South Africa
1962	Oywello. George	Uganda
1966	Kini. William	New Zealand
1970	Masanda. Benson	Uganda
1974	Meade. Neville	England
1978	Awome. Julius	England
1982	DeWit. William	Canada
1986	Peau. Jimmy	New Zealand
1990	Onyango. George	Kenya
1994	Ahmed. Omaar	Kenya
1998	Simmons. Mark	Canada

Superheavyweight Class

1986	Lewis. Lenox	Canada
1990	Kenny. Michael	New Zealand
1994	Dokiwari. Duncan	Nigeria
1998	Harrison. Audley	England

NETBALL

1998	Borlase. J.	Australia
1998	Cusack. Nicole	Australia
1998	Ellis. Elizabeth	Australia
1998	Harby. Kathryn	Australia
1998	Ilitch. Janine	Australia
1998	McKinnis. S.	Australia
1998	McMahon. Sharelle Jane	Australia
1998	O'Donnell. S.	Australia
1998	Sanders. Rebecca	Australia
1998	Sutter. Sarah	Australia
1998	Tombs. Carissa	Australia
1998	Wilson. Vicki	Australia

ROWING

Single Sculls Men

1930	Pearce. H.R. (Bobby)	Australia	
1938	Turner. Herbert J.	Australia	8.24
1950	Wood. Mervyn Thomas	Australia	7:46.8
1954	Rowlands. Donald D.	New Zealand	8:28.2
1958	McKenzie. Stuart A.	Australia	7:20.1

| 1962 | Hill. James P. | New Zealand | 7:39.7 |
| 1966 | Redgrave. Steve | England | 7:28.29 |

Light Sculls Men

| 1986 | Antonie. Peter Thomas | Australia | 7:16.43 |

Pairs Sculls Men

1930	Bole. Elswood	Canada	7:48.0
1930	Richards. Bob	Canada	7:48.0
1938	Bradley. William	England	7:29.4
1938	Pearce. Cecil	England	7:29.4
1950	Wood. Mervyn Thomas	Australia	7:22.0
1950	Riley. Murray	Australia	7:22.0
1954	Wood. Mervyn Thomas	Australia	7:54.5
1954	Riley. Murray	Australia	7:54.5
1958	Spracklen. Michael	England	6:54.4
1958	Baker. Geoffrey	England	6:54.4
1962	Justice. George C.	England	6:52.4
1962	Birkmyre. Nicholas J.	England	6:52.4
1986	Ford. Bruce	Canada	6:19.43
1986	Walter. Pat	Canada	6:19.43

Rowing Pairs Without Cox Men

1950	Lambert. Walter	Australia	7:58.0
1950	Webster. Jack	Australia	7:58.0
1954	Parker. Robert	New Zealand	8:23.9
1954	Douglas. Reginald	New Zealand	8:23.9
1958	Parker. Reginald	New Zealand	7:11.1
1958	Douglas. Reginald	New Zealand	7:11.1
1962	Farquharson. Stewart	England	7:03.7
1962	Lee-Nicholson. James	England	7:03.7
1986	Holmes. Andrew	England	6:40.48
1986	Redgrave. Steve	England	6:40.48

Light Fours Men

1986	Bates. Christopher	England	6:25.86
1986	Forbes. Stuart	England	6:25.86
1986	Haining. Peter	England	6:25.86
1986	Staite. Neil	England	6:25.86

Fours With Cox Men

Year	Name	Country	Time
1930	Brough. F.	New Zealand	
1930	Eastwood. Arthur H.	New Zealand	
1930	McDonald. John	New Zealand	
1930	Sandos. Bertram M.	New Zealand	
1930	Waters. E.A.	New Zealand	
1938	Fraser. Donald	Australia	7:16.8
1938	Elder. Stewart	Australia	7:16.8
1938	Freeth. Gordon	Australia	7:16.8
1938	Fisher. Jack	Australia	7:16.8
1938	Kerr. Harry	Australia	7:16.8
1950	Carroll. William	New Zealand	7:17.5
1950	James. William	New Zealand	7:17.5
1950	Johnson. Edward	New Zealand	7:17.5
1950	Johnstone. Charles	New Zealand	7:17.5
1950	O'Brien. John	New Zealand	7:17.5
1954	Anderson. David Rollo	Australia	7:58.3
1954	Evatt. Peter Maitland	Australia	7:58.3
1954	Robberds. Lionel Phillip	Australia	7:58.3
1954	Williamson. Geoffery	Australia	7:58.3
1954	Woods. Merfyn Thomas	Australia	7:58.3

1958	Beresord. H.M.	England	6:46.5
1958	Crosse. S.C.	England	6:46.5
1958	Porter. C.F.	England	6:46.5
1958	Vigurs. J.P.	England	6:46.5
1962	Heselwood. K.J.	New Zealand	6:48.2
1962	Patterson. G.M.	New Zealand	6:48.2
1962	Pulman. D.W.	New Zealand	6:48.2
1962	Smedley. H.W.	New Zealand	6:48.2
1962	Stephens. W.T.	New Zealand	6:48.2
1986	Cliff. Adam	England	6:08.13
1986	Cross. Martin	England	6:08.13
1986	Ellison. Adrian	England	6:08.13
1986	Holmes. Andrew	England	6:08.13
1986	Redgrave. Steve	England	6:08.13

Fours Without Cox Men

1930	Boardman. H.C.	England
1930	Edwards. H.R.H.	England
1930	Fizwilliams. F.M.L.	England
1930	Harby. A.J.	England

1958	Pope. R.D.E.	England	6:34.4
1958	Redman. C.T.	England	6:34.4
1958	Shakell. K.J.	England	6:34.4
1958	Young. D.R.	England	6:34.4
1962	Beveridge. J.	England	6:31.1
1962	Clay. M.C.	England	6:31.1
1962	Davidge. C.G.V.	England	6:31.1
1962	Tilbury. J.W.	England	6:31.1
1986	Main. Crant	Canada	6:00.56
1986	Neufeld. Kevin	Canada	6:00.56
1986	Styeele. Paul	Canada	6:00.56
1986	Turner. Pat	Canada	6:00.56

Eights Men

1930		England	
1938	Beazley. Basil	England	6:29
1938	Burrough. John	England	6:29
1938	Hambridge. Rhodes	England	6:29
1938	Jackson. Peter	England	6:29
1938	Kingsford. Desmond	England	6:29
1938	Reeve. Thomas	England	6:29

1938	Sturrock. John	England	6:29
1938	Turnbull. John	England	6:29
1938	Turner. J.T.	England	6:29
1950	A'Court. Peter Holmes	Australia	6:27
1950	Barnes. J.E.	Australia	6:27
1950	Allen. William	Australia	6:27
1950	Gayzer. Phillip Arthur	Australia	6:27
1950	Goswell. Bruce Henry	Australia	6:27
1950	Langley. Eric Osborne	Australia	6:27
1950	Pain. Edward Oscar	Australia	6:27
1950	Selmad. Ross Lincoln	Australia	6:27
1950	Tinning. Robert Noel	Australia	6:27
1954	Drummond. K.J.	Canada	6:59.0
1954	Harris. Thomas M.	Canada	6:59.0
1954	MacDonald. Daryl	Canada	6:59.0
1954	Sierans. Ray	Canada	6:59.0
1954	Smith. Glen W.	Canada	6:59.0
1954	Toynbee. Thomas A.	Canada	6:59.0
1954	West. Lawrence	Canada	6:59.0
1954	Wilson. Robert A.	Canada	6:59.0
1954	Zloklikovitis. H.J.	Canada	6:59.0

1958	Arnold. D.J.	Canada	5:55.1
1958	Biln. S.	Canada	5:55.1
1958	D'Hondt. I.W.	Canada	5:55.1
1958	Loomer. L.K.	Canada	5:55.1
1958	MacInnon. A.A.	Canada	5:55.1
1958	McKerlich. W.A.	Canada	5:55.1
1958	Merfyn. G.A.	Canada	5:55.1
1958	Pretty. D.W.	Canada	5:55.1
1958	Wilson. R.A.	Canada	5:55.1
1962	Davies. Terrence Rodney	Australia	5:53.4
1962	Ellesworth. Ian	Australia	5:53.4
1962	Guest. Paul Marshall	Australia	5:53.4
1962	Howell. Walter Neville	Australia	5:53.4
1962	Lehman. Charles James	Australia	5:53.4
1962	McCalk. Graeme	Australia	5:53.4
1962	Palfreyman. David	Australia	5:53.4
1962	Stankovich. Dushan	Australia	5:53.4
1962	Tomanovits. Martin George	Australia	5:53.4
1986	Batten. Malcolm William	Australia	5:44.42
1986	Caterson. Dale	Australia	5:44.42
1986	Cooper. Andrew Dollman	Australia	5:44.42

1986	Doyle. Mark Andrew	Australia	5:44.42
1986	Evans. Stephen Frederick	Australia	5:44.42
1986	Galloway. Chester	Australia	5:44.42
1986	McKay. Michael Scott	Australia	5:44.42
1986	Pora. Ion	Australia	5:44.42
1986	Tomkins. James Bruce	Australia	5:44.42

Eights Women

1986	Bassett. Deborah	Australia	6:43.69
1986	Chapman-Pope. Susan C.	Australia	6:43.69
1986	Foster. Margot Elizabeth	Australia	6:43.69
1986	Fry. Kaylynn Maree	Australia	6:43.69
1986	Grey-Gardner. Robyn	Australia	6:43.69
1986	Kay. Urzula Anne	Australia	6:3.69
1986	Kidd. Marilyn Joan	Australia	6:43.69
1986	Sooner. Vicky Suzanne	Australia	6:43.69
1986	Voorthuis. Annelies	Australia	6:43.69

Fours with Cox Women

1986	Clarke. Tina	Canada	6:50.13
1986	Smith. Tricia	Canada	6:50.13
1986	Thompson. Leslie	Canada	6:50.13
1986	Tregunno. Janet	Canada	8:50.13

Singles Sculls Women

1986	Forster. Stephanie	New Zealand	7:43.22

Singles Light Sculls Women

1986	Ferguson. Adair Janella	Australia	7:45.49

Pairs Women

1986	Barr. Kathryn	Canada	7:34.51
1986	Schreiner. Andrea	Canada	7:34.51

Pairs Sculls Women

1986	Clarke. Robin	New Zealand	7:21.52
1986	Foster. Stephanie	New Zealand	7:21.52

Light Fours Women

1986	Burne. Judith	England	6:54.70
1986	Clark. Lyn	England	6:54.70
1986	Forbes. Alexa	England	6:54.70
1986	Hodges. Gillian	England	6:54.70

RUGBY SEVENS

1998	Rush. Eric	New Zealand
1998	Lomu. Jonah	New Zealand
1998	Seymour. Dallas	New Zealand
1998	Ralph. Caleb	New Zealand
1998	Reihana. Bruce	New Zealand
1998	Cullen. Christian	New Zealand
1998	Randle. Roger	New Zealand
1998	Vidiri. Joeli	New Zealand
1998	Gear. Rico	New Zealand
1998	Amasio. Valence	New Zealand

SHOOTING

50 m Sport Rifle Three Position Individual Women

| 1998 | McCreadie. Susan | Australia | 667.3 |

50 m Sport Rifle Individual Women

| 1998 | Unnikrishnan. Roopa | India | 590 |

25 m Sport Pistol Individual Women

| 1998 | Trefry. Christine | Australia | 672.8 |

10 m Air Pistol Individual Women

| 1998 | Forder. Annemarie | Australia | 480.6 |

10 m Air Rifle Individual Women

| 1998 | Baharin. Nurul Hudda | Malaysia | 494.8 |

10 m Air Pistol Pairs Women

| 1998 | Forder. Anne Marie | Australia | 748 |
| 1998 | Trefrey. Christine | Australia | 748 |

50 m Sport Rifle Pairs Prone Lying Women

1998	Frazier. Kim	Australia	1174
1998	Quigley. Carolyn	Australia	1174

50 m Sport Rifle Pairs Three Position Women

1998	Ashcroft. Christina	Canada	1133
1998	Bowes. Sharon	Canada	1133

50 m Air Rifle Pairs Women

1998	Ashcroft. Christina	Canada	778
1998	Bowes. Sharon	Canada	778

25 m Sport Pistol Pairs Women

1998	Woodward. Annette	Australia	1140
1998	Trefry. Christine	Australia	1140

50 m Smallbore Rifle Three Position Individual Men

1982	Allan. Alister	Scotland	1146
1986	Cooper. Malcolm	England	1170
1994	Dion. Michel	Canada	1234

Fullbore Three Position Individual Men

1998	Lowndes. Timothy	Australia	1235.3

Smallbore Rifle Prone-Lying Men

1966	Boa. Gilmour	Canada	587
1974	Gowland. Yvonne	Australia	594
1978	Allan. Alister	Scotland	598
1982	Smith. Alan	Australia	1184
1986	Smith. Alan	Australia	599
1994	Petterson. Stephen	New Zealand	698.4

Fullbore Rifle Open Individual Men

| 1998 | Paton. James | Canada | 402 |

Fullbore Rifle Individual Men

1966	*Swansea. Lord*	*Wales*	*394*
1974	Gordon. Maurice	New Zealand	387.26
1978	Vamplew. Desmond G.	Canada	391
1982	Clarke. Arthur	Scotland	387
1986	Golinsky. Stanley John	Australia	396
1990	Mallett. Colin	Jersey	394
1994	Calvert. David Peter	Northern Ireland	398

Fullbore Rifle Team Men

| 1982 | Affleck. Keith | Australia | 572 |
| 1982 | Ayling. Geoffrey | Australia | 572 |

Centre Pistol Individual Men

1966	Lee. James	Canada	576
1982	Cooke. John	England	580
1986	Northaver. Robert	England	583
1990	Pandit. Ashok	India	583

| 1994 | Rana. Jaspal | India | 581 |
| 1998 | Rana. Jaspal | India | 581 |

Centre Rapid Pistol Pairs   Men

| 1998 | Rana. Jaspal | India | 1154 |
| 1998 | Pandit. Ashok | India | 1154 |

Trap Pairs Men

| 1998 | Singh. Manavjit | India | 192pts. |
| 1998 | Singh. Mansher | India | 192 pts. |

Fullbore Rifle Three Position Pairs Men

| 1998 | Sorensen. Wayne | Canada | 2276pts. |
| 1998 | Dion. Michel | Canada | 2276pts. |

Air Pistol Men

1982	Darling. George	England	576 pts.
1986	Yelavich. Gregory	New Zealand	575 pts.
1990	Sandstrom. Bengt Olov	Australia	580 pts.
1994	Huot. Jean-Pierre	Canada	672.4 pts.
1998	Gault. Michael	England	679.9 pts.

Free Pistol Individual Men

1966	Sexton. Charles	England	585pts.
1974	Sobrian. Jules	Canada	549 pts.
1978	Trempe. Yvon	Canada	543 pts.
1982	Guinn. Thomas	Canada	553 pts.
1986	Yelavich. Gregory	New Zealand	551 pts.
1990	Adams. Phillip	Australia	554pts.
1994	Gault. Michael	England	654.1pts.
1998	Gault. Michael	England	646.3pts.

Rapid Fire Pistol Individual Men

1966	Clark. Anthony	England	585 pts.
1974	Hare. William	Canada	586 pts.
1978	Sobrian. Jules	Canada	587 pts.
1982	Lee. Solomon	Hong Kong	583 pts.
1986	Murray. Patrick	Australia	591 pts.
1990	Breton. Adrian	Guernsey	583 pts.
1994	*Jay. Michael*	*Wales*	*670.7 pts.*
1998	Igorov. Metodi	Canada	674.8 pts.

Rapid Fire Pistol Pairs Men

1998	Murray. Patrick Brian	Australia	1138pts.
1998	Giustinano. Michael A.	Australia	1138pts.

25 m Rapid Pistol for Teams Men

1982	Heuke. Peter	Australia	1160pts.
1982	Taransky. Alexander	Australia	1160pts.
1986	Turner. Terry	England	1169pts.
1986	Girling. Brian Edward	England	1169pts.
1990	Favell. B.	Australia	1153pts.
1990	Murray. Patrick	Australia	1153pts.
1994	Murray. Patrick	Australia	1148pts.
1998	Murray. Patrick Brian	Australia	1138pts.
1998	Giustinano. Michael A.	Australia	1138pts.

10 m Air Pistol Pairs Men

1998	Gault. Michael	England	1145pts.
1998	Baxter. Nick	England	1145pts.

Individual Trap Men

| 1998 | Diamond. Michael | Australia | 144pts. |

Individual Skeet Men

1974	Willsie. Harry	Canada	194pts.
1978	Woolley. Lawrence	New Zealand	193pts.
1982	Woolley. Lawrence	New Zealand	197pts.
1986	Kelly. Nigel	Isle of Man	196 pts.
1990	Harman. Kenneth	England	187 pts.
1994	Hale. Ian Maxwell	Australia	144 pts.
1998	*Davies. Desmond*	*Wales*	*145 pts.*

Fullbore Rifle Prone-Lying Men

| 1998 | Petterson. Stephen | New Zealand | 697.4 pts. |

Free Rifle Three Position Individual Men

| 1990 | Klepp. Mart | Canada | 1157pts. |

Free Rifle Three Position Team Men

| 1990 | Klepp. Mart | Canada | 2272pts. |
| 1990 | Senecal. Jean-Francois | Canada | 2272pts. |

238

Free Rifle Prone-Lying Individual Men

| 1990 | Harvey. Roger | New Zealand | 591 pts. |

Skeet Pairs Men

| 1998 | Stratis. Costas | Cyprus | 188 pts. |
| 1998 | Nicolaides. Antonis | Cyprus | 188 pts. |

Air Rifle Pairs Men

| 1998 | Wallace. Nigel | England | 1173 pts. |
| 1998 | Hector. Chris | England | 1173 pts. |

Fullbore Rifle Prone-Lying Pairs Men

| 1998 | Van Rhyn. Gavin | South Africa | 1189 pts. |
| 1998 | Thiele. Michael | South Africa | 1189 pts. |

Fullbore Open Pairs   Men

| 1998 | Calvert. David | Northern Ireland | 595 pts. |
| 1998 | Millar. Martin | Northern Ireland | 595 pts. |

Smallbore Rifle Three Position Team Men

| 1982 | Cooper. Malcolm | England | 2301pts |

1982	Dagger. Barry	England	2301pts.
1986	Cooper. Malcolm	England	2278pts.
1986	Cooper. Malcolm	England	2278pts.
1994	Sorensen. Wayne	Canada	2300pts
1994	Dion. Michel	Canada	2300pts.

Smallbore Prone-Lying Men

1982	Cooper. Malcolm	England	1187pts.
1982	Sullivan. Mike	England	1187pts.
1986	Stewart. Gale	Canada	1175pts.
1994	Petterson. Stephen	New Zealand	1181pts.
1994	Arthur. Lindsay	New Zealand	1181pts.

Free Pistol Pairs Men

1982	Adams. Philip	Australia	1077pts.
1982	Tremelling. John	Australia	1077pts.
1986	Guinn. Thomas	Canada	1099pts.
1986	Beaulieu. Claude	Canada	1099pts.
1990	Adams. Philip Maxwell	Australia	1106pts.
1990	Sandstrom. Bengt Olaf	Australia	1106pts.
1994	Adams. Philip Maxwell	Australia	1104pts.
1994	Sandstrom. Bengt Olaf	Australia	1104pts.

| 1998 | Baxter. Nick | England | 1093pts. |
| 1998 | Gault. Michael | England | 1093pts. |

Centre Pistol Team Men

1982	Ryan. Noel	Australia	1151pts.
1982	Taransky. Alexander	Australia	1151pts.
1986	Adams. Philip Maxwell	Australia	1165pts.
1986	Hack. Roderick Douglas	Australia	1165pts.
1990	Adams. Philip Maxwell	Australia	1155pts.
1990	Quick. Bruce James	Australia	1155pts.
1994	Rana. Jaspel	India	1168pts.
1994	Pandit. Ashok	India	1168pts.

Free Rifle Prone-Lying Team Men

1990	Pettersen. Stephen	New Zealand	1185pts.
1990	Harvey. Roger	New Zealand	1185pts.
1982	Gabriel. Brian	Canada	191 pts.
1982	Altmann. Fred	Canada	191 pts.
1986	Neville. Joseph Martin	England	195 pts.
1986	Harman. Kenneth	England	195 pts.
1990	Marsden. Ian	Scotland	189pts

1990	Dunlop. James	Scotland	189pts.
1994	Andreou. Antonis	Cyprus	189 pts.
1994	Kourtellas. Christos	Cyprus	189 pts.
1998	Stratis. Costa	Cyprus	188 pts.
1998	Nicolades. Antonis	Cyprus	188 pts.

10 m Air Pistol Team   Men

1982	Adams. Philip	Australia	1128pts.
1982	Colbert. Gregory	Australia	1128pts.
1986	Leatherdale. Paul	England	1143pts.
1986	Reid. Ian	England	1143pts.
1990	Rahman. Ateequr	Bangladesh	1138pts.
1990	Sattar. Abdus	Bangladesh	1138pts.
1994	Guistiniano. Michaelangelo	Australia	1137pts.
1994	Sandstrom. Bengt Olov	Australia	1137pts.

SQUASH

Singles Men

1998	Nicol. Peter	Scotland

Pairs Men

1998	Johnson. Paul	England
1998	Chaloner. Mark	England

Singles Women

1998	Martin. Michelle	Australia

Pairs Women

1998	Wright. Sue	England
1998	Jackmlan. Cassie	England

Mixed Pairs

1998	Martin. Michelle	Australia
1998	Rowland. Craig	Australia

WRESTLING

Light Flyweight Class

1970	Prakash. Ved	India
1974	Kawasaki. Mitchell	Canada

| 1978 | Kumar. Ashok | India |

Flyweight Class

1970	Kumar. Sudesh	India
1974	Kumar. Sudesh	India
1978	Takahashi. Ray	Canada

Bantamweight Class

1938	Purcell. Edward	Australia
1970	Sadar. Mohd.	Pakistan
1974	Nat. Prem	India
1978	Singh. Sathir	India

Featherweight Class

1938	Purchase. Roy	England
1970	Saeed. Mohammad	Pakistan
1974	Beiliador. Egon	Canada
1978	Beiliador. Egon	Canada

Lightweight Class

1938	Garrard. Richard	Australia
1970	Chand. Udey	India
1974	Singh. Jagrup	India
1978	Kelevitz. Zigmund	Australia

Welterweight Class

1938	Trevaskis. Thomas	Australia
1970	Singh. Mukhtiar	India
1974	Pawar. Raghunath	India
1978	Singh. Rajinder	India

Middleweight Class

1938	Evans. Terry	Canada
1970	Chandra. Harish	India
1974	Aspin. David A.	New Zealand
1978	Deschatelets. Richard	Canada

Lightheavyweight Class

1938	Scarf. Eddie	Australia
1970	Faiz. Muhammed	Pakistan

| 1974 | Paice. Terry E. | Canada |
| 1978 | Danier. Stephen | Canada |

Heavyweight Class

1938	Knight. Jack	Australia
1970	Millard. Edward H.	Canada
1974	Pilon. Claude A.	Canada
1978	Wishart. Wyatt	Canada

Superheavyweight Class

1970	Ilahi. Ikram	Pakistan
1974	Benko. William A.	Canada
1978	Gibbons. Robert	Canada

PART 2

WALES

CHAPTER FIVE

COMMONWEALTH GAMES COUNCIL FOR WALES

THE BEGINNING IN WALES

1933 was a hot dry year, and the climate on the twentieth of June was warm and summery.

Mr R.P. Green's step was light as he made his way towards City Hall, Cardiff on this special Tuesday evening. He had persuaded Charles Fletcher Sanders J.P. the Lord Mayor of Cardiff to welcome a small group of men with a penchant for sport to a special meeting at the City Hall at 6.30 pm that evening.

R.P. Green, M.M.

First Secretary, British Empire Games Council For Wales

Apparently R.P. Green was most reluctant to disclose his full name. I spent quite some time endeavouring to find what the R.P. stood for, but all in vain. I know his postal address was 23 Charles Street, Cardiff as this appeared on the notepaper of the Welsh Amateur Swimming Association, as he was its Secretary. R.P. Green was ambitious to form a British Empire Games Council for Wales.

The Lord Mayor of Cardiff welcomed everyone to the meeting and wished them well in their deliberations, before leaving for another commitment.

Mr Harry Parker, from Chepstow was appointed as Chairman. Harry Packer had won seven international rugby caps for Wales, and had been a Manager of the Lions Rugby Team in 1924. He had also been President of the International Cross Country Union on two occasions. The committee agreed to accepts the invitation from the British Empire Games Federation for Wales to participate in the next Games and noted that the sports to be contested were, Athletics. Lawn Bowls. Swimming. Boxing. Cycling. and Wrestling.

At the meeting the following were elected officers of the Council:-

Chairman	Harry Parker	Amateur Athletics Association of Wales
Vice-Chairman	T.Harry Peach	Welsh Lawn Bowls Association
Secretary	R.P. Green, M.M.	Welsh Amateur Swimming Association
Treasurer	John A. Wood	Welsh Amateur Boxing Association

The affiliation fee was set at £1-1-0 for the year. On the 19th July 1933, Wrestling was accepted but under the wing of Gymnastics. The Prince of Wales was invited to be President of the Council. On the 14th February

Harry Parker resigned as Chairman and the Vice-Chairman, T. Harry Peach accepted the Chair with E.W. O'Donnell moving to Vice-Chairman.

The Prince of Wales, declined the position of President and it was agreed to invite the Earl of Plymouth as President which he accepted.

CHAPTER SIX

OFFICIALS OF THE COMMONWEALTH GAMES COUNCIL FOR WALES IN THE 20TH CENTURY

The Council did not function between 19th April 1939 and 3rd March 1948, due to World War 2. R.P. Green would have been delighted to know that no less than 499 individual representatives from the various member sports had been present at meetings of the Council in the 20th Century. **(Index 4)**

It should be noted that Fred Howell the Cycling representative had attended 229 of the main committees. He had also been present on numerous sub - committees as well.

PATRONS

1969   Jenour, T.D.,J.P., D.L. Sir Maynard

1969   Llewellyn, C.B., C.B.E., MC.,T.D.,J.P.,D.L. Colonel Sir Godfrey

VICE- PATRONS

1969   Aberdare. Lord

1969   Berry, M.P. The Hon. Anthony

1969   Brooks, C.B.E., J.P. Sir Richard

1969   Cole, J.P. C.N.D.

1969   Harding. The Hon. Judge Rowe

1969   Heycock, C.B.E.,J.P., O.St.J., D.L., LL.D. Lord

1969   Traherne. T.D., J.P. Colonel Sir Cennydd

1969   Vaughan, C.B.E., J.P. Dr. D.W.

1969	Wheeler, K.B.E. Sir Charles
1972-1973	Thomas. David
1973	Newcombe. John

PRESIDENTS

1934. 25 April -1937. 24 March	Earl Plymouth
1937. 24 March -1939	Lord Aberdare
1948. 03 March -1958.06 January	Lord Aberdare
1952. 26 January - 1983.22 March	Howell. Cyril M.
1983. 22 March - 1995. 20 March	Rees. D. Thomas

Sitting -Tommy Rees (President), and Myrddin John
(Secretary)

1995. 20 March - 1999	Wright. Maurice A.(Mike)
1999 - 2000	Williams. Averil M.
2000 -	Griffiths, M.B.E. Dr Wayne

LIFE VICE - PRESIDENTS

1967 -	Prater, LVO. Edward H.
	Appointed Deceased
1967 - 1969	Rees, OBE. W. Russell
	Appointed Deceased
1967 - 1967	Salmon. Arthur H.
	Appointed Resigned
1967 - 1970	Taylor. A. Gus
	Appointed Deceased
1969 -	Reynolds. Mrs Jackie
	Appointed
1970 - 1976	Ingledew. Kenneth H.
	Appointed Deceased
1971 -	Fearnley. Charles E.
	Appointed Deceased
1971 - 1973	Hopkins. Edward (Ted)
	Election Deceased

1972 -	Howell. Fred
	Election
1973 -	Hooper. Berenice
	Election
1974 -	Cox. Reg A.
	Election Deceased
1976 -	John, M.B.E. Myrddin
	Election
1977 - 1983	Maidment, M.B.E. Walter
	Election Deceased
1983 - 1995	Howell. Cyril M.
	Election Deceased
1983 -	Jones, O.B.E. Raymond E.
	Election
1984 -	George. Basil
	Election
1990 - 1996	Jones. Wyndham H.
	Election Deceased
1995 - 1996	Rees. D. Thomas (Tommy)
	Election Deceased

1996 -	Jones-Pritchard. John A.
	Election
1996 -	Keitch. Mrs Rita
	Election
1996 -	Williams. Averil
	Election

VICE-PRESIDENTS

1959 - 1963	Chapman. Herbert M.
1959 - 1963	Green, M.M. R.P.
1959 - 1967	Prater, B.A. Edward (Ted)
	Elevated to Life Vice President
1959 - 1967	Rees, O.B.E. W. Russel
	Elevated to Life Vice President
1959 - 1967	Salmon. Arthur H.
	Elevated to Life Vice President
1959 - 1967	Taylor, M.M. A. Gus
	Elevated to Life Vice President
1963 - 1965	Jones. Wyndham W.
	Deceased
1963 - 1964	Matthews. Ivor
	Deceased
1964 - 1968	Reynolds.Jackie
	Elevated to Life Vice President

1966 - 1970	Ingledew, O.St.J. Kenneth H.
	Elevated to Life Vice President
1967 - 1971	Fearnley. Charles E.
	Elevated to Life Vice President
1967 - 1968	Jones, O.B.E. Raymond E.
1968 - 1972	Howell. Fred
	Elevated to Life Vice President
1969 - 1973	Hooper. Berenice
	Elevated to Life Vice President
1969 - 1971	Hopkins. Edward (Ted)
	Elevated to Life Vice President
1969 - 1977	Maidment, M.B.E. Walter G.
	Elevated to Life Vice President
1970 -	Cox. Reg A. Deceased
1971 - 1976	John, M.B.E. Myrddin
	Elevated to Life Vice President
1971 - 1975	Parfitt, M.B.E. Vernon J.
1974 -	Williams. Glen G.
1975 - 1976	Hooper. Wilf
	Deceased
1975 -	Pine. Gordon

1976 -	Davies. Sonia
1977 - 1979	Evans. Ron B.
1977 - 1990	Jones. Wyndham H.
	Elevated to Life Vice President
1978 -	Evans. Raye
1979 - 1978	Botting. Norman
	Resigned
1979 -	Llewellyn. John
	Deceased
1983 - 1984	George. Basil
	Elevated to Life Vice President
1983 - 1996	Keitch. Rita
	Elevated to Life Vice President
1984 - 1996	Jones-Pritchard. John A.
	Elevated to Life
1994 -1996	Williams. Averil
	Elevated to Life
1996 -	Parker, M.B.E. Linda
1996 -	Williams. Dave
	Deceased
1996 -	Williams. T. Peter

1996 -   Griffiths, M.B.E. Dr Wayne

CHAIRMEN

1933. 20 June - 1934. 14 February   Parker. Harry

                                             Athletics

1934. 14 February-1939.19 April   Peach. T.Harry

                                             Lawn Bowls

1948. 03. March - 1948.19 April   Peach.T. Harry

                                             Lawn Bowls

1948. 19 April - 1949.20 July   O'Donnell. Eddie W.

                                             Athletics

1949. 20 September - 1952. 25 January Taylor, M.M. A. Gus

                                             Swimming

1952. 25 January - 1959. 26 January   Howell. Cyril.

                                             Athletics

Following this the Chairman became President

VICE-CHAIRMEN

1933 - 1934   Peach. T.Harry
                                             Bowls

1934 - 1939   O'Donnell. Eddie W.

                                             Athletics

1948 - 1950	Taylor, M.M. A. Gus
	Swimming
1950 - 1952	Howell. Cyril
	Athletics
1952 -	Braddick. Reg Kenneth
	Cycling

SECRETARIES

1933. 20, June-1937.24, March	Green. R.P.
	Swimming
1937. 24, March- 1939. 19, April	Matthews. Ivor
	Boxing
1948.19, April -1959. 26, January	Prater, Ted
	C.C.P.R.
1959.26, January-1973.19, August	Williams, M.B.E. Jack
	Athletics
1974. 01, August-1975.01, August	Jones. Wyndham H.
	Rowing
1976.29, January -1976. 22, September	Hooper. Wilf
	Swimming

1976. 22, September - 1977.26, January	Jones. Wyndham H.
	Rowing
1977.26, January-1983. 22, March	Turner. D. Robert (Bob)
	Fencing
1983. 22, March -	John, M.B.E. Myrddin
	Weightlifting

TREASURERS

1933.20, July- 1939.19, April	Wood. John A.
	Boxing
1948.03, March- 1948.14, July	Wood. John A.
	Boxing
1948.03, September-1951.29, January	Swarbrick. Lieut.Colonel Ernest
	Swimming
1951. 29, January-1954.04, October	Prater. Edward H. C.C.P.R.
1954. 04, October-1955. 02,.May	Cox. Reg A.
	Bowls
1955. 07, November-1957. 01 May	Fisher. William E.
	Athletics

1958. 06, January-1961. 10, April	Jenkins. Emlyn
	Weightlifting
1961. 03, July-1983.22, March	Jones. Wyndham H.
	Rowing
1983. 22, March-	Jones-Pritchard. John A. Swimming

MEDICAL ADVISERS

08.06.53	Wilson. Dr J. Greenwood
04.10.54	Powell-Phillips. Dr D.W.
26.01.59	Grant. Dr Graham
30.01.63	Lloyd. Dr Kenneth
31.01.79	Williams. Dr J.P.R.
10.06.81	Griffiths, M.B.E. Dr Wayne
2000	Jones. Dr Gareth Lloyd

CHAPTER SEVEN

TEAM OFFICIALS

CHEF DE MISSION

1966	Howell. Cyril M.
1970	Howell. Cyril M.
1974	Howell. Cyril M.
1978	Howell. Cyril M.
1982	Jones. Wyndham H.
1986	Rees. Tommy
1990	Rees. Tommy
1994	John, M.B.E. Myrddin
1998	Jones-Pritchard. John A.

GENERAL TEAM MANAGERS

	General Team Manager	Deputy
1930	With English Team	
1934	Green, M. M. R. P.	
1938	With English Team	
1950	With English Team	
1954	Prater. Edward (Ted)	
1958	Hopkins. Edward (Ted)	

General Team Manager	Deputy
1962 Hopkins. Edward (Ted)	
1966 Hopkins. Edward (Ted)	
1970 Jones, O.B.E. Raymond E.	Jones. Wyndham H.
1974 Jones, O.B.E. Raymond E.	Jones. Wyndham H.
1978 Jones, O.B.E. Raymond E.	Jones. Wyndham H.
1982 Jones, O.B.E. Raymond E.	Pine. Gordon
1986 John, M.B.E. Myrddin	Williams. Averil
1990 John, M.B.E. Myrddin	George. Basil
1994 Jones-Pritchard. John A.	Williams. Averil. Howell. Fred
1998 Keitch. Rita	Williams. Peter. Perrins. John. Phelps. Bill

Myrddin John, General Team Manager Tîm 1986 and Averil Williams,
Deputy General Team Manager

TEAM ATTACHÉ

1954   Howard. Bruce   Vancouver

1962   Hughes. R.   Perth

1966   Evans. Clifford   Kingston

1970	Evans. Elis	Edinburgh
1974	McVeigh. Charles E.	Christchurch
1978	Russell. Dr Kelvin	Edmonton
1982	Wruck. Leon	Brisbane
1986	Hopkins. Elgar	Edinburgh
1990	Davies. Richard	Auckland
1994	Richards. Gwerfyl	Victoria
1998	Ibrahim. Alias	Kuala Lumpur

XVIᵀᴴ COMMONWEALTH GAMES KUALA LUMPUR 1998
WALES WEIGHTLIFTING

L to R Back Row:
Arfon Roberts, David Morgan, Robert Earwicker, Marius Hardiman, Jonathan Roberts.

Front Row:
Delfrig John, Neil Taylor, Gareth Hives, Simon Roach, Tony Morgan, Alan Lee.

CHAPTER EIGHT

WELSH TEAMS IN THE TWENTIETH CENTURY

M – Male   F - Female

Athlete	Sex	Discipline

1930

Headquarters

Wales did not have an Headquarters. England agreed to look after Valerie Davies.

Swimming

Athlete	Sex	Discipline
Davies. E. Valerie	F	100 yards Freestyle
		100 yards Backstroke
		400 yards Freestyle

1934

Headquarters

Athlete	Sex	Discipline
Green. R. P.	M	General Team Manager

Athletics

Athlete	Sex	Discipline
Alford. J. W. L. (Jim)	M	800 yards
Cupid. Cyril G.	M	100 yards
Evans. G.J.	M	Hop Step & Jump

Fer. P. M. G.	M	440 yards
Harris. Ken W. B.	M	1 mile
Short. Wilf	M	Marathon
Tongue. Len W.	M	3 mile
Williams. C.	M	100 yards

Lawn Bowls

Davies. Thomas R.	M	Pairs
Holloway. P.	M	Singles
Kemp. W.G.	M	Fours
Manweeler. M.	M	Fours
Rees. J.	M	Fours (Skip)
Weaver. Stan	M	Pairs(Skip)
Williams. R.	M	Fours

Boxing

Barnes. Albert	M	Bantamweight
Jones. J.D.	M	Featherweight
Pottinger. Jackie	M	Flyweight
Taylor. N. Frank	M	Lightweight

Swimming

| Capon. S.H. | M | 4 x 200 yards Relay |
| Davies. E.G. | M | 4 x 200 yards Relay |

Davies. E. Valerie	F	100 yards Backstroke. 4 x 100 yards Relay. Medley Relay
Evans. I.	F	4 x 100 yards Relay
Evans. R.	M	4 x 200 yards Relay
Gold. P.	F	4 x 100 yards Relay
Greenland. Joanne	F	4 x 100 yards Relay & Medley Relay
Perkins. E.	F	4 x 100 yards Medley Relay
Perrow. A. E.	M	High Diving
Street. K.	M	4 x 200 yards Relay

1938

Headquarters

Wales did not have an Headquarters. England agreed to look after the Welsh Team.

Athletics

Alford. James W.L.	M	880 yards. 1 mile

Cycling

Braddick. Reg Kenneth	M	100 km Massed Start.
		10 mile Track

Swimming

Browning. Shelagh	F	440 yards Freestyle
Greenland. Joanne	F	110 yards Freestyle
		110 yards Backstroke
		440 yards Freestyle
Huxtable. Grahame R	M	110 yards Backstroke
		110 yards Freestyle
		440 yards Freestyle

Boxing

Reardon. Denis Patrick	M	Middleweight

1950

Headquarters

Wales did not have an Headquarters. England agreed to look after the Welsh Team.

Athletics

Richards. Tom J.	M	Marathon

Swimming

Brockway. John W.	M	110 yards Backstroke

Cycling

Campbell. Malcolm T.	M	4,000 m Individual Pursuit. 100km Road Race

1954

Headquarters

Prater. Edward (Ted)	M	General Team Manager

Athletics

Disley. John Ivor	M	3 mile. 1 mile
Jones. Ken J.	M	100 yards. 220 yards
Phillips. Peter	M	440 yards. 880 yards
Roberts. J. Clive	M	Javelin
Shaw. Robert Douglas	M	120 yards Hurdles. 440 yards Hurdles
Williams. Hywel Lloyd	M	Discus

Lawn Bowls

Devonald. R.S.	M	Fours
Hopkins. O.B.	M	Fours
Thomas. A	M	Fours

| Thomas. A. Ivor | M | Fours |
| Thomas. Alfred (Fred) | M | Singles |

Fencing

| Harding. Aileen G. M. | F | Foil |
| Reynolds. E.O.Robert | M | Foil. Épée. Sabre |

Weightlifting

| Jenkins. Ron | M | Featherweight |
| Evans. Alwyn | M | Midheavyweight |

Swimming

| Brockway. William John | M | 110 yards Backstroke |
| Linton. Phyllis Margaret | F | 110 yards Freestyle.
440 yards Freestyle |

Boxing

| Collins. Malcolm | M | Featherweight |

Cycling

Campbell. Malcolm T.	M	4,000 m Individual Pursuit.10 mile.1,000 m Time Trial. 100 km Road Race
Skene. Donald	M	1,000 m Sprint.1,000m Time Trial. 10mile Track. 100 km Road Race
Waring. P.R.	M	4,000 m Individual Pursuit. 10 m mile.1,000 m Time Trial. 100 km Road Race

1958

Headquarters

| Hopkins. Edward (Ted) | M | General Team Manager |
| Seaborne.Mrs H. | F | Administrator |

Athletics

Cook. M. J.	F	Team Manager
Jones. K.	M	Team Manager
Alford. Jim W.	M	Coach
Barnett. Jackie	F	220 yards
Billington. T. Ray	M	880 yards
Davies. John R.	M	Shot
Davies. Rhys B.	M	Marathon
Dewar. Neil	M	Pole Vault

Disley. John	M	3 mile
Dodd. Richard	M	Triple Jump
Fletcher. Colin K.	M	Pole Vault
Franklin. Ron G.	M	Marathon
Gazard. Ray	M	Long Jump
Grainger. E.	F	4 x 100 yards Relay
Hall. LGoldie M.	M	Hammer
Horrell. A.Norman	M	880 yards
Jones. Bonnie F. yards	F	100 yards. Long Jump. 4 x 100 Relay
Jones. D.H.	M	440 yards
Jones. John C.	M	220 yards.
Jones. Ron	M	100 yards. 4 x 100 yards. Relay
Jones. Sally	F	Long Jump
Lewis. Gwyneth	F	100 yards. 220 yards. 4 x110 yards Relay
Lewis. Sheila L.	F	80 m Hurdles
Merriman. John L.	M	3 mile. 6 mile
Morgan. John E.P.	M	100 yards. 4 x 100 yards. Relay
Morgan. Terence	M	High Jump
Oliver. J. Wynne	M	220 yards
Pemberton. Malcolm W.	M	Discus

Phillips. Kevin M.	M	High Jump
Pumfrey. Anthony F.	M	1 mile
Rees. Dyfrig	M	Marathon
Richards. David Y.H.	M	3 mile
Roberts. David W.	M	100 yards. 4 x100 yards Relay
Sexton. Brian G.	M	Javelin
Shaw. Robert D.	M	440 yards Hurdles
Tawton. Haydn G.	M	880 yards
Thomas. Carol M.	F	80 m Hurdles
Turner. B.	F	100 yards
Watkins. Norman D.	M	Javelin
Whitehead. Jean A.	F	100 & 220 yards. 4 x 100 yards Relay
Whitehead. Neville J.(Nick)	M	100 & 220 yards. 4 x 100 yards Relay
Williams. Daphne H.	F	220 yards
Williams. Hywel L.	M	Discus. Shot.
Williams. John M.	M	880 yards
Wood. Tom C.	M	Marathon
Woolley. J. Bryan	M	Long Jump

Lawn Bowls

Yeoman. T.	M	Manager
Griffiths. Jack A.	M	Rinks
Hill. Len	M	Rinks
John. Wilfred	M	Pairs
Jones. Evan	M	Rinks
Lewis. Jack H.	M	Pairs
Prosser. Danny	M	Rinks
Williams. A.Bernard	M	Singles

Fencing

Lloyd. J.E.	M	Manager
Evans. J. John	M	Foil. Épee.Team Foil
Kerslake. Malcolm V.	M	Sabre. Team Foil.Team Sabre
King. J. M.	F	Foil
Lucas. T.R.	M	Sabre. Team Sabre
McCombe. J.	M	Foil. Team Foil
Maunder. Roger A.	M	Épée. Sabre. Team Épée. Team Foil. Team Sabre
Preston. John	M	Foil. Team Foil.Team Sabre
Waters. M.	F	Foil
Williams. J.L.	M	Épée. Team Épée

Weightlifting

Kelly. T.Eddie	M	Manager
Barnett. Melville J.	M	Midheavyweight
Evans. Alwyn	M	Midheavyweight
Evans. W. Iorrie	M	Middleweight
Heywood. John	M	featherweight
Jenkins. Ronald	M	Lightweight
John. Myrddin	M	Bantamweight
Newman. Gordon	M	Middleweight

Swimming

Hooper. Berenice	F	Manager
Marshall. R.	F	Official
Beavan. J.E.	M	220 yards Breastsroke. 440 yards Relay Medley.
Booth. C.C.	M	110 yards Backstroke.
Brockway. W. John	M	110 yards Backstroke. 440 yards Medley Relay
Davies D.	F	110 yards Backstroke
Dixon. J.	F	110 yards Backstroke. 440 yards Medley Relay

Edwards. E.M.	M	440 yards Freestyle. 1650 yards. Freestyle.880 yards Freestyle Relay
Evans. R.A.	M	220 yards Butterfly. 440 yards Medley Relay
Flook. B.	M	440 yards Freestyle. 880 yards Freestyle Relay
Francis. G. M.	F	110 yards Butterfly. 440 yards Freestyle Relay . 440 yards Medley Relay
Glasenbury. D.	M	880 yards Freestyle Relay
Hansard. C.J.	M	1650 yards Freestyle
Hewitt. J.C.	M	220 yards Breaststroke
Hooper. Jocelyn C.	F	110 yards Freestyle. 440 yards Freestyle. 440 yards Freestyle Relay . 440 yards Medley Relay
Howells. Miss G.	F	220 yards Breaststroke. 440 yards Freestyle Relay . 440 yards Medley Relay
Jenkins. R.H.	M	220 yards Breaststroke
Lemare. Miss J.	F	220 yards Breaststroke
Linguard. W.	M	High Diving
Morgan. G.C.	M	110 yards Freestyle. 880 yards Freestyle Relay
Newman. B.F.	M	110 yards Freestyle. 440 yards Medley Relay

O'Brien. N.	M	220 yards Butterfly
Roberts. A.	M	Diving Springboard
Shaddick. C.E.	F	220 yards Breaststroke
Stevens. A.J.	M	110 yards Backstroke
Townsend. J.M.	F	110 yards Freestyle. 440 yards Freestyle Relay

Boxing

Llewellyn. John	M	Manager
Manning. W.H.	M	Coach
Waters. W.	M	Coach
Williams. K.A.	M	Chief Coach
Braithwaite. Donald G.	M	Flyweight
Brown. W.G.	M	Light Middleweight
Collins. Malcolm	M	Featherweight
Higgins. A.Robert	M	Lightheavyweight
Phillips. W.G.	M	Welterweight
Pleace. Robert	M	Heavyweight
Robson. J.B.	M	Lightweight
Waters. G. M.	M	Middleweight
Winstone. Howard	M	Bantamweight

Rowing

Thomas. M.L.	M	Manager
Williams. Dr. K.A.	M	Coach
Brown. G.H.	M	Fours
Edwards. David C.	M	Pairs. Fours Without Cox
Edwards. John H. M.	M	Pairs. Fours Without Cox
Page. John L.	M	Fours Without Cox
Pritchard. David L.	M	Fours Without Cox

Cycling

Davies. T.R.H.	M	Manager
Bodman. W.H.C.	M	1,000 m Sprint. 1,000 m Time Trial
Evans. D.S.	M	4,000 m Individual Pursuit. 10 Mile Scratch
Hooper. N.	M	120 mile Road Race
Hughes. C.	M	120 mile Road Race
Humphreys. G.	M	4,000 m Individual Pursuit. 10 m mile Scratch
Morgan. D. M.	M	120 mile Road Race
Rees. C.	M	1,000 m Sprint. 1,000 m Time Trial
Richards. R.W.	M	4,000 m Individual Pursuit

Roach. R.S.	M	120 mile Road Race
Skene. Donald	M	1,000 m Sprint. 1,000 m Time Trial. 10 mile Scratch

Wrestling

Harvey. E.	M	Manager & Heavyweight
Bailey. Geoffrey	M	Middleweight
Dodd. J.B.	M	Lightheavyweight
Griffiths. S.	M	Flyweight
Scott. A.	M	Welterweight
Yates. R.D.	M	Lightweight

1962

Headquarters

Hopkins. Edward (Ted)	M	General Team Manager

Athletics

Barnett. Jackie	F	880 yards
Davies. Lynn	M	100 yards. Long Jump.
England. Dave M.	M	220 yards. 4 x 110 yards Relay
Jones. T.Berwin	M	100 yards 4 x 110 yards Relay
Jones. Ron	M	100 yards. 4 x 110 yards Relay

Hall. LGoldie M.	M	Shot. Hammer
Harris. Anthony J.	M	880 yards
Merriman. John L.	M	6 mile. Marathon
Whitehead. Neville (Nick)	M	100 yards. 220 yards. 4 x 110 yards Relay

Lawn Bowls

Evans. A.E.	M	Singles. Fours
Griffiths. T.	M	Pairs. Fours
Probert. E.L.	M	Pairs. Fours
Stephens. C.L.V.	M	Fours

Fencing

Ellis. Vivienne	F	Foil
Evans. J.J.	M	Foil. Sabre. Team Foil. Team Épée. Team Sabre
Maunder. R.A.	M	Foil. Sabre. Team Foil. Team Épée. Team Sabre
McCombe. J.	M	Sabre. Team Foil. Team Épée. Team Sabre
Reynolds. B.A.	F	Foil
Reynolds. R.G.	M	Foil. Épée. Team Épée

Weightlifting

Arthur. Peter	M	Lightheavyweight
Johnson. Horace A.	M	Middleweight
Owen. Ieuan W.	M	Lightweight

Swimming

Beavan. J.L.	M	110 & 220 yards Breaststroke
Hooper. Jocelyn C.	F	110 yards Freestyle. 110 yards Breaststroke. 440 yards Individual Medley
Jenkins. B.	M	110 & 220 Yards Butterfly. 440 yards Individual Medley
Jones. R.	M	110 & 220 yards Backstroke
Phillips. Glenda May	F	110 yards Freestyle. 110 yards Breaststroke. 110 yards Butterfly
Shaddick. C.	F	110 & 220 yards Breaststroke

Boxing

James. L.G.(Rocky)	M	Heavyweight
Lendrum. R.J.	M	Featherweight
Paley. D.R.	M	Lightheavyweight
Rees. G.W.	M	Light Welterweight

| Renney. B.V. | M | Lightweight |

Cycling

Davies. M. J.	M	4,000 m Individual Pursuit. 120 Mile Road Race. 10 mile Scratch
Hutchins. A.P.	M	4,000 m Individual Pursuit. 120 mile Road Race. 10 mile Scratch
Skene. D.J.C.	M	1,000 m Sprint. 1,000m Time Trial. 10 mile Scratch

Rowing

Edwards. D.C.	M	Pairs. Without Cox Fours
Edwards. J.H.M.	M	Pairs. Without Cox Fours
Luke. J.C.	M	Without Cox Fours
Luke. R.T.	M	Without Cox Fours

1966

Headquarters

Hopkins. Ted	M	General Team Manager
Williams. J.D.B.	M	Administrator
Fearnley. C.E.	M	Administrator

Athletics

Pickering. Ron J.	M	Coach
Appleby. Thelwyn	F	100, 220 & 440 yards. 4 x 110 yards Relay
Davies. Howard G.	M	220 & 440 yards
Davies. Lynn	M	Long Jump. 100 yards. 4 x 110 yards Relay
Davies. Terrence	M	100 & 220 yards. 4 x 110 yards Relay
Dourass. Gloria	F	100, 220 & 440 yards. 4 x 110 yards Relay
Gill. Elizabeth A.	F	100 yards. 220 yards. 4 x 10 yards Relay
Harris. Anthony J.	M	880 yards. 1 mile
Hart. Roy A.	M	20 mile Walk
Jones. Ronald	M	100 yards. 4 x 110 yards Relay
Jones. William K.	M	100 yards. 220 yards. 4 x 110 yards Relay
Longe. Clive C.	M	Decathlon
Parsons. Elizabeth M.	F	100 yards. 220 yards. 4 x 110 yards Relay

Badminton

Jennings. Howard R.	M	Singles. Pairs
Seaman. Peter A.	M	Singles. Pairs

Fencing

Davis. Julia M.	F	Foil. Team Foil
Julian. Angela M.	F	Foil. Team Foil
McGrath. John N.	M	Épée.Team Épée. Sabre. Team Foil
Reynolds. Andrew S.	M	Foil. Team Foil. Sabre. Team Sabre
Reynolds. Frances R.	F	Foil. Team Foil
Reynolds. Robert G.	M	Foil. Épée. Team Foil. Team Épée. Team Sabre
Turner. D. Robert(Bob)	M	Foil. Épée. Sabre. Team Foil. Team Épée. Team Sabre

Weightlifting

Acocks. Jack	M	Manager
Arthur. Peter J.	M	Lightheavyweight
Chung Kum Weng	M	Featherweight
Johnson. Horace A.	M	Middleweight
Owen. Ieuan W.	M	Lightweight
Perdue. Terence	M	Heavyweight

Swimming

Bevan. Julia Lynne	F	110 yards Breaststroke. 220 yards Breaststroke
Haswell. Madeline	F	Diving Springboard. High Diving

Jenkins. Ronald H.	M	110 yards Breaststroke. 220 yards Breaststroke.440 yards Medley
Jones. Roderick S.	M	110 yards Backstroke. 220 yards Backstroke. 440 yards Relay Medley .440 yards Freestyle Relay
Lewis. Alan	M	110 yards Freestyle. 440 yards Freestyle Relay
Moran. Kevin	M	110 yards Freestyle. 440 yards Freestyle Relay
Phillips. Glenda May	F	110 yards Freestyle. 110 yards & 220 yards Butterfly
Priestley. David	M	Diving Springboard. Diving Platform
Rees. Keith D.	M	110 yards Freestyle. 440 yards C Relay Medley. 440 yards Freestyle Relay
Ross. K.	M	110 yards Freestyle
Woodroffe. Martyn J.	M	110 yards Butterfly. 220 yards Butterfly. 440 yards Medley. 440 yards Medley Relay

Boxing

Whelan. R.J.	M	Coach
Aldridge. Maurice A.	M	Flyweight
Cranswick. Donald G.	M	Middle Lightweight

Cutts. Ian G.	M	Light Welterweight
Dwyer. Thomas H.	M	Featherweight
Perry. Reginald D.	M	Lightweight

Shooting

Lewis. T.V.	M	Coach
Williams. G.G.	M	Coach
Dunn. Thomas W.	M	Smallbore Rifle
Dyer. Douglas D.	M	Smallbore Rifle
Hassell. Robert S.	M	.22 Rapid Fire Pistol. Centre Pistol
Pryor. John	M	.303 Rifle
Swansea. Lord		
John	M	.303 Rifle

Cycling

Dyer. John	M	1,000 m Sprint Without Handicap. 10 mile Without Handicap. 1,000 m Time Trial
Lewis. Colin	M	4,000 m Pursuit. 120 miles Road Race

Pratt. Roger T.	M	4,000 m Pursuit. 120 mile Road Race
Smart. Edward C.	M	4,000 m Pursuit. 10 mile Without Handicap. 120 m mile Road Race.1,000 m Time Trial. 1,000 m Sprint Without Handicap

1970

Headquarters

Howell. Cyril M.	M	Commandant
Jones. Raymond E.	M	General Team Manager
Reynolds. Jackie	F	Deputy General Team Manager
Jones. Wyndham H.	M	Treasurer
Williams, M.B.E. J.D.B.	M	Secretary
Fearnley. Charles E.	M	Administrator

Jack Williams Secretary

Medical Staff

Lloyd. Dr Kenneth   M   Medical Officer

Burge. T.C.	M	Physiotherapist
Edwards. Marilyn J.	F	Physiotherapist
Holley. Tom P.J.	M	Physiotherapist

Athletics

Evans. Raye M.	F	Manager
Hopkins. Edward.(Ted)	M	Manager
Lay. Peter A.	M	Coach
Adams. Robert S. (Bob)	M	800 m
Ashton. Anthony F.(Tony)	M	5,000 m
Bateman. Thelwyn	F	800 m 1,500 m
Craig. Christine S.	F	High Jump
Davies. D. Hedydd	D	Marathon
Davies. Hilary	F	100 m 200 m
Davies. Howard G.	M	400 m 4 x 100 m Relay
Davies. M.B.E. Lynn.	M	Long Jump.100 m 4 x100 m Relay
Davies. Maurice G.(Mal)	M	Hammer
Davies. Terry	M	200 m 4 x 100 m Relay
Davis. Gwynne C.	M	1,500 m 5,000 m
Dourass. Gloria	F	400 m 800 m
Greatrex. John M.	M	800 m
Griffiths. D. Gwynne	M	400 m

Griffiths. Peter J.L.	M	3,000 m Steeplechase
Hayward. Bernard L.	M	3,000 m Steeplechase
Hirst. A. June	F	Pentathlon
James. Alun A.	M	110 m Hurdles
Jones. Ronald	M	100 m 200 m 4x100 m Relay
Joslyn. Alan L.	M	5,000 m 10,000 m
Lease. David N.	M	Pole Vault
Leigh. Cyril T.	M	Marathon
Lewis. Phillip J.	M	800 m
Martin-Jones. Ruth	F	100 m 200 m Pentathlon
Maplestone. Robert N.	M	1,500 m
McAndrew. Ronald	M	3,000 m Steeplechase
Pearce. Maureen L.	F	Shot Put
Plain. Bernard John	M	5,000 m 10,000 m
Price. Berwyn	M	110 m Hurdles
Richardson. Roger C.	M	400 m Hurdles
Rosser. R. David	M	20 mile Walk
Rowland. Michael	M	Marathon
Sherlock. Nigel E.	M	Javelin
Shiels. Patrice Margaret	F	100 m 200 m
Smith. Michele	F	100 m 200 m

Thomas. Phillip L.	M	1,500 m
Walters. E. John	M	Shot. Discus
Webb. Graham	M	Triple Jump
Williams. Averil Muriel	F	Javelin
Williams. Gwynfryn J.	M	Long Jump
Williams. John J.	M	100 m 200 m 4 x 100 m Relay

Badminton

Pine. S. Gordon	M	Manager
Colmer. W. David	M	Singles. Pairs
Gully. Stephen J. (Steve)	M	Singles. Pairs. Pairs Medley
Hughes. Susan (Sue)	F	Singles. Pairs. Pairs Medley
Jennings. Howard R.	M	Singles. Pairs. Pairs Medley
Morgan. J.	M	Singles. Pairs
Stockden. Julie	F	Singles. Pairs. Pairs Medley

Lawn Bowls

Toms. Trevor	M	Manager
Howells. Gwyn	M	Pairs
Jenkins. D. Leighton	M	Pairs
John. E. Aeron	M	Fours

Jones. A. Roy	M	Fours
Pattimore. William E.	M	Fours
Thompson. C.Henry	M	Fours
Wilkins. J. David	M	Singles

Weightlifting Team 1970 <u>Left to Right</u> Peter Arthur, Terry Bennett, Peter Nitsch, Horace Johnson, Terry Perdue, Ieuan Owen, Robert Wrench, Meurin Williams, John Jones. Front Row Myrddin John, Chung Kum Weng

<u>Weightlifting</u>

John, M.B.E. Myrddin	M	Coach
Jones. John G.	M	Manager

Arthur. Peter J.	M	Lightheavyweight
Bennett. Terry	M	Middleweight
Chung. Kum Weng	M	Featherweight
Johnson. Horace A.	M	Middleweight
Owen. Ieuan W.	M	Lightweight
Nitsch. Peter J.	M	Midheavyweight
Perdue. Terry R.J.	M	Superheavyweight
Williams. D. Meurin	M	Bantamweight
Wrench. Robert	M	Middleweight

Fencing

Pearson. K.	M	Coach
Reynolds. Glyn S.	M	Manager
Barkley. Julia	F	Foil. Team Foil
Brown. Lynda	F	Foil. Team Foil
Edwards. Ian Llewellyn	F	Foil. Sabre. Team Sabre
Lucas. Derek J.	F	Épée. Team Épée
McGrath. John N.	M	Team Épée
Reynolds. Andrew S.	M	Foil. Sabre. Team Sabre
Reynolds. Frances R.	F	Foil. Team Foil
Reynolds. Robert. G.	M	Foil. Épée. Team Foil. Team Sabre
Turner. D. Robert	M	Épée. Team Épée

Swimming

Eady. Roger J.	M	Coach
Hooper. Berenice H.	F	Manager
Bowen. Bernadette	F	200 m 400 m & 800 m Freestyle. 4 x100 m Freestyle
Bryce. Donald	M	Diving Springboard
Comins. Jacqueline L.	F	100 m Butterfly. 200 m & 400 m Individual Medley. 4 x100 m Relay Medley
Davies. Christine	F	100 m & 200 m Breaststroke. 4 x 100 m Relay Freestyle. 4 x 100 m. Relay Medley
Davies. Vivian J.	M	100 m & 200 m Breaststroke. 200 m Individual Medley
Edwards. Ceinwen B.	F	100 m & 200 m Breaststroke
Godfrey. Peter Charles	M	100 m & 200 m Butterfly
Hamilton. Jane F.	F	Diving Springboard. Diving Platform
Hurn. Sally A.	F	200 m Freestyle
Johnson. Nigel R.	M	100 m & 200 m Breaststroke
Jones. G. Rowland	M	400 m Individual Medley. 200 m Backstroke
Jones. Susan	F	200 m 400 m & 800 m Freestyle. 4 x100 m Freestyle Relay
Lewis. Clive M.	M	100 m Backstroke

Maher. Sean L.	M	100 m Butterfly. 200 m & 400 m Individual. 100 m & 400 m Freestyle. 4 x100 m & 4 x 200 m Freestyle Relay
Moran. Kevin	M	100 m Freestyle. 4 x100 m Freestyle Relay. 4 x 100 m Medley Relay
Morgan. Trevor G.	M	100 m & 200 m Breaststroke
Parsons. Janice	F	Diving Springboard. Platform Diving
Price. Stephanie R.	F	100 m Freestyle. 4 x 100 m Freestyle Relay. 4 x 100 m Medley Relay
Richards. Martin	M	400 m & 1,500 m Freestyle. 4 x 100 m & 4 x 200 m Freestyle Relay. 4 x100 m Medley Relay
Richards. Michael J.	M	100 m & 200 m Backstroke
Simpson. Nigel K.	M	100 m & 200 m Backstroke. 4 x 200 m Freestyle Relay
Stephens. Gail F.	F	100 m & 200 m Backstroke. 4 x 100 m Medley Relay
Thomas. Cheryl	F	100 m Freestyle
Wells. Pat C.	F	100 m & 200 m Breaststroke

Williams. Alan	M	100 m 200 m & 400 m Freestyle. 4 x 100 m & 4 x 200 m Freestyle Relay
Woodroffe. Martyn J.	M	200 m & 400 m Individual Medley 100 m & 200 m Butterfly. 4 x 100 m Medley Relay

Boxing

Llewellyn. John P	M	Manager
Hawksworth. L.J.	M	Coach
Roberts. E. M.	M	Coach
Davies. Anthony	M	Lightflyweight
Davies. David I.	M	Lightwelterweight
Davies. Phillip	M	Bantamweight
Phillips. Martin	M	Lightweight
Lloyd. Peter. M	M	Middle Lightweight
May. William James	M	Middleweight
McCluskie. Michael	M	Welterweight
O'Sullivan. Maurice A.	M	Flyweight
Pritchard. Edward V.	M	Featherweight
Roberts. Anthony M.	M	Lightheavyweight

Cycling

Richards. R.W.	M	Manager
Williams. Sam J.	M	Manager

Beswick. John M.	M	1,000 m Sprint Scratch. 2000 m Tandem Sprint
Davies. John (Cornelly)	M	4,000 m Individual Pursuit. 10 mile Scratch
Davies. John (Rhondda)	M	1,000 m Time Trial. 10 mile Scratch
Hatfield. John T.	M	1,000 m Sprint Scratch. 2000 m Tandem Sprint. 10 mile Scratch
Jenkins. Graeme J.	M	102 mile Road Race
Mery. Roland E. R.	M	102 mile Road Race
Milward. Andrew R.	M	4,000 m Individual Pursuit. 1,000 m. Time Trial. 10 mile Scratch
Pritchard. John	M	4,000 m Individual Pursuit. 1,000 m. Time Trial
Russell. David J.	M	1000 m Sprint Scratch

1974

Headquarters

Howell. Cyril M.	M	Commandant
Jones. Raymond E.	M	General Team Manager
Jones. Wyndham H.	M	Deputy General Team Manager
Hooper. Berenice	M	Chaperone
Pine. S. Gordon	M	Administrator

| Rees. Ann | F | Administrator |
| McVeigh. Charles | M | Attaché |

Medical

| Lloyd. Dr Kenneth | M | Chief Medical Officer |
| Holley. Tom | M | Physiotherapist |

Athletics

Snow. Reg C.G.	M	Manager
Clemo. Anthony (Tony)	M	Coach
Davies. John	M	3,000 m Steeplechase. 1,500 m 5,000 m
Delaney. Michael	M	200 m 400 m
Dourass. Gloria	F	400 m 800 m
Hayward. Bernard	M	3,000 m Steeplechase. 800 m 1,500 m
James. Susan	F	Javelin
Lease. David	M	Pole Vault
Lewis. Philip	M	800 m
Leyshon. Wynford	M	400 m Hurdles. 400 m
Lockhead. Jean	F	800 m 1,500 m
Martin-Jones. Ruth	F	Long Jump
Minty. Gordon	M	5,000 m 10,000 m
O'Neil. Colin	M	400 m Hurdles

Plain. Bernard	M	10,000 m. Marathon
Price. Berwyn	M	110 m Hurdles
Thomas. Malcolm	M	Marathon

Badminton

Alfieri. Susan (Sue)	F	Singles. Pairs Mixed
Jennings. Howard	M	Singles. Pairs Mixed

Lawn Bowls

Toms. Trevor	M	Manager
Evans. Maldwyn (Mal)	M	Singles
Evans. Russell	M	Pairs
Humphreys. Gareth	M	Fours
Jenkins. D. Leighton	M	Fours
Richards. David	M	Fours
Stanbury. Ellis	M	Pairs
Sutherland. Ian	M	Fours

Weightlifting

Evans. W. Iorrie	M	Manager
Bennett. Terence	M	Middleweight
Brown. Michael (Mike)	M	Heavyweight
Burns. John	M	Midheavyweight
Chung. Kum Weng	M	Featherweight

Owen. Ieuan W.	M	Lightweight
Perdue. Terry	M	Superheavyweight
Williams. D. Meurin	M	Featherweight
Wrench. Robert	M	Middleweight
Nitsch. Peter	M	Midheavyweight

Swimming

Huxtable. Grahame	M	Manager
Hooper. Berenice	F	Coach
Adams. Anne W.	F	Butterfly 100 m. Individual Medley 200 m & 400 m
Beavan. Patricia (Pat)	F	Breaststroke 100 m & 200 m. Individual Medley 200 m
Culverwell. Nigel J.	M	Backstroke 100 m & 200 m
Davies. Vivian J.	M	Breaststroke 100 m & 200 m. Individual Medley 400 m
Davis. Elizabeth (Liz)	F	Backstroke 100 m & 200 m
Hurn. Sally A. Butterfly	F	Freestyle 100 m & 200 m 200 m
John. Penelope (Penny) R.	F	Butterfly 200 m. Freestyle 400 m. Individual Medley 400 m
Jones. G. Rowland	M	Backstroke 100 m & 200 m. Individual Medley 400 m
Lewis. Clive	M	Freestyle 100 m & 200m. Backstroke 100 m

Maher. Sean	M	Butterfly 100 m. Individual Medley 200 m
Moran. Kevin	M	Freestyle 100 m
Parry. Judith	F	Breaststroke 100 m & 200 m. Individual Medley 400 m
Walker. Kim	F	Backstroke 100 m & 200 m. Freestyle 100 m

Boxing

Davies. John	M	Manager
Evans. Gwilym	M	Coach
Allen. William (Billy)	M	Middleweight
Bennett. Wayne	M	Lightweight
Davies. Christopher	M	Featherweight
Griffiths. Bryn	M	Flyweight
McKenzie. Errol	M	Welterweight

Shooting

Williams. Glen	M	Manager
George. Basil	M	Assistant Manager
Whittaker.O.B.E. T.W.Gilbert	M	Assistant Manager
Bevan. Ronald	M	Shooting Clay Trap
Cross. Richard	M	Free Pistol
Gray. Stanley	M	Fullbore Rifle

Harris. Colin T.	M	Smallbore Rifle
Hassall. Robert	M	Pistol Rapidfire. Free Pistol
Lewis. Phillip	M	Shooting Clay Trap
O'Dwyer. Terence	M	Rapidfire Pistol
Rees. Roger J	M	Skeet Shooting
Swansea. Lord.	M	Fullbore Rifle
Watkins. William H.	M	Smallbore Rifle

Cycling

Williams. John (Johnny)	M	Manager
Demery. Thomas Edwin	M	114 mile Road Race
Hatfield. John	M	1,000 m 2,000 m Tandem. 10 mile. Team Pursuit
James. John	M	114 mile Road Race
Pritchard. John	M	Time Trial Kilo. Individual Pursuit . 10 mile. Team Pursuit
Smith. Barrie (Jingles)	M	114 mile Road Race. Individual Pursuit. Team Pursuit
Taylor. Phillip Pursuit	M	Time Trial Kilo. Individual 10 mile. Team Pursuit.
Thornton. Colin	M	114 mile Road Race. Individual Pursuit . Team Pursuit
Tudor. John	M	1,000 m 2,000 m Tandem. 10 mile

<u>Top</u> Wales Team 1978

<u>Bottom</u> - Staff Headquarters Wales 1978 <u>Left to right</u> Tony Clemo, Tom Holley,
Dr Ken Lloyd, Ruth Howell, Raymond Jones, Pat Beavan, Cyril Howell, Berwyn
Price, Fred Howell, Gordon Pine, Bob Turner

312

1978

Headquarters

Howell. Cyril M.	M	Commandant
Jones. Raymond E.	M	General Team Manager
Jones. Wyndham H.	M	Deputy General Team Manager
Pine. Gordon	M	Administrator
Howell. Fred	M	Administrator
Turner. Robert	M	Administrator
Farnel. Jodi (Canada)	F	Office Clerk
Beavan. Pat	F	Chaperone
Lloyd. Dr Kenneth	M	Medical
Clemo. Tony	M	Transport Officer
Russell. Dr Kelvin	M	Attaché

Athletics

Snow. Reg	M	Manager
Williams. Averil	F	Manager
Arnold. Malcolm	M	Coach
Davies. John	M	3,000 m Steeplechase. 5,000 m
Delaney. Michael	M	400 m 4 x 400 m Relay
Evans. John	M	Triple Jump

Grant. Glen Arthur B.	M	800 m 1,500 m
Critchley. Michael J.	M	Marathon
James. Steve	M	4 x 400 m Relay
Griffiths. Jeffrey Stephen	M	200 m 400 m. 4 x 400 m Relay
Head. Vennissa Ann	F	Discus. Shot
Hollick. Hilary Jane	F	1,500 m
Howell. Ruth	F	Long Jump. Pentathlon
Jones. Stephen Henry	M	1,500 m
Phillips. David	M	Triple Jump
Price. Berwyn	M	110 m Hurdles. 4 x 400 m Relay
Roberts. David Lloyd	M	100 m 200 m
Rowlands. Michael J.	M	Marathon
Simmons. Anthony Derrick	M	5,000 m 10,000 m
Zaslona. Jacqueline	F	Javelin

Badminton

Hawkes. Graham	M	Manager
Blake. Linda	F	Singles. Pairs. Mixed Team
Brimble. Susan	F	Singles. Pairs. Mixed Pairs. Medley Team
Jones. Brian	M	Singles. Pairs. Mixed Team
Lim. Yim Chong	M	Singles. Pairs. Mixed Pairs. Mixed Team

Lawn Bowls

Toms. Trevor	M	Manager
Evans. Gwyn	M	Fours
Evans. John Russell	M	Singles
Morgan. James	M	Pairs
Stanbury. Ellis	M	Fours
Sutherland. Ian	M	Fours
Thompson. John	M	Fours
Williams. Raymond	M	Pairs

Weightlifting

John. Myrddin	M	Manager
John. Delfrig	M	Coach
Bennett. Terry	M	82.5 kg Class
Brown. David	M	90 kg Class
Brown. James Michael	M	110+kg Class
Bryce. Jeffrey	M	56 kg Class
Burns. John Robert	M	100 kg Class
Locking. Alan Wilson	M	90 kg Class
McCreadie. John N.	M	67.5 kg Class
Owen. Ieuan Wyn	M	67.5 kg Class
Shepherd. Robert Michael	M	60 kg Class

Gymnastics

Jones. Vyvyan	M	Manager
Keitch. Rita	F	Coach
McCarthy. Bob	M	Coach
Bernard. Linda	F	Individual All round. Team Competition
Hallam. Andrew Julian	M	Team Competition
Higgins. Michael Joseph	M	All round Individual. Team Competition
Jones. Robert	M	Individual All round. Team Competition
Pocock. Christina	F	Individual All round. Team Competition
Preedy. Paul	M	Individual All round. Team Competition
Surringer. Linda	F	Individual All round. Team Competition
Vokes. Jacqueline	F	Individual All round . Team Competition

Swimming

Crosswaite. Rosina	F	Manager
Hooper. Berenice	F	Coach

Adams. Wilma Anne	F	100 m Breaststroke. 100 m Butterfly. 200 m Individual Medley. 4 x100 m Freestyle Relay. 4 x100 m Medley Relay
Atkinson. Leigh	M	200 m Breaststroke. 4 x100 m Relay Medley
Bullock. Venissa Jane	F	4 x100 m Freestyle Relay
James. Amanda	F	100 m Backstroke. 4 x100 m Medley Relay.
Jones. Melanie Anne	F	100 m Backstroke. 200 m Backstroke. 4 x100 m Relay
Morris. Peter	M	100 m Butterfly. 200 m Butterfly. 400 m Individual Medley
Motly. Lindsey Adriene	F	100 m Backstroke. 100 m Freestyle. 4 x 100 m Freestyle Relay. 4 x 100 m Medley Relay
Roberts. David	M	Disable 100 m
Roberts. Michael	M	100 m Backstroke. 4 x 100 m Relay Freestyle. 4 x 100 m Medley Relay
Sadler. Grahame	M	200 m Freestyle. 400 m Freestyle. 4 x100 m Medley Relay
Taylor. Mark Grahame	M	200 m Freestyle. 4 x100 m Medley Relay
Thomas. Mark Morgan	M	200 m Individual Medley

Boxing

Llewellyn. John	M	Manager
Grieves. Jerry	M	Coach
Feal. Anthony	M	67 kg Class
George. David	M	54 kg Class
Jones. Russell	M	51 kg Class

Cycling

Clarke. J.H.	M	Manager
Walker. H.	M	Coach
Hamilton. Peter	M	4,000 m Individual Pursuit. 183 km Road Race
Hodge. Neil	M	183 km Road Race
Patten. David	M	1,000 m Time Trial
Pritchard. John	M	4,000 m Individual Pursuit. 183 km Road Race
Thornton. Colin	M	4,000 m Individual Pursuit
Taylor. Phillip	M	1,000 m Time Trial
Tudor. John	M	1,000 m Sprint. 1,000 m Time Trial

Shooting

Williams. Glen G.	M	Manager
George. Basil	M	Coach

Phelps. Bill	M	Coach
Whittaker. O.B.E. Lt.-Colonel	M	Coach
Bowden. Tony	M	Rapid Fire Pistol
Breeze. Emyr	M	Trap Clay Pigeon
Brown. Dennis	M	Trap Clay Pigeon
Griffiths. Robert	M	Skeet
Morley. Howell	M	Fullbore Rifle Queens Prize Pair
Rees. Roger	M	Skeet
Swansea. Lord John	M	Fullbore Rifle Queens Prize Pair
Watkins. William	M	50 m Rifle Prone
Williams. Peter	M	50 m Free Pistol

1982

Headquarters

Jones. Wyndham	M	Commandant
Jones. Raymond E.	M	General Team Manager
Pine. Gordon	M	Deputy General Team Manager
Clemo. Tony	M	Transport Manager
Howell. Fred	M	Administrator
Keitch. Rita	F	Administrator
Speck. Terry	M	Administrator

Wruck. Leon	M	Attaché

Medical

Griffiths. Dr Wayne	M	Chief Medical Officer
Russell. Dr Kelvin	M	Doctor
McKenzie. Jack	M	Physiotherapist

Athletics

Snow. Reg	M	Manager
Williams. Averil Muriel	F	Manager
Arnold. Malcolm	M	Coach
Barry. Steven	M	30 km Walk
Fowles. Dennis	M	5,000 m 10,000 m
Fryar. Diane	F	400 m Hurdles
Hackney. Roger	M	3,000 m Steeplechase
Head. Venissa	F	Shot. Discus
Hollick. Hilary	F	3,000 m 5,000 m
Jones. Stephen	M	5,000 m 10,000 m
Llewelyn. Trevor	M	High Jump
Lock. Kim	F	800 m 1,500 m 3,000 m
McDermot. Kirsty	F	400 m 800 m
Norgate. Philip	M	800 m
Owen. Sarah	F	Heptathlon

Price. Berwyn	M	110 m Hurdles
Reagan. Gillian	F	Long Jump
Rowe. Sarah	F	Heptathlon
Scutt. Michelle	F	100 m 400 m
Smart. Carmen	F	100 m 200 m

Badminton

Brimble. John	M	Manager
Richards. Mark	M	Singles. Pairs
Sutton. Philip	M	Singles. Pairs

Lawn Bowls

Stephens. Charles	M	Manager
Parker. Linda	F	Manager
Ackland. Janet	F	Triples
Miles. Gill	F	Triples
Morgan. James	M	Fours
Perkins. Lyn	M	Pairs
Pomeroy. Margaret	F	Triples
Thomas. Alun	M	Fours
Williams. Cliff	M	Fours

| Williams. Ray | M | Fours |
| Wilshire. Spencer | M | Pairs |

Weightlifting

John. Myrddin	M	Manager
Welch. Dennis	M	Coach
Bryce. Jeffrey	M	62 kg Class
Burns. John	M	110 kg Class
Easton. Paul	M	92 kg Class
Lee. Ronald	M	56 kg Class
Locking. Alan	M	92 kg Class
Morgan. David	M	69 kg Class
Shepherd. Robert	M	75 kg Class
Taylor. Gary	M	100 kg Class
Wilson. Steven	M	105 kg Class

Swimming

Jones-Pritchard. John A.	M	Manager
Williams. Bryn	M	Coach
Adkins. Karl	M	200 m Individual Medley. 4 x100 m Freestyle Relay
Atkinson. Leigh	M	100 m Breaststroke. 4 x 100 m Medley Relay

Day. Anthony	M	1.500 m Freestyle. 4 x 200 m Freestyle Relay
Gwilt. Peter	M	100 m Breaststroke. 4 x 100 m Freestyle Relay 4 x 100 m Medley Relay
Morgan. Robert	M	Diving. Springboard & Platform
Morris. Peter	M	200 m Butterfly. 4 x 200 m Freestyle Relay
Perry. Bruce	M	200 m Individual Medley. 4 x 200 m Freestyle Relay
Roberts. Stuart	M	100 m Freestyle. 4 x 100 m Freestyle Relay.4 x 100 m Medley Relay
Taylor. Mark	M	100 m & 200 m Freestyle. 4 x 100m & 4 x 200 m Freestyle Relay 100 m Medley Relay
Tucker. Clare	F	Swimmer

Boxing

Carro. Wilfred	M	Manager
Pearson. Charles	M	Coach
Alsop. Jonathan	M	60 kg
Lewis. Paul	M	71 kg

Shooting

George. Basil	M	Manager
Gilbertson. Richard	M	Fullbore Manager
Monk. Tony	M	Smallbore Manager
Arnold. David	M	Smallbore Rifle & Air Rifle 3 Position Individual & Team
Bowden. Anthony	M	Air Rifle Individual & Team
Edwards. John	M	Shooter
Harris. Colin	M	Prone Lying Rifle Team
Llewellyn. Phil	M	Skeet
O'Leary. Dion	M	Fullbore Team
Pelopida. Peter	M	Trap Team
Swansea. Lord John	M	Fullbore Team
Watkins. William	M	Prone Lying Rifle Individual & Team

Archery

Mansel-Edwards. Digby	M	Manager
Bluck. C.	M	Coach
Lewis. Anthony	M	Round FITA Double
Workman. Marion	F	Round FITA Double

Welsh Team Edinburgh 1986

1986

Headquarters

Rees. Tommy	M	Commandant
John. Myrddin	M	General Team Manager
Williams. Averil M.	F	Deputy General Manager
Evans. John	M	Administrator
Howell. Fred	M	Administrator
Keitch. Rita	F	Administrator
Hopkins. Elgar	M	Attaché

Medical

Griffiths. Dr Wayne	M	Chief Medical Officer
Phillips. Nicola	F	Physiotherapist
Phillips. Jacqueline	F	Physiotherapist

Welsh Athletics Team, Edinburgh 1986

Athletics

Williams. David	M	Manager
Elgie. Margaret	F	Manager
Arnold. Malcolm	M	Coach
Edwards. Malcolm	M	800 m
Ellis. Ieuan	M	Marathon
Evans. A.	F	400 m Hurdles

Hackney. Roger	M	3,000 m Steeplechase
Head. Venissa	F	Discus
Horsfield. Neil	M	1,500 m
Hough. Karen	F	Javelin
Jackson. Nigel	M	110 m Hurdles
Johnson. Stephen	M	30 km Walk
Jones. Steve	M	10,000 m
McKenzie. Colin	M	Javelin
Miles. Helen	F	100 m 4 x 100 m Relay .
Morley. Kay	F	100 m Hurdles. 4 x 100 m Relay .
Morris. Sharon	F	400 m
Morris. Sian	F	200 m 4 x 100 m Relay
Newnham. Tim	M	Javelin
Pickering. Shaun	M	Hammer. Discus. Shot
Reagan. Gillian	F	Long Jump
Short. Sally-Anne	F	100 m 200 m
Smart. Carmen	F	100 m 200 m. 4 x 100 m Relay
Tooby. Angela	F	10,000 m
Tooby. Susan	F	10,000 m

Vandendrook-Evans. Alyson	F	400 m Hurdles
Wade. Kirsty	F	800 m 1.500 m
Walker. Nigel	M	110 m Hurdles
Wood. David	M	Triple Jump
Williams. P.	M	800 m

Badminton

Fifield. Richard	M	Manager
Doody. Sarah	F	Singles. Pairs. Mixed Pairs
Rees. Christopher	M	Singles. Pairs
Roberts. Lesley	F	Singles. Mixed Pairs. Pairs
Sutton. Philip	M	Singles. Mixed Pairs
Williams. Lyndon	M	Pairs. Mixed Pairs

Lawn Bowls

Hubbard. Victor	M	Manager
Ackland. Janet	F	Pairs
Dainton. Ann	F	Singles
Evans. Linda	F	Fours
Hill. Ray	M	Singles
Jones. Rita	F	Fours
Parker. Linda	F	Fours

Perkins. Lyn	M	Pairs
Pomeroy. Margaret	F	Pairs
Rickets. Joan	F	Fours
Thomas. Hafod	M	Fours
Thomas. William	M	Fours
Weale. Robert	M	Fours
Wilshire. Spencer	M	Pairs

Welsh Weightlifting Team Edinburgh 1986.

Front Row Left to Right - Myrddin John, Den Welch, Jeff Bryce, Neil Taylor, Ray Williams, David Morgan, Chris Edwards, Arthur Jenkins. **Back Row** - Gareth Hives, Andrew Davies, Steve Wilson, Ken Webster

Weightlifting

Jenkins. Arthur	M	Manager
Welch. Den	M	Coach
Bryce. Jeffrey	M	60 kg
Davies. Andrew	M	100 kg
Edwards. Chris	M	56 kg
Hives. Gareth	M	82.5 kg
Morgan. David	M	82.5 kg
Taylor. Neil	M	67.5 kg
Webster. Ken	M	+110 kg
Williams. Raymond	M	60 kg
Wilson. Steve	M	110 kg

Swimming

James. Robert	M	Manager
Williams. Bryn	M	Coach
Budd. Andy	M	Diving Platform
Cumbers. Nicky	F	100. 200. 400 & 800 m Freestyle. 200 & 400m Individual Medley. 4 x 100m Freestyle Relay
Day. Anthony	M	200. 400. & 1,500 m Freestyle. 400 m Individual Medley. 4 x 100 & 4 x 200 m Freestyle Relay

Gwynne. Steven	M	200. 400 & 1,500 m Freestyle. 100 & 200 m Butterfly. 4 x 100 m & 200 m Freestyle Relay. 4 x 100m Medley Relay .
Lewis. Samantha	F	100 m Freestyle. 100 m Breaststroke 200 m Butterfly. 200 m Individual Medley. 100 m Individual Medley. 4 x 100 m Medley Relay
McKinnell. Maxine	F	100 & 200 m Freestyle. 100m Butterfly. 2 x 100 m Individual M Medley. 4 x 100 m Medley Relay 4 x 100 m Freestyle.
Morgan. Robert	M	Diving Platform. 3 m Springboard
Perry. Bruce	M	100 & 200 m Breaststroke. 100 & 200 m Individual Medley 4 x 100 m & 4 x 200 m Freestyle Relay
Reeve. Claire	F	100 & 200 m Breaststroke. 4 x 100 m Medley Relay
Rosser. Ian	M	400 m Freestyle. 100 & 200 m Freestyle. 200 & 400 m Individual Medley. 4 x 100 m Relay Freestyle 4 x 100 m Medley Relay

Tucker. Clare	F	100 & 200 m Breaststroke. 4 x 100 m Freestyle Relay 4 x 100 m Medley Relay
Williams. Gareth	M	100 & 200 m Backstroke. 100 m Butterfly. 400 m Individual Medley

Boxing

Turner. Robert	M	Manager
Dyer. Roy	M	Coach
Alsop. Jonathan	M	Light Welterweight
Khan. Tony	M	Featherweight
Haddock. Neil	M	Lightweight
Lewis. Paul	M	Middleweight
McCormack. Kevin	M	91 kg
Piper. C	M	67 kg
Pullen. Byron	M	81 kg
Thomas. Glyn	M	57 kg
Webber. Kerry	M	Flyweight

Welsh Rowing Team 1986

Rowing

Hartland. John	M	Manager
Collingwood. Dave	M	Coach
Woods. Alexander	M	Equipment Manager
Davies. Rhian	F	Singles Sculls. Singles Light Sculls
Edwards. Jeremy	M	Light Fours
Gregory. Philip	M	Fours
Hartland. Nicholas	M	Singles. Fours with Cox. Eights
Hartland. Katherine	F	Fours with Cox. Fours Without Cox
Hancock. Richard	M	Pairs Sculls
Hnatiw. Michael		D Fours. Eights
Howell. Chris		D Singles Sculls

Hyndman. Martin	D	Light Fours
Jenkins. Christopher	D	Fours with Cox. Eights with Cox
Jones. Chris	D	Fours Without Cox.
Kidwell. David	D	Light Fours
Kingsley. Louise	M	Fours with Cox. Fours without Cox
Lloyd. Ivor	D	Singles. Fours with Cox. Eights
Luke. Robert	D	Sculls Pairs
McCann. Sarah	M	Light Fours
Partridge. Michael	D	Singles. Fours with Cox. Sixes without Cox
Price. Fiona	M	Fours with Cox
Redwood. Stephen	D	Light Fours
Roberts. Iestyn	D	Fours. Eights
Roberts. Robin	D	Fours. Eights
Taylor. Paul	D	Fours with Cox. Fours without Cox. Eights
Thomas. Guy	D	Fours. Eights
Trigwell. Lorna	M	Fours with Cox. Fours without Cox
Williams. Robin	D	Singles Light Sculls

Shooting

Speck. Terry	D	Manager
Gilbertson.		
Colonel Gilbert	D	Coach
Monk. Tony	D	Coach
Clubb. David	M	Coach
Arnold. David	D	Smallbore Rifle 3 Position
Clubbe. Stuart	D	Olympic Trap
Fox. Albert	D	Free Pistol
Griffiths. Terry	D	Skeet
Harris. Colin	D	Smallbore Rifle Prone Lying
Hockley. Christopher	D	Fullbore Rifle
Irving. Gareth	D	Rapidfire Pistol

Welsh Cycling Team 1986

<u>Cycling</u>

Friswell. John	M	Manager
Williams. Bob	M	Coach
Coles. Stuart	M	100 km Team Time Trial. 105 mile Road Race
Davies. Norton	M	Time Trial Team kilo. 4,000m Team Pursuit Track 10 m mile Track

Davies. Tim	M	10 mile Track. 4,000 m Individual Pursuit.4,000 m Team Pursuit Track
Evans. John	M	100 km Time Trial Team 105 mile Road Race
Hughes. Norman	D	100 km Time Trial Team 105 mile Road Race
Jones. Keith	D	100 km Time Trial Team. 105 mile Road Race
Murphy. Mike	D	Sprint. 4.000 m Pursuit Team Track
Paulding. Steve	D	Time Trial kilo. Sprint. 10 mile Track
Westwood. Mark	D	4,000m Individual Pursuit. 4,000m Pursuit Track Team.10 mile Track

1990

Headquarters

John.M.B.E. Myrddin	D	General Team Manager
George. Basil	D	Deputy General Team Manager
Jones-Pritchard. John A.	D	Administrator
Howell. Fred	D	Administrator
Keitch. Rita	M	Administrator

Medical Staff

Griffiths. M.B.E. Dr Wayne	M	Chief Medical Officer
Munson (Phillips). Nicola	F	Physiotherapist
Phillips. Jacqueline	F	Physiotherapist

Athletics

Elgie. Margaret	F	Manager Women
Williams. David	M	Manager Men
Arnold. Malcolm	M	Coach
Bevan. Nigel	M	Javelin
Brace. Steve	M	Marathon
Edwards. Paul	M	Shot. Discus
Hackney. Roger	M	3,000 m Steeplechase
Hamer. Ian	M	1,500 m 5,000 m
Horsfield. Neil	M	800 m 1,500 m
Jackson. Colin	M	110 m Hurdles
Jones. Stephen	M	10,000 m Marathon
Miles. Helen	F	100 m 200 m. 4 x 110 m Relay
Morley. Kay	F	100 m Hurdles. 4 x 100 m Relay

Short. Sallyanne	F	100 m 200 m. 4 x100 m Relay
Smart. Carmen	F	100 m. 4 x100 m Relay
Tooby. Angela	F	10,000 m
Walker. Nigel	M	110 m Hurdles
White. Caroline	F	Javelin

Badminton

Ford. Mike	M	Manager
Rees. Christopher	M	Singles. Pairs Mixed
Williams. Sarah	F	Singles. Pairs Mixed

Cycling

Williams. Robert	D	Manager
Jones. Phillip	D	Coach
Evans. John	D	120 mile Road Race. 100 km Road Race Team Trial
Greenwood. Claire	F	3,000 m Pursuit. 60 km Road Race
Hughes. Norman	D	120 mile Road Race. 100 km Road Race Team Trial
Hughes. Richard	D	4,000 m Team Pursuit 10 mile Track.120 mile Road Race.
Jones. Louise	F	1,000 m Sprint. 60 km Road Race
McKenzie. Sally	F	300 m Pursuit. 60 km Road Race

| Paulding. Steven | M | 1,000 m Sprint. 1.000 m Time Trial. 10 mile Track. 50 km Points |
| Postle. Matthew | M | 120 mile Road Race. 100 km |

Lawn Bowls

Calnan. John	M	Manager
Parker. M.B.E. Linda	F	Manager
Ackland. Janet	F	Singles
Beer. Alan	M	Fours
Dainton. Ann	F	Fours
Evans. Linda	F	Fours
Griffiths. Pamela	F	Pairs
Hughes. Mary	F	Pairs
Jones. Rita	F	Fours
Mounty. Trevor	M	Fours
Oliver. Stella	F	Fours
Price. John	M	Singles
Thomas. William	M	Pairs
Vowles. David	M	Fours
Weale. Robert	M	Pairs
Wilkins. David	M	Fours

Weightlifting

Phillips. Gordon	M	Manager
Welch. M.B.E. Dennis	M	Coach
Arnold. Aled	M	110 kg Class
Bryce. Jeffrey	M	60 kg Class
Chaplin. Ricky	M	75 kg Class
Davies. Andrew	M	110+ kg Class
Hives. Gareth	M	100 kg Class
Jones. Karl	M	75 kg Class
Morgan. David	M	82.5 kg Class
Roach. Mark	M	67.5 kg Class
Williams. Raymond	M	67.5 kg Class
Wilson. Steven	M	110 kg Class

Gymnastics

Jones. Leigh	M	Manager
Black. Lisa	F	Coach
Clubb. David	M	Coach
Bennion. Catherine	F	Artistic. Artistic Team
Buffin. David	M	Artistic
Griffiths. David	M	Artistic. Artistic Team

| Morris. Andrew | M | Artistic. Artistic Team |
| Sloman. Peter | M | Artistic. Artistic Team |

Judo

Farthing. Glyn	M	Manager
Duston. Noel	M	Coach
Charles. James	M	Extra Lightweight
Davies. Daniel	M	Half Middleweight
Duston. Helen	F	Extra Lightweight
Griffiths. Lisa	F	Half Lightweight
Jenkins. Andrew	M	Lightweight
Knowles. Philippa	F	Halfheavyweight
Sutton. Moira	F	Lightweight
Thomas. Dafydd	M	Halflightweight
Woods. Simon	M	Middleweight

Swimming

James. Robert	M	Manager
Atkinson. Leigh	M	Coach
Squire. Peter	M	Coach Diving
Brown. Richard	M	100 & 200 m Breaststroke
Clark. Olivia	F	Diving 10 m Platform. 3 m & 1m Springboard

Day. Anthony	M	400 & 1,500 m Freestyle. 400 m Relay
Evans. Joanne	F	100 m Freestyle. 100 & 200 m Backstroke
Henwood. Julia	F	100 & 200 m Breaststroke
Jones. Debbie	F	100.200.400 & 800 m Freestyle
Jones. Mark	M	50 & 100 m Freestyle. 100 m Butterfly
Lock. Maxine	F	50 & 100 m Freestyle. 100 m Butterfly. 200 m Medley
Mansfield. Helen	F	100 & 200 m Freestyle. 200 m Medley
Morgan. Robert	M	Diving 3 m Platform. 3 & 1m Springboard
Rosser. Ian	M	100 & 200 m Backstroke. 200 & 400 m Medley
Watkins. Michael	M	200 m Freestyle. 100 & 200 m Butterfly. 200 m Medley

Boxing

Allen. Ray	M	Manager
Watts. Gerry	M	Coach

Mathews. Jason	M	Lightweight
McCormack. Kevin	M	Superheavyweight
Smyth. Michael	M	Lightwelterweight
Williams. John	M	Featherweight

Shooting

Speck. Terry	M	Manager
Osborne. John	M	Coach
Birkett – Evans. Chris	M	Pellet Gun Individual & Pairs Olympic Trench
Dallimore. John	M	Individual & Pairs Smallbore Rifle 50 m
Evans. Colin	M	Pellet Gun Individual & Pairs Olympic Trench
Davies. Desmond	M	Pellet Gun Individual & Pairs S Skeet
Hockley. Christopher	M	Individual & Pairs Fullbore Rifle
Jay. Michael	M	Rapid Fire Pistol. Individual & Pairs Centre Pistol
Lewis. Anthony	M	Pellet Gun. Individual & Pairs Skeet
O'Leary. Dion	M	Individual & Pairs Smallbore Rifle
Pengelly. Stephen	M	Rapid Fire Pistol. Individual Individual & Pairs Centre Pistol
Wakefield. Terence	M	Smallbore Prone Lying Pairs 50 m

Headquarters Staff in Edmonton 1994 <u>Left to Right</u>-Ray Allen, John Jones-Pritchard, Dr Nicola Phillips, Dr Wayne Griffiths, Averil Williams, Malcolm Stammers, Fred Howell, Russell Davison, Linda Parker

1994

Headquarters

John, M.B.E. Myrddin	M	Chef de Mission
Jones-Pritchard. John A.	M	General Team Manager
Howell. Fred	M	Deputy General Team Manager
Williams. Averil	F	Deputy General Team Manager
Allen. Ray	M	Administrator
Parker, M.B.E. Linda	F	Administrator
Richards. Gwerfyl	M	Attaché

Staff Medical

Griffiths, M.B.E. Dr Wayne	M	Chief Medical Officer
Davison. Russell	M	Physiotherapist
Phillips. Nicola	F	Physiotherapist

Public Relations

Rees. Allan	M	Officer
Stammers. Malcolm	M	Chief Officer

Athletics

Davies. Delyth	F	Manager
Perks. Steve	M	Coach
Baulch. James	M	200 a 400 m 4 x 400 m Relay
Bevan. Nigel	M	Javelin
Chaston. Justin	M	3,000 m Steeplechase
Dawson. Catherine	F	800 m
Gibbs. Lisa	F	Heptathlon
Gray. Paul	M	110 m Hurdles. 4 x 400 m Relay
Harries. Philip	M	400 m Hurdles. 4 x 400 m Relay
Hobbs. Justin	M	5,000 m 10,000 m
Ingram. Steve	M	Long Jump. 4 x 400 m Relay
Jackson, M.B.E. Colin	M	110 m Hurdles
Maitland. Peter	M	100 m 200 m 4 x 400 m Relay
Nash. Hayley	F	Marathon
Rixon. Dale	M	Marathon
Thomas. Iwan	M	400 m. 4 x 400 m Relay
Wiltshire. Lee	M	Shot
Winter. Neil	M	Pole Vault

Athletics Wheelchair

Hallam. Chris	M	800 m
Harris. John	M	800 m
Powell. Richard	M	Marathon

Badminton

Clark. Dennis	M	Manager
Lewis. Geraint	M	Singles. Pairs Mixed. Team
Morgan. Kelly	F	Singles. Pairs. Pairs Mixed. Team
Phipps. Rachel	F	Singles. Pairs. Pairs Mixed. Team
Rees. Christopher	M	Singles. Pairs. Team
Tonks. David	M	Pairs. Pairs Mixed.Team

Cycling

Jones. Phil	M	Manager
Owen. Bill	M	Coach
Colloby. Stephen	M	4,000 m Individual Pursuit. 4,000 m Team Pursuit. 40 km Points. 1,000 km Team Road Race Trial
Greenwood. Clare	F	3,000 m Individual Pursuit. 25 km Points. Road Race
Hodge. Sally	F	25 km Points. Road Race

Hughes. Richard	M	4,000 m Individual Pursuit. 4,000 m Team Pursuit. 10 mile Track.40 km Points
Owen. Alun	M	4,000 m Team Pursuit. 10 mile Track.40 km Points. 100 km Time Trial Team Road Race
Postle. Matthew	M	4,000 m Individual Pursuit. 4,000 m Team Pursuit. 10 mile Track. 100 km Time Trial Team Road Race. Road Race
Wedley. Daniel	M	Road Race
Wooles. Richard	M	100 km Time Trial Team Road Race. Road Race
Wright. Will	M	1,000 m Time Trial. Road Race

LAWN BOWLS

Flemming. Barry	M	Manager
Griffiths. Pamela	F	Manager
Ackland. Janet	F	Pairs
Dainton. Ann	F	Pairs
Davies. Mary	F	Fours
Evans. Linda	F	Fours
Hoskins. Jim	M	Fours
Howell. Valerie	F	Fours
Jones. Rita	F	Singles
Matthews. Wyn	M	Fours

Morgan. Betty	F	Fours
Price. John	M	Pairs
Rowlands. Philip	M	Fours
Thomas. William	M	Singles
Weale. Robert	M	Pairs
Wilkins. David	M	Fours

LAWN BOWLS VISUALLY IMPAIRED

Hopkins. Ken	M	Director
Hopkins. Gloria	F	Singles
Edmunds. Glenys	F	Director
Edmunds. George	M	Singles

WEIGHTLIFTING

Welch, M.B.E. Dennis	M	Manager
Roach. Lynne	M	Coach
Goswell. Andrew	M	70 kg Class
Hives. Gareth	M	99 kg Class
Morgan. David	M	76 kg Class
Morgan. Tony	M	70 kg Class
Perdue. Terry (Iau)	M	110+ kg Class
Richard. Paul	M	64 kg Class
Roach. Mark	M	70 kg Class

Taylor. Neil	M	83 kg Class
Thomas. Rhodri	M	83 kg Class
Williams. Gary	M	91 kg Class

GYMNASTICS

Keitch. Rita	F	Manager
Burton. Neil	M	Coach
Davies. Gareth	M	Artistic
Hamer. Clare	F	Artistic
Irwin. Gareth	M	Artistic
Lawrence. Sonia	F	Artistic
Mortimer. Janine	F	Artistic
Powell. Bethan	F	Artistic
Tombs. Andrew	M	Artistic

SWIMMING

Rosser. Gary	M	Manager
Ayres. Andrew	M	Coach/100 & 200 m Breaststroke
Hale. Victoria	F	200 & 400 m Freestyle. 400 m Medley.
Hopkins. Sara	F	50 m Freestyle.100 m Freestyle
Jones. Christopher	M	200 m Freestyle. 100 & 200 m Backstroke. 200 & 400 m Medley

Jones. Mark	M	50 & 100 m Freestyle. 100 m Butterfly
Lock. Maxine	F	50 & 100 m Freestyle. 100 m Butterfly
Lundie. Ian	M	200 & 400 m Freestyle
Melhuish. Philip	M	100 & 200 m Breaststroke 4 x 100 m Relay Medley
Morgan. Robert	M	Diving Springboard 1m & 3 m Platform Diving
Niblett. Charlotte	F	200 & 400 m Individual Medley
Watkins. Michael	M	200 m Freestyle. 100 & 200 m Butterfly

BOXING

Smith. Terry	M	Manager
Braithwaite. Don	M	Coach
Teague. Billy	M	Coach
Briggs. Grant	M	Middleweight
Cook. Jason	M	Featherweight
Lawrence. Gareth	M	Lightweight
McCormack. Kevin	M	Superheavyweight
Robinson. Andrew	M	Light Welterweight
Thomas. Karl	M	Welterweight

Vowles. Richard	M	Bantamweight

SHOOTING

Osborne. John	M	Manager
Dallimore. John	M	Coach
Hockley. Christopher	M	Coach
Birkett-Evans. James	M	Individual & Pairs Trap Shooting
Craven. Richard	M	Individual & Pairs Pistol Centre Shooting 25 m Individual & Pairs. Rapid Fire Pistol
Davies. David	M	Individual & Pairs Fullbore Rifle
Davies. Desmond	M	Individual & Pairs Skeet Shooting
Evans. Mark	M	Individual & Pairs Trap Shooting
Hartop. Susan	FF	Individual & Pairs Air Rifle 10m. Smallbore Rifle Prone Lying 50 m. Smallbore Rifle 3 Position 50 m
James. Jonathan	M	Individual & Pairs Fullbore Rifle
Jay. Michael	M	Individual & Pairs Pistol Shooting Centre 25 m & Rapid Fire Pistol
Lewis. Tony	M	Individual & Pairs Skeet Shooting
Malcolm. Julie	F	Individual & Pairs Air Rifle 10 m. Smallbore Rifle Prone Lying. Smallbore Rifle 3 Position 50 m
Morris. Adrian	M	Air Rifle 10 m

Top-Left to Right Malcolm Stammers, Office, Steve Gallagher, Office. Front- Peter Williams, John Jones-Pritchard, Rita Keitch, John Perrins, Bill Phelps.

Bottom-Officials and Visitors at the Kuala Lumpur Headquarters

354

1998

HEADQUARTERS

Jones-Pritchard. John A.	D	Chef de Mission
Keitch. Rita	M	General Team Manager
Perrins. John	D	Deputy General Team Manager
Phelps. Bill	D	Deputy General Team Manager
Williams. T. Peter	D	Deputy General Team Manager
Stammers. Malcolm	D	Public Relations
Gallagher. Steve	D	Transport Officer

Dr Nicola Phillips, Welsh Chief Physiotherapist

MEDICAL STAFF

Griffiths, M.B.E. Dr. Wayne	D	Chief Medical Officer
Jones. Dr. Gareth Lloyd	D	Doctor
Morrison. Dr. Linda	M	Doctor
Phillips. Dr. Nicola	M	Chief Physiotherapist

Anderson. Graham	D	Physiotherapist
Blair. Saskia	M	Physiotherapist
Coales. Philippa	M	Physiotherapist
Davies. Mark	D	Physiotherapist
Morris. Lyn	D	Physiotherapist
Zaslona. Jackie	M	Physiotherapist

Dr Nicola Phillips addressing the Management Team.

Welsh Athletics Team 1998

ATHLETICS

Davies. Delyth	F	Manager
Delaney. Michael	M	Manager
Banning. Phil	M	Coach
Thomas. Adrian	M	Coach
Baulch. Jamie	M	400 m 4 x 100 m Relay .4 x 400 m Relay
Bevan. Nigel	M	Javelin
Brace. Steve	M	Marathon
Clarke. Rhian	F	Pole Vault
Crane. Julie	F	High Jump

Davies. Emma	F	800 m 1,500 m 4 x 400 m Relay
Elias. Matthew	M	400 m Hurdles.4 x 400 m Relay
Gray. Paul	M	110 m Hurdles. 400 m Hurdles. 4 x 400 m Relay
Henthorn. Jamie	M	100 m 200 m 4 x100 m Relay 4 x 400 m Relay
Jackson. Colin	M	110 m Hurdles. 4 x 100 m Relay
King. Rachel	F	100 m Hurdles
Layzell. Alyson	F	400 m Hurdles. 4 x 400 m Relay
Mair. Angharad	F	Marathon
Malcolm. Christian	M	100 a 200 m 4 x 100 m Relay
Moore. Sarah	F	Hammer
Nash. Hayley	F	10,000 m
Newcombe. Rachel	F	800 m 4 x 400 m Relay
Newman. Lee	M	Discus
Pickering. Shaun	M	Shot
Rixon. Dale	M	Marathon
Roles. Philippa	F	Discus
Stephenson. Christian	M	1,500 m. 3,000 m Steeplechase

Thomas. Iwan	M	400 m 4 x 400 m Relay
Turner. Douglas	M	200 m 4 x 100 m Relay
Williams. Kevin	M	100 m 4 x 100 m Relay

BADMINTON

Ford. Michael	M	Manager
Rees. Chris	M	Coach
Ashworth. Robyn	F	Mixed Pairs
Groves-Burke. Andrew	M	Mixed Pairs
Groves-Burke. Natasha	F	Singles
Howell. Katy	F	Singles. Pairs
Hughes. Matthew	M	Singles
Leung. John	M	Singles. Pairs
Lewis. Geraint	M	Singles. Pairs
Morgan. Kelly	F	Singles
Osborne. Gail	F	Singles. Pairs
Vaughan. Richard	M	Singles

CYCLING

Jones. Phil	M	Manager
Cosgrove. Matt	M	Coach
Sutton. Shane	M	Coach

Taylor. Simon	M	Coach
Beckett. Mathew	M	184 km Road Race. Men
Esposti. Paul	M	184 km Road Race. Men
Greenwood. Clare	F	24 km Points. 28 km IRTT.92 km Road Race
Hughes. Megan	F	24 km Points.28 km IRTT. 92 km Road Race
Jones. Louise km	F	3,000 m Individual Pursuit. 24 Points. 28 km IRTT. 92 km Road Race
Jones. Sion	M	4,000 m Individual Pursuit. 4,000 m Team Pursuit
Malarczyk. Tony	M	184 km Road Race
Owen. Alun	M	1,000 m IRTT. 4,000 m Individual Pursuit 4,000 m Team Pursuit.20 km Scratch
Postle. Matthew	M	42 km IRTT
Pritchard. Ceri	M	4,000 m Individual Pursuit. 42 km IRTT
Pritchard. Huw	M	4,000 m Individual Pursuit. 4,000 Team Pursuit. 20 km Scratch
Rand. David	M	184 km Road Race
Sheppard. Paul	M	4,000 m Individual Pursuit. 4.000 m Team Pursuit

Williams. Chris	M	184 km	Road Race
Winn. Julian	M	184 km	Road Race

TENPIN BOWLING

Chamberlain. Laura	F	Manager
Parker. Alan	M	Coach
Ball. Geoffrey	M	Player
Fortt. Cynthia	F	Player
Outrim. Patricia	F	Player

SQUASH

Evans. Andrew	M	Manager
Robertson. Chris	M	Coach
Benjamin. Matthew	M	Singles. Pairs
Davies. Gareth	F	Pairs. Pairs Mixed
Evans. David	M	Pairs. Pairs Mixed
Hogan. Katrina	F	Pairs.Pairs Mixed
Johnson. Sian	F	Pairs.Pairs Mixed
Tippings. Greg	M	Singles. Pairs Mixed

Welsh Lawn Bowls Team 1998

LAWN BOWLS

Humphreys. Gareth	M	Manager
Parker, M.B.E. Linda	F	Manager
Anstey. Mark	M	Fours
Jones. Rita	F	Pairs
Mansbridge. Sarah	F	Fours
Miles. Gillian	F	Fours
Morgan. Betty	F	Fours

Pearce. Kathy	F	Fours
Sutherland. Ann	F	Pairs
Price. John	M	Singles
Rees. Neil	M	Fours
Slade. Ian	M	Fours
Thomas. William	M	Pairs
Watson. Judith	F	Singles
Weale. Robert	M	Pairs
Wilkins. David	M	Fours

WEIGHTLIFTING

John. Delfrig	M	Manager
Lee. Alan	M	Coach
Roach. Simon	M	Coach
Earwicker. Robert	M	95 kg
Roberts. Arfon	M	77kg
Hardiman. Marius	M	85 kg
Hives. Gareth	M	105 kg
Morgan. David	M	77 kg
Morgan. Tony	M	69 kg
Roberts. Jonathan	M	95 kg
Taylor. Neil	M	85 kg

GYMNASTICS

John. Sue	F	Manager
Burton. Neil	M	Coach
Coombs. Joanne	F	Coach
Still. Colin	M	Coach
Cotter. Jeanette	F	Rhythmic Women
Davies. Gareth	M	Artistic Men
Eaton. David	M	Artistic Men
Irwin. Gareth	M	Artistic Men
Lawrence. Sonia	F	Artistic Women
Lucitt. Natalie	F	Artistic Women
Macleod. Emma	F	Artistic Women
Maunton-Gardiner. Jennifer	F	Rhythmic Women
Morris. Paul	M	Artistic Men
Mortimer. Janine	F	Artistic Women
Wink. Jason	M	Artistic Men

HOCKEY MEN

Gilbody. Martin	M	Manager
Lindley. Martin	M	Deputy Manager
Bunyan. David	M	Coach
Ashcroft. Chris	M	Player

Carruthers. Alistair	M	Player
Colclough. Tony	M	Player
Edwards. Paul	M	Player
Egan. Graeme	M	Player
Griffiths-Jones. Owen	M	Player
Grimes. Andrew	M	Player
Hughes-Rowlands. Ian	M	Player
Hacker. David	M	Player
Jones. Zak	M	Player
Lindley. Martin	M	Player
Markham. Richard	M	Player
Moore. Tyrone	M	Player
Organ. Simon	M	Player
O'Sullivan. Clive	M	Player
Priday. Kevin	M	Player
Williamson. Michael	M	Player

HOCKEY WOMEN

Edwards. Margaret	F	Manager
Lawrence. Jan	F	Coach
Medlow. Margaret	F	Coach
Bevan. Ann	F	Player

Daltry. Michelle	F	Player
Ellis. Louise	F	Player
Thomas. Michelle	F	Player
James. Emma	F	Player
Jones. Caroline	F	Player
Williams. Justine	F	Player
Williams. Laurden	F	Player

BOXING

Jones. Jim	M	Manager
Lewis. Steve	M	Coach
Ross. Bill	M	Coach
Gammer. Ralph	M	Coach
Connors. William	M	57 kg
Donaldson. Stephen	M	81 kg
Evans. Kevin	M	91 kg
Flynn. Mark	M	91+ kg
Hall. Ceri	M	60 kg
Hayde. Darren	M	51 kg
Pepperall. Sean	M	75 kg
Powell. Vince	M	63.5 kg

Short. Kevin	M	71 kg
Thomas. Karl	M	67 kg

NETBALL

Handley. Ann	F	Manager
Roper. Avril	F	Coach
Allen. Janet	F	Player
Battle. Ceri	F	Player
Donovan. Dawn	F	Player
Evans. Mair	F	Player
Hawkins. Clare	F	Player
Jackson. Kara	F	Player
Jones. Rhian	F	Player
Kendrick. Claire	F	Player
Phillips. Leanne	F	Player
Rees. Elizabeth	F	Player
Walker. Pam	F	Player
Weston. Helen	F	Player

RUGBY SEVENS

Ryan. John	M	Manager
Hopkins. Kevin	M	Coach
Cooper. Gareth	M	Player

Gibbs. Scott	M	Player
Howley. Robert	M	Player
James. Dafydd	M	Player
Ringer. Jamie	M	Player
Robinson. Matthew	M	Player
Thomas. Gareth	M	Player
Warlow. Craig	M	Player
Wyatt. Chris	M	Player
Wyatt. Gareth	M	Player

SHOOTING

Osborne. John	M	Manager
Mumford. Patricia	F	Coach
Davies. Gwyn	M	Coach
George. David	M	Coach
Grey. Paul	M	Coach
Edwards. Dr. Richard	M	Coach
Allen. Malcolm	M	Pairs Skeet
Birkett-Evans. James	M	Pairs Trap
Blake. Martyn	M	Smallbore Free 3 Position. 50 m Pairs. 50 m Pairs Air Rifle
Brekke. Johanne	F	Smallbore Rifle. Sport Rifle Prone Lying 50 m Pairs

Brown. Fred	M	Pairs 50 m Smallbore Rifle Prone Lying
Craft. Steve	D	Pairs 10 m Air Pistol. 25 m Free Centre Pistol
Craven. Richard	F	Pairs 25 m Rapid Pistol
Davies. David	M	Pairs Open Fullbore Rifle
Davies. Desmond	M	Individual & Pairs Skeet
Davies. Gwyn	M	Coach
Davies. Robert	M	Pairs Trap
Daltry. Stuart	M	Pairs Air Rifle 10 m Pairs Smallbore Free Rifle 3 Position
Harris. Ian	M	Pairs 10 m Air Pistol
Hockley. Chris	M	Pairs Fullbore Rifle. Individual Fullbore Rifle
Malcolm. Julie	F	Pairs Air Rifle 10 m Pairs Sport Rifle Smallbore Prone Lying. Smallbore Prone Lying 50 m Smallbore Rifle Prone Lying 50 m 3 Position
Pengelly. Steve	M	Pairs Shooting Pistol 25 m Centre & Rapid Fire
Wakefield. Terry	M	Pairs Smallbore Rifle Free Prone Lying 50 m
Wyke. Rhian	F	Air Rifle

SWIMMING

Rosser. Gary	M	Manager
Haller. David	M	Coach
Roberts. Mike	M	Coach
Ayres. Andrew	M	100, 200m Breaststroke. 4 x 100m Freestyle Relay
Coleman. Leighton	M	50m F/style. 4 x 100m F/style R.
Coole, Bethan	F	100, 200m Backstroke. 200m F/style. 4x100m & 4x200m F/style Relay
Davies. Catrin	F	50,100m F/style. 4x100 & 200m F/styleRelay. 4x100m Medley R
Davies. Martyn	M	50 & 100m F/style. 4x100m F/style Relay
Flook. Suzanne	F	100 & 200 Butterfly. 4x100m Medley Relay
Hale. Victoria	F	50.100 &200m F/style. 4 & 200m F/style Relay
Hopkins. Sara	F	50 & 100m F/style. 4x100 & 200m F/style Relay

Johnson. Adam	M	50 & 100m F/style. 4x100m F/style R..4x100m Medley Relay
Jones. Chris	M	100m Back stroke. 200m Medley. 4x100m Medley Relay
Jones. Mark	M	100m F/Style.100m Butterfly. 4x100m Freestyle Relay.
Lewis. Jonathan	M	100 &200m Breaststroke.4x100m Medley Relay
Morgan. Robert	M	Platform Diving
Niblett. Charlotte	F	200m Butterfly. 200 & 400m Medley
Warren. Caroline	F	100 & 200m Breaststroke. 4x100m Medley Relay
Watkins. Michael	M	100 & 200m Butterfly. 4x100m Medley Relay

CHAPTER NINE

MEDALS

MEDALS WON BY WALES IN COMMONWEALTH GAMES

1930 -1998

M – Male F - Female

Year	Athlete	Sex	Discipline	Gold	Silver	Bronze
Athletics						
1938	Alford. James (Jim) William.	M	1,500 m	1		
1954	Jones. Kenneth	M	200 m			1
1958	Shaw. Robert	M	400 m Hurdles			1
1958	Merriman. John	M	10,000 m		1	
1962	England. David M.	M	4 x100 m Relay			1
1962	Jones. Ronald	M	4 x100 m Relay			
1962	Jones. T. Berwin	M	4 x100 m Relay			
1962	Whitehead. Neville J.	M	4 x100 m Relay			
1966	Longe. Clive	M	Decathlon		1	
1966	Davies. Lynn	M	Long Jump	1		
1970	Davies. Lynn	M	Long Jump	1		
1974	Martin-Jones. Ruth	F	Long Jump			1
1974	Davies. John	M	3,000 m Steeplechase		1	

Year	Athlete	Sex	Discipline	Gold	Silver	Bronze
1974	Price. Berwyn	M	110 m Hurdles		1	
1978	Price. Berwyn	M	110 m Hurdles	1		
1982	Scutt. Michelle	F	400 m		1	
1982	McDermott. Kirsty	F	800 m	1		
1982	Barry. Steve	M	30 km Walk	1		
1986	Wade(McDermott). Kirsty	F	800 m	1		
1986	Wade(McDermott). Kirsty	F	1,500 m	1		
1986	Miles. Helen	F	4 x100 m Relay			1
1986	Morris. Sian	F	4 x100 m Relay			
1986	Short. Sally Anne	F	4 x100 m Relay			
1986	Smart. Carmen	F	4 x100 m Relay			
1986	Head. Venissa	F	Discus		1	
1986	Tooby. Angela	F	10,000 m			1
1986	Hackney. Roger	M	3,000 m Steeplechase		1	
1986	Jones. Steve	M	10,000 m			1
1986	Jackson. Colin	M	110 m Hurdles			
1990	Morley. Kay	F	100 m Hurdles	1		
1990	Jackson. Colin	M	110 m Hurdles	1		
1990	Hamer. Ian	M	5,000 m			1

Year	Athlete	Sex	Discipline	Gold	Silver	Bronze
1990	Edwards. Paul	M	Shot Put			1
1994	Jackson. Colin	M	110 m Hurdles	1		
1994	Grey. Paul	M	110 m Hurdles			1
1994	Winter. Neil	M	Pole Vault	1		
1998	Thomas. Iwan	M	400 m	1		
1998	Malcolm. Christian	M	200 m		1	
1998	Pickering. Shaun	M	Shot Put			1
1998	Grey. Paul	M	4 x 400 m Relay			1
1998	Baulch. Jamie	M	4 x 400 m Relay			
1998	Turner. Doug	M	4 x 400 m Relay			
1998	Thomas. Iwan	M	4 x 400 m Relay			
Lawn Bowls						
1934	Davies. Thomas. R.	M	Pairs			1
1934	Weaver. Stan	M	Pairs			
1978	Evans. John	M	Singles			1
1978	Morgan. James	M	Pairs			1
1978	Williams. Ray	M	Pairs			
1982	Perkins. Lyn	M	Pairs		1	
1982	Wilshire. Spencer	M	Pairs			
1986	Evans. Linda	F	Fours	1		
1986	Rickets. Joan	F	Fours			
1986	Jones. Rita	F	Fours			

Year	Athlete	Sex	Discipline	Gold	Silver	Bronze
1986	Parker. Linda	F	Fours			
1986	Morgan. James	M	Fours	1		
1986	Thomas. Hafod	M	Fours			
1986	Thomas. William	M	Fours			
1986	Weale. Robert	M	Fours			
1994	Jones. Rita	F	Singles		1	
1994	Hopkins. Gloria	F	Singles-Visually Impaired		1	
1994	Ackland. Janet	F	Pairs			1
1994	Dainton. Ann	F	Pairs			
1994	Weale. Robert	M	Pairs		1	
1994	Price. John	M	Pairs			
1998	Price. John	M	Singles		1	
1998	Jones. Rita	F	Pairs			1
1998	Sutherland. Ann	F	Pairs			
1998	Thomas. William	M	Pairs		1	
1998	Weale. Robert	M	Pairs			
1998	Rees. Nei5l	M	Fours			1
1998	Slade. Ian	M	Fours			
1998	Anstey. Mark	M	Fours			
1998	Wilkins. David	M	Fours			
Badminton						

377

Year	Athlete	Sex	Discipline	Gold	Silver	Bronze
1998	Morgan. Kelly	F	Singles	1		
Fencing						
1954	Harding. Aileen	F	Foil			1
1958	Evans. J. John	M	Foil Team			1
1958	Maunder. Roger A.	M	Foil Team			
1958	McCombe. J.	M	Foil Team			
1958	Kerslake. Malcolm V.	M	Sabre Team			1
1958	Maunder. Roger A.	M	Sabre Team			
1958	Preston. John	M	Sabre Team			
1958	Reynolds. E.O. Robert	M	Épée			1
Weightlifting						
1954	Jenkins. Ronald	M	60 kg			1
1962	Owen. Ieuan W.	M	60 kg		1	
1962	Johnson. Horace A.	M	75 kg			1
1962	Arthur. Peter J	M	82.5 kg		1	
1966	Chung. Kum Weng	M	60kg	1		
1966	Owen. Ieuan W.	M	67.5 kg		1	
1966	Johnson. Horace A.	M	75 kg			1
1970	Owen. Ieuan W.	M	67.5 kg		1	
1970	Arthur. Peter	M	82.5 kg			1
1970	Perdue. Terry	M	110+ kg		1	

Year	Athlete	Sex	Discipline	Gold	Silver	Bronze
1974	Owen. Ieuan W.	M	67.5 kg		1	
1974	Wrench. Robert	M	75 kg			1
1974	Perdue. Terry	M	110+ kg			1
1978	Bryce. Jeffrey	M	56 kg			1
1978	Burns. John	M	100 kg	1		
1982	Morgan. David	M	67.5 kg	1		
1982	Burns. John	M	110 kg	1		
1986	Williams. Raymond	M	60 kg	1		
1986	Bryce. Jeffrey	M	60 kg			1
1986	Taylor. Neil	M	75 kg			1
1986	Morgan. David	M	82.5 kg	1		
1986	Davies. Andrew	M	110 kg			1
1990	Roach. Mark	M	67.5 kg Snatch			1
1990	Roach. Mark	M	67.5 kg Total			1
1990	Jones. Karl	M	75 kg Snatch		1	
1990	Morgan. David	M	82.5 kg Snatch	1		
1990	Morgan. David	M	82.5 kg Jerk	1		
1990	Morgan. David	M	82.5 kg Total	1		
1990	Wilson. Steve	M	110 kg Snatch			1
1990	Arnold. Aled	M	110 kg Jerk			1
1990	Arnold. Aled	M	110 kg Total			1
1990	Davies. Andrew	M	110+kg Snatch	1		

Year	Athlete	Sex	Discipline	Gold	Silver	Bronze
1990	Davies. Andrew	M	110+kg Jerk	1		
1990	Davies. Andrew	M	110+kg Total	1		
1994	Morgan. David	M	76 kg Snatch	1		
1994	Morgan. David	M	76 kg Jerk		1	
1994	Morgan. David	M	76 kg Total	1		
1994	Hives. Gareth	M	100 kg Snatch			1
1994	Hives. Gareth	M	100 kg Jerk			1
1994	Hives. Gareth	M	100 kg Total			1
1998	Morgan. Tony	M	67.5 kg Snatch			1
1998	Morgan. David	M	77 kg Snatch		1	
Gymnastics						
1994	Lawrence. Sonia	F	Vault		1	
Judo						
1990	Duston. Helen	F	48 kg		1	
1990	Griffiths. Lisa	F	52 kg			1
1990	Sutton. Moira	F	56 kg			1
1990	Knowles. Philippa	F	72 kg			1
1990	Charles. James	M	60 kg			1
Swimming						
1930	Davies. E. Valerie	F	100 m yards Freestyle			1
1930	Davies. E. Valerie	F	100 m yards		1	

Year	Athlete	Sex	Discipline	Gold	Silver	Bronze
			Backstroke			
1930	Davies. E. Valerie	F	400 m yards Freestyle		1	
1934	Davies. E. Valerie	F	100 yards Backstroke			1
1938	Greenland. Joanne	F	110 yards Backstroke		1	
1950	Brockway. John	M	100 m Backstroke		1	
1970	Richards. Michael J.	M	100 m Backstroke		1	
1970	Woodroffe. Martyn	M	200 m Butterfly Ind. Medley		1	
1970	Richards. Michael J.	M	4 x 400 m Relay Medley			1
1970	Johnson. Nigel R.	M	4 x 400 m Relay Medley			
1970	Woodroffe. Martyn	M	4 x 400 m Relay Medley			
1970	Moran. Kevin	M	4 x 400 m Relay Medley			
1970	Richards. Michael J.	M	200 m Backstroke	1		
1974	Beavan. Pat	F	200 m	1		

Year	Athlete	Sex	Discipline	Gold	Silver	Bronze
			Breaststroke			
1986	Morgan. Robert	M	Diving			1
1990	Morgan. Robert	M	Diving	1		
Boxing						
1934	Pottinger. Jackie	M	Flyweight			1
1934	Barnes. Albert	M	Bantamweight		1	
1934	Jones. J.D.	M	Featherweight		1	
1934	Taylor. Frank	M	Lightweight		1	
1938	Reardon. Dennis P.	M	Middleweight	1		
1954	Collins. Malcolm	M	Featherweight		1	
1958	Braithwaite. Donald	M	Flyweight			1
1958	Winstone. Howard	M	Bantamweight	1		
1958	Collins. Malcolm	M	Lightweight		1	
1958	Brown. W.G.	M	Lightmiddle wt			1
1958	Higgins. Robert	M	Lightheavywt.		1	
1958	Pleace. Robert	M	Heavyweight			1
1970	Davies. Dai J.	M	Lightwelterwt.		1	
1974	McKenzie. Errol	M	Welterweight		1	
1978	Friel. Anthony	M	Welterweight			1
Rowing						
1958	Edwards. D.C.	M	Fours Without Cox			1

Year	Athlete	Sex	Discipline	Gold	Silver	Bronze
1958	Page. J.L.	M	Fours Without Cox			
1958	Pritchard. D.L.	M	Fours Without Cox			
1958	Edwards. J.H.M	M	Fours Without Cox			
1962	Edwards. D.C.	M	Fours Without Cox		1	
1962	Edwards. J.H.M	M	Fours Without Cox			
1962	Luke. R.T.	M	Fours Without Cox			
1962	Luke. J.C.	M	Fours Without Cox			
Shooting						
1966	Swansea. .Lord John	M	Rifle .303	1		
1974	Lewis. Philip	M	Trap Clay Target			1
1974	Watkins. William (Bill)	M	Smallbore Rifle		1	
1982	Watkins. William (Bill)	M	Smallbore Rifle Prone			1
1982	Swansea. Lord John	M	Fullbore Rifle		1	
1982	Harris. Colin	M	Smallbore		1	

Year	Athlete	Sex	Discipline	Gold	Silver	Bronze
			Team Prone			
1982	Watkins. William (Bill)	M	Smallbore Team Prone			
1986	Phillips. Rowland	M	Trap			1
1986	Wakefield. Terry	M	Smallbore Team Prone			1
1986	Harries. Colin	M	Smallbore Team Prone			
1990	Evans. Colin	M	Pairs Trench Gun		1	
1990	Birkett-Evans. James	M	Pairs Trench Gun			
1990	Jay. Michael	M	25 m Rapid Fire Pistol			1
1994	Craven. Richard	M	Pairs Rapid Fire Pistol		1	
1994	Jay. Michael	M	Pairs Rapid Fire Pistol			
1994	Jay. Michael	M	Singles Rapid Fire Pistol	1		
1998	Davies. Desmond	M	Skeet	1		
Squash						

Year	Athlete	Sex	Discipline	Gold	Silver	Bronze
1998	Gough. Alex	M	Singles			1
Cycling						
1954	Skene. Donald	M	10 mile Track			1
1958	Skene. Donald	M	10 mile Track			1
1970	Hatfield. John	M	Sprint Tandem			1
1970	Beswick. John M	M	Sprint Tandem			
1990	Jones. Louise	F	1,000 m Sprint	1		
1994	Hodge. Sally	F	25 km		1	

(Index 1)

WELSH SPORTS WHO WON MEDALS AT THE GAMES IN THE TWENTIETH CENTURY

Sport	Number of Games	Medals			Total
		GOLD	SILVER	BRONZE	
Archery	1	0	0	0	0
Athletics	16	13	9	12	34
Badminton	9	1	0	0	1
Boxing	16	2	11	9	22
Cricket	1	0	0	0	0
Cycling	14	1	1	3	5
Fencing	6	0	0	4	4
Gymnastics	4	0	1	0	1
Hockey	1	0	0	0	0
Judo	1	0	1	4	5
Lawn Bowls	15	2	6	6	14
Netball	1	0	0	0	0
Rowing	7	0	1	1	2
Rugby 7 a side	1	0	0	0	0
Shooting	8	2	6	5	13
Squash	1	0	0	1	1
Swimming	16	4	6	5	15
Tenpin Bowling	1	0	0	0	0
Weightlifting	13	13	11	19	43
Wrestling	13	0	0	0	0

INDIVIDUAL WELSH MEDALLISTS AT COMMONWEALTH GAMES IN THE TWENTIETH CENTURY

Index 1

GOLD MEDALS David Morgan- Most Medals for Wales

Name	Sport	Nº

GOLD MEDALS

Name	Sport	Nº
Morgan. David	Weightlifting	7
Davies. Andrew	Weightlifting	3
Wade (McDermott). Kirsty	Athletics	3
Burns. John	Weightlifting	2
Davies. O.B.E. Lynn	Athletics	2
Jackson. Colin	Athletics	2
Arthur. Jamie	Boxing	1
Alford. Jim	Athletics	1
Beavan. Pat	Swimming	1
Chung. Kum Weng	Weightlifting	1
Evans. Linda	Lawn Bowls (4s)	1
Jay. Michael	Shooting	1
Jones. Rita	Lawn Bowls (4s)	1
Jones. Louise	Cycling	1
Morgan. James	Lawn Bowls (4s)	1
Morgan, M.B.E. Kelly	Badminton	1
Morgan. Robert	Swimming (Diving)	1

Morley. Kay	Athletics	1
Parker. M.B.E. Linda	Lawn Bowls (4s)	1
Price. Berwyn	Athletics	1
Reardon. Dennis P.	Boxing	1
Richards. Michael J.	Swimming	1
Rickets. Joan	Lawn Bowls (4s)	1
Swansea. Lord John	Shooting	1
Thomas. Hafod	Lawn Bowls (4s)	1
Thomas. Iwan	Athletics	1
Thomas. William	Lawn Bowls (4s)	1
Weale. Robert	Lawn Bowls (4s)	1
Williams. Raymond	Weightlifting	1
Winstone. Howard	Boxing	1
Winter. Neil	Athletics	1

SILVER MEDALS

Owen. Ieuan W.	Weightlifting	3
Collins. Malcolm	Boxing	2
Davies. E. Valerie	Swimming	2
Morgan. David	Weightlifting	2

Price. John	Lawn Bowls	2
Watkins. Bill	Shooting	2
Weale. Robert	Lawn Bowls	2
Arthur. Peter J.	Weightlifting	1
Barnes. Albert	Boxing	1
Birkett-Evans. James	Shooting Pairs	1
Brockway. John	Swimming	1
Cave. Leanda	Triathlon	1
Cook. Jason	Boxing	1
Craven. Richard	Shooting Pairs	1
Davies. Dai	Boxing	1
Davies. John	Athletics	1
Duston. Helen	Judo	1
Edwards. D.C.	Rowing Without Cox 4s	1
Edwards. J.H.M	Rowing Without Cox 4s	1
Evans. Aneurin	Boxing	1
Evans. Colin	Shooting Pairs	1
Elias. Matthew	Athletics	1
Greenland. Joanne	Swimming	1
Hackney. Roger	Athletics	1
Haddock. Neil	Boxing	1

Head. Venissa	Athletics	1
Higgins. Robert	Boxing	1
Hodge. Sally	Cycling	1
Hopkins. Gloria	Lawn Bowls(Vision Impaired)	1
Jackson. Colin	Athletics	1
Johnson. Horace A.	Weightlifting	1
Jones. J.D	Boxing	1
Jones. Karl	Weightlifting	1
Jones. Rita	Lawn Bowls	1
Lawrence. Sonia	Gymnastics	1
Longe. Clive	Athletics	1
Luke. J.C.	Rowing Without Cox 4s	1
Luke. R.T.	Rowing Without Cox 4s	1
Malcolm. Christian	Athletics	1
McKenzie. Errol	Boxing	1
Merriman. John	Athletics	1
Perdue. Terry	Weightlifting	1
Perkins. Lyn	Lawn Bowls	1
Price. Berwyn	Athletics	1
Richards. Mike	Swimming	1
Scutt. Michelle	Athletics	1

Taylor. Frank	Boxing	1
Weale. Robert	Lawn Bowls	1
Wilshire. Spencer	Lawn Bowls	1
Woodroffe. Martyn	Swimming	1

BRONZE MEDALS

Hives. Gareth	Weightlifting	3
Arnold. Aled	Weightlifting	2
Davies. Valerie E.	Swimming	2
Gray. Paul	Athetics	2
Maunder. Roger A.	Fencing	2
Roach. Mark	Weightlifting	2
Skene. Donald	Cycling	2
Ackland. Janet	Lawn Bowls	1
Anstey. Mark	Lawn Bowls	1
Arthur. Peter J.	Weightlifting	1
Baulch. Jamie	Athletics	1
Beswick. John M.	Cycling	1
Braithwaite. Donald	Boxing	1
Brown. W.G.	Boxing	1

Bryce. Jeffery	Weightlifting	1
Dainton. Ann	Lawn Bowls	1
Davies. Andrew	Weightlifting	1
Davies. Thomas R.	Lawn Bowls	1
Edwards. D.C.	Rowing	1
Edwards. J. M.	Rowing	1
Edwards. Paul	Athletics	1
England. David M.	Athletics	1
Evans. John	Lawn Bowls	1
Evans. John J.	Fencing	1
Freal. Anthony	Boxing	1
Gough. Alex	Squash	1
Griffiths. Lisa	Judo	1
Hamer. Ian	Athletics	1
Harding. Aileen	Fencing	1
Harries. Colin	Shooting	1
Hatfield. John	Cycling	1
James. Charles	Judo	1
Jay. Michael	Shooting	1
Jenkins. Ronald	Weightlifting	1
Johnson, Horace	Weightlifting	1

Johnson. Nigel R.	Swimming	1
Jones. Berwyn	Athletics	1
Jones. Kenneth	Athletics	1
Jones. Rita	Lawn Bowls	1
Jones. Ronald	Athletics	1
Jones. Steve	Athetics	1
Kerslake. Malcolm	Fencing	1
Knowles. Philippa	Judo	1
Lewis. Philip	Shooting	1
Martin-Jones. Ruth	Athletics	1
McCombe. J.	Fencing	1
Miles. Helen	Athletics	1
Moran. Kevin	Swimming	1
Morgan. Anthony	Weightlifting	1
Morgan. James	Lawn Bowls	1
Morgan. Robert	Swimming (Diving)	1
Morris. Sian	Athletics	1
Owen. Ieuan	Weightlifting	1
Page. D.L.	Rowing	1
Perdue. Terry	Weightlifting	1
Phillips. Rowland	Shooting	1

Pickering. Shaun	Athletics	1
Pleace. Robert	Boxing	1
Pottinger. Jackie	Boxing	1
Preston. John	Fencing	1
Pritchard. D.L.	Rowing	1
Rees. Neil	Lawn Bowls	1
Reynolds. E.O. Robert	Fencing	1
Richards. Michael J.	Swimming	1
Shaw. Robert	Athletics	1
Short. Sally Anne	Athletics	1
Slade. Ian	Lawn Bowls	1
Smart. Carmen	Athletics	1
Sutherland. Ann	Lawn Bowls	1
Sutton. Moira	Judo	1
Taylor. Neil	Weightlifting	1
Thomas. Iwan	Athletics	1
Thomas. William	Lawn Bowls	1
Tooby. Angela	Athletics	1
Turner. Douglas	Athletics	1
Wakefield. Terry	Shooting	1
Watkins. William	Shooting	1

Weaver. Stan	Lawn Bowls	1
Whitehead. Neville	Athletics	1
Wilkins. David	Lawn Bowls	1
Williams. Ray	Lawn Bowls	1
Wilson. Steve	Weightlifting	1
Woodroffe. Martyn J.	Swimming	1
Wrench. Robert	Weightlifting	1

FIRST MEDAL FOR WALES

Davies. E. Valerie	Swimming	Bronze	1930

FIRST GOLD MEDAL FOR WALES

Reardon. Dennis	Boxing	1938

FIRST SILVER MEDAL FOR WALES

Davies. E. Valerie	Swimming	1930

FIRST BRONZE MEDAL FOR WALES

Davies. E. Valerie	Swimming	1930

FIRST MEDAL FOR THEIR SPORT

Athletics	GOLD	Alford. Jim	1938
	SILVER	Merriman. John	1958
	BRONZE	Jones. Ken	1954
Badminton	GOLD	Morgan. Kelly	1998
Cycling	GOLD	Jones. Louise	1994
	SILVER	Hodge. Sally	1994
	BRONZE	Skene. Donald	1954
Bowling (F)	GOLD	Evans. Linda	1986
	GOLD	Jones. Rita	1986
	GOLD	Parker. Linda	1986
	GOLD	Rickets. Joan	1986
	SILVER	Jones. Rita	1994
	BRONZE	Ackland. Janet	1994
Bowling (M)	GOLD	Morgan. James	1986
	GOLD	Thomas. Hafod	1986
	GOLD	Thomas. William	1986
	GOLD	Weale. Robert	1986
	SILVER	Perkins. Lyn	1982
	SILVER	Wilshire. Spencer	1982

	BRONZE	Davies. Thomas R.	1934
	BRONZE	Weaver. Stan	1934
<u>Fencing</u>	**BRONZE**	Harding. Aileen	1954
<u>Weightlifting</u>	**GOLD**	Chung. Kum Weng	1966
	SILVER	Owen. Ieuan	1962
	BRONZE	Jenkins. Ron	1954
<u>Gymnastics</u>	**SILVER**	Lawrence. Sonia	1994
<u>Judo</u>	**SILVER**	Duston. Helen	1990
	BRONZE	Griffiths. Lisa	1990
<u>Swimming</u>	**GOLD**	Brockway. John	1950
	SILVER	Davies. E. Valerie	1930
	BRONZE	Davies. E. Valerie	1930
<u>Boxing</u>	**GOLD**	Reardon. Dennis	1938
	SILVER	Barnes. Albert	1934
	BRONZE	Pollinger. Jackie	1934
<u>Rowing</u>	**SILVER**	Edwards. David C.	1962
	SILVER	Edwards. John H. M.	1962
	SILVER	Luke. Richard T.	1962
	SILVER	Luke. J.C.	1962
	BRONZE	Edwards. David C.	1958

	BRONZE	Edwards. John H. M	1958
	BRONZE	Page. J.L.	1958
	BRONZE	Pritchard. D.L.	1958
<u>Shooting</u>	**GOLD**	Swansea. Lord John	1966
	SILVER	Birkett-Evans. James	1990
	SILVER	Evans. Colin	1990
	BRONZE	Lewis. Philip	1974
<u>Squash</u>	**BRONZE**	Gough. Alex	1998

Note when calculating number of medals that only one medal should be counted for sports involving more than one person e.g. Team, Pairs, Relays etc.

COUNTRIES THAT HAVE WON MEDALS AT THE GAMES

Some countries have changed their names, some have amalgamated with other countries and some have left the Commonwealth.

Old Name	Present Name
Aden	Left the Commonwealth
Dominica	Left the Commonwealth
British Honduras	Belize
Gold Coast	Ghana
British Guyana	Guyana
Malaya	Malaysia
Sarawak	Malaysia
Sabah	Malaysia
Ireland	Northern Ireland
Ceylon	Sri Lanka
Tanganyika	Tanzania
Northern Rhodesia	Zambia
Southern Rhodesia	Zimbabwe
Newfoundland	Canada

G – Gold   **S** – Silver   **B** - Bronze

1930		G	S	B	Sum
1	England	25	23	13	61
2	Canada	20	15	19	54
3	South Africa	6	4	7	17
4	New Zealand	3	4	2	9
5	Australia	3	4	1	8
6	Scotland	2	3	5	10
7	*Wales*	*0*	*2*	*1*	*3*
8	British Guyana	0	1	1	2
9	Northern Ireland	0	1	0	1

1934		G	S	B	Sum
1	England	29	20	24	73
2	Canada	17	25	9	51
3	Australia	8	4	2	14
4	South Africa	7	10	5	22
5	Scotland	5	4	17	26
6	New Zealand	1	0	2	3
7	British Guyana	1	0	0	1
8	*Wales*	*0*	*3*	*3*	*6*

9	Northern Ireland	0	1	2	3
10	Jamaica	0	1	1	2
11	Southern Rhodesia	0	0	2	2
12	India	0	0	1	1

1938		**G**	**S**	**B**	**Sum**
1	Australia	24	19	22	65
2	England	15	14	10	39
3	Canada	13	16	15	44
4	South Africa	10	10	6	26
5	New Zealand	5	7	12	24
6	***Wales***	*2*	*2*	*0*	*4*
7	Ceylon	1	0	0	1
8	Scotland	0	2	3	5
9	Rhodesia	0	0	2	2
10	British Guyana	0	1	0	1

1950		**G**	**S**	**B**	**Sum**
1	Australia	34	27	19	80
2	England	19	16	13	48
3	New Zealand	10	22	21	53

4	Canada	8	9	14	31
5	South Africa	8	4	7	19
6	Scotland	5	2	3	10
7	Malaysia	2	1	1	4
8	Fiji	1	2	2	5
9	Ceylon	1	2	1	4
10	Nigeria	0	1	0	1
10	Rhodesia	0	1	0	1
12	*Wales*	*0*	*1*	*0*	*1*

1954		**G**	**S**	**B**	**Sum**
1	England	23	24	20	67
2	Australia	20	11	17	48
3	South Africa	16	7	12	35
4	Canada	9	20	14	43
5	New Zealand	7	6	6	19
6	Scotland	6	2	5	13
7	Trinidad & Tobago	2	2	0	4
8	Southern Rhodesia	2	1	0	3
9	Northern Ireland	2	1	0	3
10	Northern Rhodesia	1	5	4	10
11	Nigeria	1	3	3	7

12	Pakistan	1	3	2	6
13	*Wales*	*1*	*1*	*5*	*7*
14	Jamaica	1	0	0	1
15	Hong Kong	0	1	0	1
16	Uganda	0	1	0	1
17	Barbados	0	1	0	1
18	British Guyana	0	0	0	1

1958		**G**	**S**	**B**	**Sum**
1	England	29	22	29	80
2	Australia	27	2	17	66
3	South Africa	13	10	8	31
4	Scotland	5	5	3	13
5	New Zealand	4	6	9	19
6	Jamaica	4	2	1	7
7	Pakistan	3	5	2	10
8	India	2	1	0	3
9	Singapore	2	0	0	2
10	Canada	1	10	16	27
11	*Wales*	*1*	*3*	*7*	*11*
12	Northern Ireland	1	1	3	5

13	Bahamas	1	1	0	2
13	Barbados	1	1	0	2
15	Malaya	0	2	0	2
16	Nigeria	0	1	1	2
17	British Guyana	0	1	0	1
17	Uganda	0	1	0	1
19	Southern Rhodesia	0	0	3	3
20	Kenya	0	0	2	2
21	Ghana	0	0	1	1
21	Trinidad & Tobago	0	0	1	1
21	Isle of Man	0	0	1	1

1962		**G**	**S**	**B**	**Sum**
1	Australia	38	36	31	105
2	England	29	22	27	78
3	New Zealand	10	12	10	32
4	Pakistan	8	1	0	9
5	Canada	4	12	15	31
6	Scotland	4	7	3	14
7	Ghana	3	5	1	9
8	Jamaica	3	1	1	5

9	Kenya	2	2	1	5
10	Singapore	2	0	0	2
11	Uganda	1	1	4	6
12	Rhodesia	0	2	5	7
13	*Wales*	*0*	*2*	*4*	*6*
14	Bahamas	0	1	0	1
15	Fiji	0	0	2	2
15	Trinidad & Tobago	0	0	2	2
17	Barbados	0	0	1	1
17	British Guyana	0	0	1	1
17	Northern Ireland	0	0	1	1
17	Jersey	0	0	1	1
17	Malaysia	0	0	1	1
17	Papua New Guinea	0	0	1	1

1966		G	S	B	Sum
1	England	33	24	23	80
2	Australia	23	28	22	73
3	Canada	14	20	23	57

4	New Zealand	8	5	13	26
5	Ghana	5	2	2	9
5	Trinidad & Tobago	5	2	2	9
7	Pakistan	4	1	4	9
8	Kenya	4	1	3	8
9	India	3	4	3	10
9	Nigeria	3	4	3	10
11	*Wales*	*3*	*2*	*2*	*7*
12	Malaysia	2	2	1	5
13	Scotland	1	4	4	9
14	Northern Ireland	1	3	3	7
15	Isle of Man	1	0	0	1
16	Jamaica	0	4	8	12
17	Bahamas	0	1	0	1
17	Bermuda	0	1	0	1
17	Guyana	0	1	0	1
17	Papua New Guinea	0	1	0	1
21	Uganda	0	0	3	3
22	Barbados	0	0	1	1

1970		G	S	B	Sum
1	Australia	36	24	22	82
2	England	27	25	32	84
3	Canada	18	24	24	66
4	Scotland	6	8	11	25
5	Kenya	5	3	6	14
6	India	5	3	4	12
7	Pakistan	4	3	3	10
8	Jamaica	4	2	1	7
9	Uganda	3	3	1	7
10	Northern Ireland	3	1	5	9
11	*Wales*	*2*	*6*	*4*	*12*
12	New Zealand	2	6	6	14
13	Ghana	2	3	2	7
14	Nigeria	2	0	0	2
15	Malaysia	1	1	1	3
16	Hong Kong	1	0	0	1
17	Trinidad & Tobago	0	4	3	7
18	Zambia	0	2	4	4
19	Singapore	0	1	1	2

20	Barbados	0	1	0	1
20	Tanzania	0	1	0	1
22	Fiji	0	0	1	1
22	Gambia	0	0	1	1
22	Guyana	0	0	1	1
22	Malawi	0	0	1	1
22	St. Vincent	0	0	1	1
22	Isle of Man	0	0	1	1

1974		**G**	**S**	**B**	**Sum**
1	Australia	29	29	25	83
2	England	28	31	22	81
3	Canada	25	18	18	61
4	New Zealand	9	8	18	35
5	Kenya	7	2	9	18
6	India	4	8	3	15
7	Scotland	3	5	10	18
8	Nigeria	3	3	4	10
9	Northern Ireland	3	1	2	6
10	Uganda	2	4	3	9
11	Jamaica	2	1	0	3

12	*Wales*	*1*	*5*	*4*	*10*
13	Ghana	1	3	5	9
14	Zambia	1	1	1	3
15	Malaysia	1	0	3	4
16	Tanzania	1	0	1	2
17	St. Vincent	1	0	0	1
18	Western Samoa	0	1	1	2
18	Trinidad & Tobago	0	1	1	2
20	Lesotho	0	0	1	1
20	Singapore	0	0	1	1
20	Swaziland	0	0	1	1

1978		**G**	**S**	**B**	**Sum**
1	Canada	45	31	33	109
2	England	27	29	31	87
3	Australia	24	33	27	84
4	Kenya	7	6	5	18
5	New Zealand	5	5	10	20
6	India	5	4	6	15
7	Scotland	3	6	5	14
8	Jamaica	2	2	3	7

9	*Wales*	*2*	*1*	*5*	*8*
10	Northern Ireland	2	1	2	5
11	Hong Kong	2	0	0	2
12	Malaysia	1	2	1	4
13	Ghana	1	1	1	3
13	Guyana	1	1	1	3
15	Tanzania	1	1	0	2
16	Zambia	0	2	2	4
16	Trinidad & Tobago	0	2	2	4
18	Papua New Guinea	0	1	0	1
19	Western Samoa	0	0	3	3
20	Isle of Man	0	0	1	1

1982		**G**	**S**	**B**	**Sum**
1	Australia	39	39	29	107
2	England	38	38	32	108
3	Canada	26	23	33	82
4	Scotland	8	6	12	26
5	New Zealand	5	8	13	26
6	India	5	8	3	16

7	Nigeria	5	0	8	13
8	*Wales*	*4*	*4*	*1*	*9*
9	Kenya	4	2	4	10
10	Bahamas	2	2	2	6
11	Jamaica	2	1	1	4
12	Tanzania	1	2	2	5
13	Malaysia	1	0	1	2
14	Fiji	1	0	0	1
14	Hong Kong	1	0	0	1
14	Zimbabwe	1	0	0	1
17	Northern Ireland	0	3	3	6
18	Uganda	0	3	0	3
19	Zambia	0	1	5	6
20	Guernsey	0	1	1	2
21	Bermuda	0	0	1	1
21	Singapore	0	0	1	1
21	Swaziland	0	0	1	1

1986		G	S	B	Sum
1	England	52	42	49	143
2	Canada	51	34	30	115

3	Australia	40	46	33	119
4	New Zealand	8	16	14	38
5	*Wales*	*6*	*5*	*12*	*23*
6	Scotland	3	12	18	33
7	Northern Ireland	2	4	9	15
8	Isle of Man	1	0	0	1
9	Guernsey	0	2	0	2
10	Swaziland	0	1	0	1
11	Hong Kong	0	0	2	2
11	Malawi	0	0	2	2
13	Botswana	0	0	1	1
13	Jersey	0	0	1	1
13	Singapore	0	0	1	1

1990		**G**	**S**	**B**	**Sum**
1	Australia	52	54	56	162
2	England	47	40	42	129
3	Canada	35	41	37	113
4	New Zealand	17	14	27	58
5	India	13	8	11	32
6	*Wales*	*10*	*3*	*12*	*25*

7	Kenya	6	9	3	18
8	Nigeria	5	13	7	25
9	Scotland	5	7	10	22
10	Malaysia	2	2	0	4
11	Jamaica	2	0	2	4
12	Uganda	2	0	2	4
13	Northern Ireland	1	3	5	9
14	Nauru	1	2	0	3
15	Hong Kong	1	1	3	5
16	Cyprus	1	1	0	2
17	Bangladesh	1	0	1	2
18	Jersey	1	0	1	2
19	Bermuda	1	0	0	1
20	Papua New Guinea	1	0	0	1
20	Guernsey	1	0	0	1
22	Zimbabwe	0	2	1	3
23	Ghana	0	2	0	2
24	Tanzania	0	1	2	3
25	Zambia	0	0	3	3
26	Bahamas	0	0	2	2
26	Western Samoa	0	0	2	2

28	Guyana	0	0	1	1
28	Malta	0	0	1	1

1994		**G**	**S**	**B**	**Sum**
1	Australia	88	34	43	184
2	Canada	41	43	49	133
3	England	31	45	51	127
4	Nigeria	11	13	13	37
5	Kenya	7	4	8	19
6	India	6	12	7	25
7	Scotland	6	3	11	20
8	New Zealand	5	16	21	42
9	*Wales*	*5*	*8*	*6*	*19*
10	Northern Ireland	5	2	3	10
11	Nauru	3	0	0	3
12	South Africa	2	4	5	11
13	Jamaica	2	4	2	8
14	Malaysia	2	3	2	7
15	Cyprus	2	1	2	5
16	Sri Lanka	1	2	0	3
17	Zambia	1	1	2	4

18	Namibia	1	0	1	2
19	Zimbabwe	0	3	3	6
20	Papua New Guinea	0	1	0	1
20	Samoa	0	1	0	1
22	Hong Kong	0	0	4	4
23	Pakistan	0	0	3	3
24	Ghana	0	0	2	2
24	Trinidad & Tobago	0	0	2	2
24	Uganda	0	0	2	2
27	Bermuda	0	0	1	1
27	Botswana	0	0	1	1
27	Guernsey	0	0	1	1
27	Seychelles	0	0	1	1
27	Tanzania	0	0	1	1
27	Tonga	0	0	1	1
27	Norfolk Islands	0	0	1	1

1998		**G**	**S**	**B**	**Sum**
1	Australia	82	61	57	200
2	England	36	47	52	135
3	Canada	30	31	40	101

4	Malaysia	10	14	12	36
5	South Africa	9	11	14	34
6	New Zealand	8	6	20	34
7	India	7	10	8	25
8	Kenya	7	5	4	16
9	Jamaica	4	2	0	6
10	*Wales*	*3*	*4*	*8*	*15*
11	Scotland	3	2	7	12
12	Nauru	3	0	0	3
13	Northern Ireland	2	1	1	4
14	Zimbabwe	2	0	3	5
15	Ghana	1	1	3	5
16	Mauritius	1	1	2	4
17	Cyprus	1	1	1	3
17	Tanzania	1	1	1	3
17	Trinidad & Tobago	1	1	1	3
20	Bahamas	1	1	0	2
20	Mozambique	1	1	0	2
22	Barbados	1	0	2	3
23	Lesotho	1	0	0	1
24	Cameroon	0	3	3	6

25	Namibia	0	2	1	3
26	Seychelles	0	2	0	2
27	Sri Lanka	0	1	1	2
28	Bermuda	0	1	0	1
28	Fiji	0	1	0	1
28	Pakistan	0	1	0	1
28	Isle of Man	0	1	0	1
32	Papua New Guinea	0	0	1	1
32	Zambia	0	0	1	1
32	Uganda	0	0	1	1

Table Indicating The Progression Of Wales In The Games And The Number Of Medals Won

	Rank	G	S	B	Sum
1930	7	0	2	1	3
1934	8	0	3	3	6
1938	6	2	2	0	4
1950	12	0	1	0	1
1954	13	1	1	5	7
1958	11	1	3	7	11
1962	13	0	2	4	6
1966	11	3	2	2	7
1970	11	2	6	4	12
1974	12	1	5	4	10
1978	9	2	1	5	8
1982	8	4	4	1	9
1986	5	6	5	12	23
1990	6	10	3	12	25
1994	9	5	8	6	19
1998	10	3	4	8	15

G - Gold   S - Silver   B - Bronze

(Index 3)

Medals Won By Wales In The Twentieth Century

Gold Medals	40
Silver Medals	52
Bronze Medals	74
Total	**166**

(Index 1)

CHAPTER TEN

THE BRITISH EMPIRE & COMMONWEALTH GAMES IN 1958

Following the Games in Sydney in 1938 the idea of bringing the Games to Wales was born in the mind of Sir Robert Wheeler but unfortunately World War II interfered with this thought. However, the result of this thinking led to Wales being invited to organise the Games in 1958. In a meeting held during the Olympic Games in Helsinki in 1952, official permission was granted for the Games to be held in Wales in 1958. This meant that Wales had six years to organise the Games. This was considerably more than the seven months given to Hamilton in 1930, although the Games were known to be much larger. .

Sir Godfrey Llewellyn was given the privilege and honour of chairing the organisation of these Games. An Executive Committee was formed that would aid Sir Godfrey Llewellyn to fulfil this project.

XVI BRITISH EMPIRE & COMMONWEALTH GAMES 1958 ORGANISING COMMITTEES

OFFICERS

Traherne. T.D., J.P. Major Cennydd G.

Lord Lieutenant of Glamorgan	President
The Lord Aberdare	Deputy General President

Morgan. O.B.E.,J.P. J.H.	Chairman
Ferrier. Alderman G.Ll.	Deputy Hon.Chairman
Llewellyn, C.B., C.B.E., MC., T.D., J.P., D.L. Sir Godfrey	Chairman
Jenour, T.D., J.P. Sir A. Meynard C.	Vice-Chairman
Newham, O.B.E. Charles E.	Director of Organisation
Vaughan, J.P. O.B.E.,M.A.	Hon. Treasurer

EXECUTIVE COMMITTEE

CHAIRMEN	COMMITTEE
Alexander, T.D., MA. Duncan	Empire Games Village
Bailey, O.B.E., D.F.C. Group Captain	Finance
Berry, M.A. Hon. Anthony	Press & Publicity
Bradburn, B.Sc. R.F	Communications
Crouch, D.L. Colonel L. Roy	Medals
Duncan, T.D., D.L. Colonel D.A.	Souvenir Book
Groves. Cllr. W.	Empire Pool
Harding. His Honour Judge Rowe	Rugby
Harris. K. M.	Tickets

Howell. Cyril M.	Technical
Howells, M.D. Dr Leonard	Medical
Hurford, M.B.E., T.D.,J.P., D.L., A.D.C.	
Brigadier E.C.	Ceremonial
Ingledew, B.C.L., B.A., O.St.J. Kenneth H.	Legal
Llewellyn, C.B., C.B.E., M.C., T.D., J.P., D.L.	
Sir Godfrey	Appeals
Owen. Major T.D. D. Glyn	London
Rhys. Group Captain R.O.	Labour & Staff
Smith, C.B.E. W.H.	Reception & Entertainment
Swift, O.B.E., M.Inst.T. H.H.	Transport
Thomas. Chief Constable W.F.	Traffic
Thorpe. Lt. Colonel V.F.A.	Contracts & Concessions
Vile, M.B.E., J.P. Major T.H.	Main Stadium
Wheeler, C.B.E. C. Robert	Lake Padarn
Williams, O.B.E., J.P., D.L. Ald. D.T.	Visitors Accommodation
Wynne-Jones, O.B.E., J.P. G.V.	National Support
Brooke. J.P., A.C.A. N.R.R.	
John. Richard	
Oaten. J.	

Oldfield-Davies, C.B.E., M.A. A.B.

Pode. J.P., A.C.A., F.C.I.S. E. Julian

Paton. J. Roy

Prater. B.A. Edward(Ted) H.

Richards, B.COM. T. Wyndham

Tapper-Jones, Ll.B. S.

Thomas. Howard

Llewellyn. Ward

Webber, J.P., D.L. Sir Robert

Altogether there were some 140 committees each having its own particular responsibility.

This work fell into a pattern that fed the Executive Committee. I was delighted to have been a member of the Weightlifting Technical Committee under the Chairmanship of Emlyn Jenkins, a headmaster from Pontypool. These committees met once a month, so that the Chairman was au fait with up to the minute knowledge of all developments

As well as these committees, the interest spread all over the country with minor committees being set up to gather funds. An example of this was the committee in Cross Hands, Carmarthenshire as can be seen from the following pamphlet: –

VIᴛʜ BRITISH EMPIRE AND COMMONWEALTH GAMES

WALES - 1958

MABOLGAMPAU'R GYMANWLAD BRYDEINIG

Dear Sir or Madam,

The Year 1958 will focus the attention of the British Empire and Commonwealth, and indeed the World, on our little Country—WALES, for between July 18th and 26th, 1958, the VIth British Empire and Commonwealth Games will be staged in our Capital City—Cardiff.

We feel certain that every Welsh man and woman will wish to uphold the standard of hospitality and sportsmanship which is part of our tradition.

It was to this end that a Public Meeting was convened at Cross Hands recently, when it was unanimously decided, by a well attended meeting, to form a Committee to be called "The Cross Hands and District Appeals Committee."

It is therefore with the greatest confidence that we make this appeal for donations, as the cost of staging the Games is estimated to be at least £350,000. This amount is so great and our resources as a small country so little that the success of the venture will depend upon the goodwill and generosity of all of us throughout the country.

Wales is not likely to see the Games for another 80 years. Let us therefore make certain that the 1958 Games will be the most memorable in its history.

All contributions, great or small, will be gratefully appreciated, and you are kindly asked to return the attached envelope containing your donation to the Headmaster of your local school, who has readily agreed to act as local Treasurer.

Who knows ? Events such as these, where the Youth of more than 24 Countries will be meeting in friendly competition, may do more than anything else towards the advancement of World Peace.

Give generously so that Mynydd Mawr will have contributed its share in ensuring the success of the Games in Wales.

We are,

Yours sincerely,

W. Davies (Chairman), Cross Hands.
T. Johns (Treasurer), Lloyds Bank, Tumble.
T. H. Richards (Hon. Secretary), Cross Hands.
D. A. Stephens, Headmaster, C.P. School, Cross Hands

T. M. Jones,	,,	,,	Gorslas
Gwynne D. Evans,	,,	,,	Nantygroes.
T. D. Jones,	,,	,,	Penygroes.
D. J. Morris,	,,	,,	Llechyfedach.
B. F. Thomas,	,,	,,	Drefach.
A. G. Jones,	,,	,,	Cefneithin.
D. P. Jones,	,,	,,	Tumble
Delme Thomas,	,,	,,	Llannon.
Gwilym Walters,	,,	,,	Cwmgwili.
W. Harries,	,,	,,	Maesybont.

The result was an overwhelming success. I well recall the immense excitement and expectation when I arrived at Swansea Railway Station resplendent in my brand new scarlet team blazer and met three others on their way on the same train to join the rest of the Welsh Team at the newly built Empire Swimming Pool, Cardiff. The three were weightlifters Yorrie Evans and John Heywood, and Wrestler, Geoff Bailey.

Left to Right: YorrieEvans, John Heywood, Myrddin John, Geoff Bailey

It was interesting to receive the following information from Wynne Oliver, from Llangennech. Seven school pupils were selected to compete for Wales at the 1958 Games. The names of the seven were:-

Men

John Davies	Shot Put
J.C. Jones	220 yards
J. Wynne Oliver	220 yards
John Williams	880 yards

Women

Bonny F. Jones	100 yards
Carol M Thomas	80 yards Hurdles
Daphne H. Williams	220 yards

To be selected to represent Wales in the Games is an honour but to be selected while still a school pupil must be an unforgettable experience.

The teams were housed at the RAF Camp in St. Athans. About twenty athletes occupied the billets at the Camp and which were subdivided into convenient areas by partitions for three or four or more single beds.

We had our meals at the camp. Having only recently emerged from the war with its stringent food rationing, it was a source of wonder to see so much food at mealtimes. Not only was there ample food but it was also so appetising and I recall eating at the same table as the Duke of Edinburgh. As well as this, and situated around the outside area were conveniently placed stands where we could sample free cold drinks and snacks.

Due to the distance between Cardiff and St. Athans, (about 15 miles) a shuttle bus service was set up throughout the day, but with a strict rule that there would be no standing on the buses. One day when returning from Cardiff to the camp Wynne Oliver found himself on a bus but with no seat. Although an outstanding sprinter Wynne was comparatively small in stature. As he made his way out of the bus in order to catch the next bus, Wynne found himself being lifted off his feet by a huge Australian wrestler who gently deposited him on the lap of Dawn Fraser the world renown swimmer from Australia and there he remained comfortably ensconced until he arrived at St. Athans having complied with the rules.

Wynne Oliver and myself recall the immense difference between the regimentation and pomp of the Opening Ceremony and the informality of the Closing Ceremony. During the Closing Ceremony the Queen's speech was read out stating that in the future, Prince Charles would be made Prince of Wales at Caernarfon. **(Index 7)**

It was a sad sight to see the workmen tearing up the track even before the athletes had finished leaving the stadium so that preparations could be made for the racing.

A farewell dance was organised at the Sophia Gardens pavilion and during the evening's merriment a competition was arranged to find the shortest male athlete dancing with the tallest female athlete. These transpired to be Wales's Wynne Oliver and Canada's Women's Discus Thrower, Marie Dupree. The tallest male, dancing with the shortest woman was Men's Champion Discus thrower Stephanus J. Du Plessis of South Africa and Welsh athlete Daphne Williams.

The Executive Committee appointed Charles Newham to head the Headquarters staff and organise the day to day organisation and answerable to the Chairman. An admirable appointment. History shows that Charles Newham was especially talented in this type of work and it would be extremely difficult to find any blemishes in his work.

As well as the organisation the competitors did not let the occasion down with 10 world records and numerous Commonwealth records being broken.

Wales won 11 medals – one Gold, three Silver and seven Bronze.

The table of Welsh medals at Commonwealth Games up to the 1958 Games was:-

1930	3
1934	6
1938	3
1950	1
1954	7
1958	11

At the completion of the Games, the Organising Committee was able to present £33,677 to the British Empire and Commonwealth Games Council for. This money was donated to enable Wales to be able to send a representative team to future Games, to preserve the Council and support it to uphold its duties as a full member of the Games Federation. The money was invested in a Trust. Each year the Council received a donation accrued from the interest, to help with the necessary expense of operating the work of the Council. The remainder was reinvested in the Trust. Over the years the value of the Trust has increased considerably. It is the solemn duty of members of the Council to be ever cautious in all matters relating to the Trust. It is incumbent on

Council members to safeguard this capital to ensure the independence of the Council and to aid future Council members to carry on their aims.

It is gratifying to note that these principles have been upheld until the present time, and that the capital is available in any emergency that the Council may encounter.

Following the Games the Duke of Edinburgh wrote:-

From every point of view the VI British Empire and Commonwealth Games at Cardiff were immensely successful, in numbers of competitors, in Standards of achievement, and, most important, in the friendly comradeship which existed throughout the Games.

All this was matched by a wonderful piece of detailed organisation by the local committee.

All who were fortunate enough to see something of the games witnessed many remarkable performances and sportsmanship at its best, and all of us have taken away our own impressions of this memorable Commonwealth occasion.

Phillip

The British Empire and Commonwealth Games Federation was highly appreciative of the success of these Games and its president, Sir Arthur Porritt wrote:-

The triumph of Wales and Cardiff in staging the Sixth British Empire and Commonwealth Games is now history – and history that will ring down the years to come. The smallest country yet to accept, the onerous responsibility of acting as host. Wales produced what, in retrospect, can only be called a masterpiece. Superb organisation, both administrative and technical, a standard of competition and sporting results comparing with the best in the world and, most important of all, a spirit of friendship and understanding engendered automatically by the traditional and spontaneous Welsh enthusiasm and warmth of hospitality – all combined to ensure an outstanding success.

Wales should be justly proud of this achievement. We of the British Empire and Commonwealth Games Federation can only express for ourselves and on behalf of all our Daughter Associations a deep and genuine gratitude for and appreciation of an unique occasion – an occasion which so amply fulfilled the highest ideals of the Empire Games movement.

Arthur Porritt

Chairman

British Empire and Commonwealth Games Federation

November 1958

THE BID FOR THE 1994 COMMONWEALTH GAMES

India, Canada, Kenya, Northern Ireland, Barbados and Wales had declared an interest in organising the 1994 Games. Following much discussion the Executive Committee of the Commonwealth Games Council for Wales agreed to make an official bid for these Games.

The attitude of the Executive Committee was disheartening and I had to raise the subject at many meetings between 1979 and July 1981 until at last permission was granted for the President, Cyril Howell and myself to meet Swansea Council to seek its support for the bid in Swansea in 1990. Swansea turned us down.

I than attempted many times to try for 1994 at Cardiff.. Eventually I succeeded once more. This time the City of Cardiff was keen to take part.

On 14 June 1984 the following bid committee was set to arrange the bid:

Chairman   Sir Cennydd Traherne
Vice-Chairman   Lord J.Brooks
Director of Organisation   Myrddin John

3 councillors from Cardiff City
3 councillors from South Glamorgan
Sports Council for Wales   Lin Tatham
Commonwealth Games Council   Tommy Rees
                                  Averil Williams
                                  Fred Howell
                                  Basil George
                                  John Jones-Pritchard
                                  Rita Keitch

For some unknown reason the Councils of Cardiff and South Glamorgan met and arranged for Lord Brooks to be replaced by Cllr Ron Watkiss as Vice-Chairman without the knowledge of the other members of the committee.. The Committee also grew by adding the following to the committee:,- Cllr. Jeff Sainsbury. Cllr. John Reynolds. Cllr. T.H. Davies. Cllr. Jenny Randerson. Cllr. P.H. Bowen. Cllr. G. M Brinks. Cllr. D.J. Selignan. W.Emrys Evans. Prys Edwards. Geoff Rich and Paul Lovelock. Peter Gill and Associates was invited to guide the bid with Brian Hoey to present the bid.

Presentations were arranged in Nairobi, Noumea, Rome, Seoul, Edinburgh and London. Lord Brooks' contribution was his excellent support behind the scenes through his worldwide connections.especially in Nairobi where we had a wonderful welcome by Mr and Mrs Clive Pulman. Clive Pulman was a Welshman and Managing Director of the Standard newspaper. Needless to say we had daily coverage in this newspaper.

Although I suggested to Cllr. Ron Watkiss that it would be advisable for visits to be made to every affiliated country of the Games Federation that had a vote, this was turned down. I was of the opinion that this was a big mistake, because although convenient dinners were organised at cities where various countries met on special occasions, this was not so impressive and effective as having made a specific effort to meet a country on home ground to seek their support.

The Committee received sponsorship from various sources such as £5.000 from Pannell, Kerr, Foster towards the cost of the bid at Seoul. Peter Gill and Partners, produced pamphlets and a special promotion film but Victoria won the bid with Delhi second and Cardiff third. This was a big disappointment as the Cardiff Bid was way ahead of that given by the others and much more professional. Wales is not considered as a country and we were handicapped by this as we did not have political clout and our leaders failed to understand this point.

Unfortunately as Wales is not a country in the world of politics, it does not hold any power in this field where favours can be brokered. It is at this level that deals can be made and if Wales aspires to make a contribution at world level where there is competition, then it goes without saying, that this problem has to be addressed and strategic plans meticulously prepared. This applies to bidding for the Commonwealth Games. If Wales wishes to win the bid for the Commonwealth Games then it is imperative that it develops a political thrust together with a policy to target every member country of the Commonwealth Games Federation.

Following the disastrous result of this bid I immediately informed the Commonwealth Games Congress that Wales would be bidding for 2014. It is unfortunate that someone thought that this was not a good idea due to the pending London Olympic Games. What a foolish decision. Years of planning simply abandoned by some idle thinking by someone with no experience in this field. It would have been relatively simple to postpone the bid at a much later date if this had become necessary. On the other hand Glasgow continued its bid and won unopposed. This could have been Wales.

I am convinced that if Wales would have been given the right to organise the 1994 Games had they continued with the bid and that Scotland would have withdrawn as Scotland had organised the Games on two occasions, in 1970 and in 1986, whereas Wales had only done so once as far back as 1958.

It could be that Wales has already lost the chance of ever organising these Games due to the way the Games are developing and with a slowly increasing realisation by countries in other continents that they would have the chance of hosting the Games providing the finance could be found. If Wales ventures to make another bid, it would be a gamble that the Games would be able to cope financially and not leave the country with large debts.

CHAPTER ELEVEN

THE OLYMPIC GAMES

The main purpose of this book is to concentrate on the achievements of Welsh athletes and officials at Commonwealth Games in the twentieth century. However, I could be accused of a degree of vacillation and indeed, maybe irresponsibility if I did not include some small comment regarding the Olympic Games in relation to Wales.

I feel that as a nation we have been brainwashed by the consequences of historical events into an unconscious feeling of inferiority because we supposedly, reside in a small country, when an examination of the population of the countries of the world **(Index 5),** will reveal that this is not so. And what about achievements? Wales as a nation has given the world accomplished and respected leaders as well as successful people in many fields such as the arts, music, literature, politics, science, etc. This book gives indication that Wales more than holds its own in comparison with other countries at Commonwealth and World level in sport.

Welsh people who have represented Britain in the Olympic Games have shown great talent and aptitude. They have won many more medals than large numbers of smaller countries and indeed many of the countries with much larger populations. The following is a list of some of our talented greats who are comfortably ensconced (or at present have seats reserved for them) in the Parthenon of Welsh sport, - Sir Harry Llewellyn, Lynn Davies, Colin Jackson, Nicole Cooke, Tanni Grey-Thompson, Chris Hallam, Dai Roberts, Valerie Davies, Paul Radmilovic, Richard Meade etc. These come easily to the mind to students of sport..

The following is a list of Welsh people who have won medals at Olympic Games in the 20th Century. This list is outstanding and far beyond the reach of some of the smaller countries that have participated at Olympic Games. Indeed, many of the world's larger countries will look with great envy at this list.

MEDALS WON BY WELSH ATHLETES IN THE OLYMPIC GAMES

GAMES	NAME	SPORT

GOLD

GAMES	NAME	SPORT
1908 London	Radmilovic Paulo	**Water Polo**
	Radmilovic Paulo	**Swimming** 4 x 200m Freestyle Relay
	Gladstone. Albert	**Rowing** Eights with Cox
1912 Stockholm	Jacobs. David	**Athletics** 4 x100 m Relay
	Steer. Irene	**Swimming** 4 x100 m Freestyle
	Radmilovic. Paulo	**Water Polo**
1920 Antwerp	Radmilovic. Paulo	**Water Polo**
	Jones. Christopher	**Water Polo**
	Griffiths. Cecil	**Athletics** 4 x100 m Relay
	Ainsworth-Davies. John	**Athletics** 4 x 400 m Relay
1932 Los Angeles	Edwards. Hugh	**Rowing** Pairs Without Cox
	Edwards. Hugh	**Rowing** Fours Without Cox
1952 Helsinki	Llewellyn. Sir Harry	**Equestrian** Team Horse Jumping

1964	Tokyo	Davies. Lynn	**Athletics** Long Jump
1968	Mexico	Meade. Richard	**Equestrian**
1972	Munich	Meade. Richard	**Equestrian** 3 Day Team Event
		Meade. Richard	**Equestrian** Individual 3 Day

Tribute is due to Paul Radmilovic for his outstanding record.

PaulRadmilovic was born in Cardiff in 1886. His father came from Greece and his mother from Ireland. Paul won four Olympic Gold medals. Three of these were for Water Polo in 1908, 1912 and 1920 with another one in Swimming in 1908 in the 4 x 200 m Freestyle Relay. He competed in five Olympic Games. Between 1901 and 1922 he won 15 Welsh titles in the 100 yards Freestyle swimming events.

SILVER

1908	London	Brookes-King. Reginald	**Archery**
1948	London	Richards. Thomas	**Athletics** Marathon
		Jones. Ken	**Athletics** 4 x100m Relay
		Davis. Ron	**Hockey**
		Griffiths. William	**Hockey**
1968	Mexico	Woodroffe. Martyn	**Swimming** 200 m
1988	Seoul	Jackson. Colin	**Athletics** 110 m Hurdles
1996	Atlanta	Baulch. Jamie	**Athletics** 4 x400m Relay

| | | Thomas. Iwan | **Athletics** 4x400 m Relay |
| 2000 | **Sydney** | Barker. Ian | **Sailing** |

BRONZE

1908	**London**	Wales	**Hockey** *
1912	**Stockholm**	Titt. William Cowhig. William	**Gymnastics** All round Team
1932	**Los Angeles**	Davies. Valerie	**Swimming** 100 m Backstroke
		Davies. Valerie	**Swimming** 4 x 100 m Freestyle Relay
1948	**London**	Llewellyn. Sir Harry	**Equestrian** Team Horse Jumping
1952	**Helsinki**	Disley. John	**Athletics** 3.000 m Steeplechase
		Dadds. Graham Taylor. John	**Hockey** **Hockey**
1960	**Rome**	Broome. David	**Equestrian** Horse Jumping
		Whitehead. Nick	**Athletics** 4 x 100 m Relay
1968	**Mexico**	Broome. David	**Equestrian** Horse Jumping

1972	**Munich**	Evans. Ralph	**Boxing** Light Flyweight
1980	**Moscow**	Probert. Michelle	**Athletics** 4 x 400 m Relay
		Wiggin. Charles	**Rowing** Pairs Without Cox
1984	**Los Angeles**	Cattrall. Robert	**Hockey**
1992	**Barcelona**	Morgan. Helen	**Hockey**

* Wales competed as Wales in the 1908 Olympic Games **(Index 2)**

As can be seen in the table 'Population of the World' **(Index 5)**, the United Kingdom is 22nd on the list, and Wales with a population of 3,063,456 is 135 on a list of 196 countries.

There are 41 countries with less than a population of 1 million e.g. Luxembourg, Qatar, Solomon Isles, Bhutan, Guyana, Fiji, etc. 30 countries have less than half a million such as Samoa, Tonga, Malta, Bahamas, Belize and Monaco etc. Further down the list we find smaller countries such as Dominica, Antigua, Lichtenstein, Seychelles, San Marino etc. with less than 100,000. Why is Wales with over 3 million people not competing alongside these at Olympic Games?

There are some 61 countries with a population which is lower than that of Wales, and the large majority of those compete in the Olympic Games. There is a strong argument that Wales should be competing as a country in the Olympic Games. People who purport to have a vision concerning sport in Wales, - and in my view unfortunately there are very few of these, should do all in their power to pressurise the I.O.C. to welcome Wales as a full member. Of course I recognise that this is a political problem and it is probable that such a request would be rejected, but such a course of action needs to be launched as early as possible. Once initiated it is then important that those involved continue with the fight. It is my opinion that perseverance is often stronger than power.

It is unfortunate that those people who occupy positions to do this have not got the necessary vision in this field or do not possess the necessary courage or the strength of mind to make any kind of gesture. Failure to do this will mean that hundreds of Welsh sportspeople in various sports will be denied the chance of becoming an Olympian, whereas athletes with lesser ability and from smaller countries, achieve this honour. Britain could still claim that its countries do well.

Readers may still be unconvinced that Wales is not good enough to compete in the Olympic Games. I would remind them that at the 2008 Olympic Games, Wales won 11% of the British medal count as well as 14% in the Paralympics. This achievement from only 5% of the population of Britain.

Unfortunately this state of affairs still persists. Hopefully the contents of this book will make readers realise that we are not a little country as our bards and politicians seem to continually emphasize, sometimes as an excuse when we lose or sometimes as a kind of remorse when Wales is successful. This situation continues to exist and is perpetuated by England when it is convenient to its argument. This kind of thinking is as a result of constant but subtle brainwashing such as Britain for some reason which eludes me, placing the word Great before its name. The British imperial mind is very cunning, and as Wales is next to England it is extremely vulnerable to this and the effect has been disastrous over the years. Why bring this argument into this book? My raison d'être for this is that Wales's athletes would produce even better results at Commonwealth Games through being able to compete at a higher level provided by the Olympic Games. Surely if Wales competes internationally it deserves to compete at Olympic Games. I was taught at school that international means between countries, - and that is what the Olympic movement is concerned with, isn't it?

It is my hope that this book will awaken a strong desire in someone to campaign vigorously and with passion not only for Welsh sport but also in other fields of interest that we excel in, so that we can participate at the highest of levels. Excellence can only be achieved when we are tested against others at the highest levels. It must be emphasized that we are not Little Wales but **GREAT WALES,** and as such deserve to be accepted as full members of the International Olympic Committee and to compete side by side with other countries on the world sporting stage. It is highly probable that other countries will be accepted as members of the IOC with Wales as usual belatedly following on about fifty years later.

Determination and Perseverance

Are the Progenitors of Success

Dyfal Donc a Dyrr y Garreg

CHAPTER TWELVE

THE COUNCIL'S INTERNATIONAL AWARD

The Commonwealth Games Council for Wales initiated an International Award, which was presented to individuals and bodies who had contributed to the betterment of Welsh sport and in particular to the work of the Council at a high level. These awards in the guise of attractive personalised plates were designed by **Dr Wayne Griffiths** and are presented during special occasions. The recipients during this period were:

1991

Les Davies-City of Cardiff Council
Sir Geraint Evans
Cllr. Wynne Evans- Dyfed County Council
Cyril Howell
John Elfed Jones – Wales Water
David Morgan
Cllr. J.V. Owen-Anglesey County Council
Allan Owen- Whitbread Welsh
Tommy Rees
Idwal Symmonds – HTV
Sir Cennydd Traherne
Malcolm Waldron
Derek Wignall

1992

Cllr. Jim Davies
Lynn Davies, M.B.E.
Fred Howell
Sir Meynard Jenour, K.T.,T.D.
A. de O Salles, C.B.E., J.P.
Bryn Thomas, B.E.M.

1993

Glyn Jones
Rita Keitch
Ieuan Owen

2000

Dr. Wayne Griffiths, M.B.E.
Myrddin John, M.B.E.
John Jones - Pritchard

INAUGURAL
INTERNATIONAL AWARDS
CEREMONY

on
FRIDAY, 28th SEPTEMBER, 1990
at
HERENSTON HOTEL, EWENNY,
BRIDGEND

Presentations by:
SIR MAYNARD JENOUR, Kt., T.D.

Grace:
HUGH THOMAS, Esq.

M.Cs:
BRYN THOMAS, B.E.M.
MYRDDIN JOHN, M.B.E.

Poster of the First Games in Hamilton, Canada

BY THE AUTHOR

I first began my interest in the sport of weightlifting at the early age of twelve by collecting magazines connected with the sport. The collecting developed slowly until I became the owner of quite a substantial library of magazines and books.

Following my selection to represent Wales in the 1958 British Empire and Commonwealth Games, I purchased the official book recording the events at these Games. Since then I became an avid collector and bought any magazine or book connected with the Commonwealth Games, that I chanced upon.

Following my friendship over the years with the late Alun Cooper of Bethlehem, Llandeilo, he persuaded me to become a serious collector in this field.when he said – "if you don't do this, who will?"

The collection has now developed into a fairly substantial sporting compendium. It specialises in Commonwealth Games, Olympic Games as well as the sport of weightlifting, consisting of books, magazines and pamphlets together will medals and badges. I have also developed a penchant for books printed by the famous Gregynnog Press.

Having written this book with facts collected from numerous sources but mainly from my own library, I appreciate another pearl from Alun who said, "the fact is correct, because I have the book".

Thank you Alun.

MJ

WINNING IS THE AIM – TAKING PART IS THE VICTORY

PART 3

INDEX 1

Individual Welsh Medals at Commonwealth Games in the Twentieth Century

Name	Sport	Number
Morgan. David	Weightlifting	7
Davies. Valerie E.	Swimming	4
Owen. Ieuan W.	Weightlifting	4
Weale. Robert	Lawn Bowling	4
Davies. Andrew	Weightlifting	3
Hives. Gareth	Weightlifting	3
Wade (McDermott). Kirsty	Athletics	3
Arnold. Aled	Weightlifting	2
Arthur. Peter J.	Weightlifting	2
Burns. John	Weightlifting	2
Collins. Malcolm	Boxing	2
Davies. Lynn	Athletics	2
Edwards. D. C.	Rowing	2
Edwards. J.H.M.	Rowing	2
Gray. Paul	Athletics	2
Jackson. Colin	Athletics	2

Johnson. Horace A.	Weightlifting	2
Jones. Rita	Lawn Bowling	2
Maunder. Roger A.	Fencing	2
Perdue. Terry	Weightlifting	2
Price. Berwyn	Athletics	2
Price. John	Lawn Bowling	2
Richards. Michael J.	Swimming	2
Roach. Mark	Weightlifting	2
Skene. Donald	Cycling	2
Watkins. Bill	Shooting	2
Woodroffe. Martyn J.	Swimming	2
Ackland. Janet	Lawn Bowling	1
Anstey. Mark	Lawn Bowling	1
Arthur. Jamie	Boxing	1
Alford. Jim	Athletics	1
Baulch. Jamie	Athletics	1
Barnes. Albert	Boxing	1
Beavan. Pat	Swimming	1
Beswick. John M.	Cycling	1
Birkett-Evans. James	Shooting	1
Braithwaite. Donald	Boxing	1

Brockway. John	Swimming	1
Brown. W.G.	Boxing	1
Bryce. Jeffrey	Weightlifting	1
Cave. Leanda	Triathlon	1
Chung Kum Weng	Weightlifting	1
Cook. Jason	Boxing	1
Craven. Richard.	Shooting	1
Dainton. Ann	Lawn Bowling	1
Davies. Dai	Boxing	1
Davies. John	Athletics	1
Davies. Thomas R.	Lawn Bowling	1
Duston. Helen	Judo	1
Edwards. Paul	Athletics	1
Elias. Matthew	Athletics	1
England. David M.	Athletics	1
Evans. Aneurin	Boxing	1
Evans. Colin	Shooting	1
Evans. John	Lawn Bowling	1
Evans. John J.	Fencing	1
Evans. Linda	Lawn Bowling	1
Freal. Anthony	Boxing	1

Gough. Alex	Squash	1
Greenland. Joanne	Swimming	1
Griffiths. Lisa	Judo	1
Hackney. Roger	Athletics	1
Haddock. Neil	Boxing	1
Hamer. Ian	Athletics	1
Harding. Aileen	Fencing	1
Harries. Colin	Shooting	1
Hatfield. John	Cycling	1
Head. Venissa	Athletics	1
Higgins. Robert	Boxing	1
Hodge. Sally	Cycling	1
Hopkins. Gloria	Lawn Bowling	1
James. Charles	Judo	1
Jay. Michael	Shooting	1
Jenkins. Ronald	Weightlifting	1
Johnson. Nigel R.	Swimming	1
Jones. Berwyn	Athletics	1
Jones. J. D.	Boxing	1
Jones. Karl	Weightlifting	1
Jones. Kenneth	Athletics	1

Jones. Steve	Athletics	1
Kerslake. Malcolm	Fencing	1
Knowles. Philippa	Judo	1
Lawrence. Sonia	Gymnastics	1
Lewis. Philip	Shooting	1
Longe. Clive	Athletics	1
Luke. J. C.	Rowing	1
Luke. R. T.	Rowing	1
Parker. Linda	Lawn Bowling	1
Rickets. Joan	Lawn Bowling	1
Thomas. Hafod	Lawn Bowling	1
Malcolm. Christian	Athletics	1
McKenzie. Errol	Boxing	1
Morgan. James	Lawn Bowling	1
Thomas. William	Lawn Bowling	1
Jay. Michael	Shooting	1
Jones. Louise	Cycling	1
Martin-Jones. Ruth	Athletics	1
McCombe. J.	Fencing	1
Merriman. John L.	Athletics	1
Miles. Helen	Athletics	1

Moran. Kevin	Swimming	1
Morgan. Anthony	Weightlifting	1
Morgan. James	Lawn Bowling	1
Morgan. Kelly	Badminton	1
Morgan. Robert	Swimming (Diving)	1
Morley. Kay	Athletics	1
Morris. Sian	Athletics	1
Page. D. L.	Rowing	1
Perkins. Lyn	Lawn Bowling	1
Phillips. Rowland	Shooting	1
Pickering. Shaun	Athletics	1
Pleace. Robert	Boxing	1
Pottinger. Jackie	Boxing	1
Preston. John	Fencing	1
Pritchard. D. L.	Rowing	1
Reardon. Dennis P.	Boxing	1
Rees. Neil	Lawn Bowling	1
Reynolds. E. O. Robert	Fencing	1
Scutt. Michelle	Athletics	1
Shaw. Robert	Athletics	1
Short. Sally Anne	Athletics	1

Slade. Ian	Lawn Bowling	1
Smart. Carmen	Athletics	1
Sutherland. Ann	Lawn Bowling	1
Sutton. Moira	Judo	1
Swansea. Lord John	Shooting	1
Taylor. Frank	Boxing	1
Taylor. Neil	Weightlifting	1
Thomas. Iwan	Athletics	1
Thomas. William	Lawn Bowling	1
Tooby. Angela	Athletics	1
Turner. Douglas	Athletics	1
Wakefield. Terry	Shooting	1
Watkins. William	Shooting	1
Weaver. Stan	Lawn Bowling	1
Whitehead. Neville	Athletics	1
Wilkins. David	Lawn Bowling	1
Williams. Ray	Lawn Bowling	1
Wilshire. Spencer	Lawn Bowling	1
Williams. Raymond	Weightlifting	1
Wilson. Steve	Weightlifting	1
Winstone. Howard	Boxing	1

Winter. Neil	Athletics	1
Woodroffe. Martyn J.	Swimming	1
Wrench. Robert	Weightlifting	1

Wales Competes in the 1908 Olympic Games.

Results of the Men's Hockey in London 1908

    1. GBR England

    2. Ireland.

    3. GBR Scotland

    3. *GBR Wales*

Although Wales is given equal third placing, I am unable to understand this as in my opinion Wales should have been fourth.

According to some sources only four countries competed in the Hockey event. Perhaps Wales and Scotland were invited to compete in order to make the competition viable. Great Britain wanted Hockey to be included in the programme no doubt aware of its superiority in the sport and therefore adding to its tally of gold medals. A ploy which succeeded. As there were no entries from other countries Wales and Scotland were considered to be countries at these Olympic Games albeit as GBR Wales, GBR Scotland and GBR England, with a German Team from one club and the French Team selected from 3 clubs as can be seen in the following report -

There seems to be much confusion as to the placing but I have been able to conclude that eventually there were 6 entries –

The final placing was:

1 England

2 Ireland

3 Wales and Scotland

5 Germany

6 France

There was no playoff for 3rd place so Scotland and Wales won a bronze medal each.

1st Round	England	10	France	1
	Scotland	4	Germany	0
Semi Final	Scotland	1	England	6
	Ireland	3	Wales	1
Final	England	8	Ireland	1

France played Germany in an 'extra' match with Germany winning 1 nil.

It is possible that some arrangement was concocted in the scoring procedure that ensured that all four home countries won a medal which explained how Wales won a bronze medal in the 1908 Olympic Games?

As this is the only time that Wales competed at the Olympic Games I feel justified in naming the players as very little notice is given to this.

WELSH HOCKEY TEAM 1908

Turnbull. W. Bruce
Richards. Edward W.G.
Shepard. Charles. W.
Lyne. Richard
Pallott. William J.
Evans. Llewellyn
Phillips. F. Gordon
Turnbull. Phillip B.
Connah. Frederick
Law. Arthur A.
Williams. James. Ralph

INDEX 3 Position of Wales at the Games

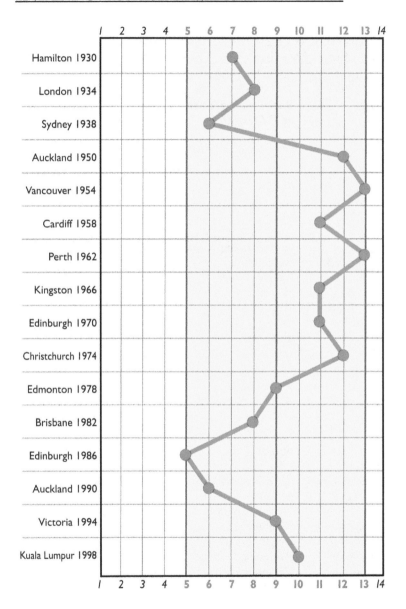

INDEX 4

Attendance At Executive And General Meetings Since The First Meeting Of The Commonwealth Games Council For Wales In 1930

Name	Representing Body at 1st Meeting	Date Of 1st Meeting	No of Meetings

A

AcklandJanet	Lawn Bowling Women	29.03 1990	1
Acocks. Jack	Weightlifting	04.06.1948	32
Aherne. A.	Rifle Shooting	20.03.1995	1
Allen. Alec L.	Hockey	29.01.1964	25
Allen. Raymond C.Boxing		13.06.1979	110
Allwood.	?	14.02.1934	1
Anderson. U.MollyBadminton		24.04.1963	1
Andrew. Fred J.	Boxing	14.02.1934	4
Arnold. G.	?	30.01.1980	1

B

Bailey. Geoffrey	Wrestling	25.011960	3
Baird. W.	?	19.07.1933	10
Banahan. David	Lawn Bowling Men	09.03.1999	1
Banning. Phil A.	Athletics	09.03.1999	1
Banwell-Clode. Mark Pistol Shooting		27.03.1985	30
Barnes. A.	Weightlifting	18.01.1954	1
Barnett. Melville	Weightlifting	28.10.1959	5
Barry. J.	Swimming	25.04.1934	3
Barton. J.A.	Gymnastics	31.03.1949	1
Batty. Gerry G.	Athletics Men	10.06.1981	11
Baxter-Wright.Tom Sports Council		16.07.1993	6
Beer. P.	Table Tennis	25.03.1988	1
Bertorelli. Frank	Rifle Shooting	27.01.1970	3
Best. John L.	Badminton	29.01.1964	3

Billing. Cyril	Gymnastics	28.01.1958	1
Bingham Cecil D.	Race Walking	14.03.1967	1
Bingham. Maurice	Race Walking	30.01.1967	7
Bird. Jack M.	Boxing	31.01.1962	4
Blake. Sally	Athletics Women	23.02.1982	5
Bluck. C.	Archery	22.03.1983	2
Blyth. Ella	Swimming	22.03.1983	12
Boaden. Ken J.	Rifle Shooting	10.06.1981	8
Booker. J.	Sailing	25.10.1967	1
Booth L.G.	?	19.01.1939	1
Botting. Norman	Rowing	29.01.1964	57
Bowsher. F.W.	Rowing	27.01.1970	6
Braddick. Reginald	Cycling	11.03.1955	24
Brock H.A.V.	Cycling	18.01.1949	6
Brown. Hilton J.	Badminton	26.04.1990	38
Brown. June	Hockey	25.10.1967	11
Brimble. John	Badminton	22.03.1983	9
Allen. Bruce	Selection Committee	26.08.1982	1
Bruce. Jeffrey	Clay Pigeon Shooting	28.01.1981	4
Bryant. David F.	Gymnastics	22.01.1968	1
Bryant-Lewis. Diana	Swimming	20.03.1995	1
Buffin. W.	Gymnastics	03.03.1948	3

C

Calnan. John	Lawn Bowling Men	01.10.1988	7
Canning. Graham	Badminton	02.02.1999	3
Carro Wilfred	Boxing	23.02.1982	2
Chadwick. Tony	Pistol Shooting	27.03.1985	4
Chamberlain. Ron	Tenpin Bowling	24.02.1997	10
Chambers.Royston.	Boxing	28.03.1996	4
Chambers. J. M.	Boxing	19.03.1998	2
Chapman. Herbert	Lawn Bowling	11.03.1955	32
Clark. Dennis A.	Badminton	27.02.1995	3
Clark. Una	Tenpin Bowling	17.06.1999	3
Clarke. P.	?	14.02.1934	4
Claypole. T.L.	Sailing	08.01.1974	19
Clemo. Tony	Athletics Men	27.01.1976	2
Clough. Jane	Badminton	25.03.1988	2
Coates. D.	Basketball	15.12.1954	1
Cocks. W.J.	?	15.12.1938	1
Cole. Walter F.	Sports Council	04.01.1984	1

Collard. Jack P.	Athletics	26.01.1965	1
Collins. Glyn	Weightlifting	28.01.1969	20
Collins. John H.	Cross Country	29.11.1978	8
Cook. Fred S.	Smallbore Rifle Shooting	28.01.1969	5
Cooper. Alun M.	Weightlifting	23.09.1992	1
Corrigan. Peter	Publicity Officer	27.01.1970	2
Coulson.Elizabeth	Rowing	25.02.1987	3
Coulthard. Terry	Lawn Bowling Men	28.03.1996	10
Courtney. Ray	Athletics Women	07.07.1981	13
Cox. Reg A.	Lawn Bowling	29.01.1951	74
Crate. Alec E.	Lawn Bowling Men	22.03.1983	1
Crimp. Graham C	Hockey Men	29.01.1975	2
Crosby. William	Rifle Shooting	29.01.1964	1
Cross. Richard W.	Pistol Shooting	25.03.1986	3
Crossling. J.	Swimming	17.02.1937	1
Crosswaite. Alfred	Swimming	26.01.1977	1
Crosswaite.Rosina	Swimming	08.01.1974	1
Crowther. Denise	Archery	31.01.1979	1
Crump. G.	?	05.12.1979	1
Cumbers. Peggy	Swimming	23.04.1986	9

D

Dallimore. John	Smallbore Rifle Shooting	19.03.1982	1
Davies. Bronwen	Gymnastics	25.03.1988	7
Davies. Clyde	Fencing	30.01.1967	5
Davies. Colin	Clay Target Shooting	22.02.1992	2
Davies. Cadfan	Sports Council	06.07.1973	4
Davies. Desmond	Gymnastics	30.01.1980	3
Davies. Delyth	Athletics	16.12.1993	28
Davies. Gordon	Weightlifting	14.06.1948	3
Davies. Graham J.	Sports Council	16.12.1993	11
Davies. G.	Shooting	19.03.1998	1
Davies. Gilbert E.	Swimming	29.01.1964	7
Davies. Gerald	Sports Council	05.02.1975	1
Davies. G.W.	Wrestling	29.05.1958	1
Davies. George W.	Swimming	29.01.1975	2
Davies. H.	Swimming	19.07.1933	21
Davies. H.E.	Boxing	31.01.1961	2
Davies. John	Boxing	10.11.1970	12
Davies. Lynn A.	Gymnastics	25.03.1987	9
Davies. L.R.J.	Smallbore Rifle Shooting	20.02.1975	1
Davies. Mary	Bowls Women	11.06.1985	1
Davies. Mari O.	Athletics	02.05.1957	25

Davies. Ormond	Lawn Bowling Men	21.03.1994	1
Davies. P.	Power Boat Racing	26.01.1977	1
Davies. P.	Gymnastics	19.03.1992	1
Davies. Ronald	Gymnastics	22.03.1983	3
Davies. Sonia	Hockey	12.02.1968	23
Davies. S.	Clay Target Shooting	21.03.1994	1
Davies. S.R.	Trampoline	04.12.1974	1
Davies. William	Boxing	22.01.1953	10
Davies. William E.	Boxing	22.01.1966	1
Davis. K.	Athletics	26.01.1959	1
Davison. Fay	Hockey Women	29.01.1975	1
Delaney. Ron	Athletics	20.03.1995	1
Denner. C. Mansel	Weightlifting	14.06.1948	1
Dennis. Donald	Weightlifting	18.01.1949	1
Dennis-Jones. Glyn	Hockey	06.01.1958	12
Drew. Albert J.	Boxing	26.10.1960	5
Duggan. Frank	Athletics	15.12.1954	7

E

Eddols. G.C.	Rowing	22.02.1992	1
Edmunds. R.J.	Trampoline	09.12.1980	2
Edwards. Mildred	Lawn Bowling Women	09.03.1999	1
Elgie. Margaret	Athletics Women	18.03.1975	26
Elliott. Geoffrey	Badminton	27.01.1970	2
Ellis. K.	Cycling	29.03.1990	1
Ellis. M. Anne	Hockey	19.09.1996	10
England. Maurice	Hockey	26.10.1960	1
England. D.	Cycling	31.01.1979	1
Enoch. Cyril J.	Archery	22.03.1983	2
Evans. Alwyn	Weightlifting	06.01.1958	8
Evans. Athol T.	Cycling	26.10.1960	2
Evans. Colin D.	Clay Pigeon Shooting	26.01.1972	1
Evans. E.N.	Rowing	29.01.1964	1
Evans. Geraint	Publicity Officer	04.01.1984	3
Evans. Glyn	Cycling	12.12.1994	20
Evans. John	Bodybuilding	30.01.1961	5
Evans. John	Coopted Member	22.10.1985	14
Evans. J.	Swimming	20.03.1995	1
Evans. J.	Archery	07.12.1953	1
Evans. Lynne	Archery	29.03.1990	1
Evans. P.	Cycling	20.03.1995	1
Evans. Ron B.	Athletics Men	05.12.1973	20
Evans. R.C.	Wrestling	24.04.1958	4

Evans. Rachel	Athletics	14.03.1967	26
Evans. Roy	Table Tennis	07.04.1981	6
Evans. W.A.L.	Athletics Men	25.01.1978	50

F

Farr. Colin	Smallbore Rifle Shooting	05.03.1984	3
Farr. Ken	Boxing	25.03.1987	4
Farthing. Glyn	Judo	29.03.1990	1
Fearnley. Charles	.Boxing	18.10.1956	50
Fifield. Richard	Badminton	11.06.1985	14
Fisher. William E.	Athletics	03.03.1948	17
Fligeltone. P.	Swimming	19.04.1948	5
Forrest. Rod	Hockey Men	27.01.1971	2
Foxwell. Gerald	Bodybuilding	26.10.1960	1
Francis. Norman	Hockey Men	26.01.1972	1
Franklin. A.G.	Rowing	25.01.1960	10
Franklyn. Ann	Appeal	22.01.1991	1
Fraser. Alan	Legal Adviser	01.06.1987	16
Friswell. John	Cycling	25.03.1987	3

G

Gage. G. M	Clerk	08.01.1974	1
Gallagher. Steve	Appeal	18.07.1995	16
Ganz. Mrs Judith	Cross Country	07.04.1981	1
Ganz. C. Robin	Cross Country	31.01.1979	1
George. Basil	Clay Target Shooting	06.10.1971	96
George. David	Shooting	19.03.1998	1
Gilbertson.Richard	Rifle Shooting 1	10.06.1981	1
Giles. Howard C.	Badminton	08.01.1974	4
Gilmore. Sidney	Lawn Bowling Men	28.01.1981	1
Gimbletie. W.	Gymnastics	03.09.1948	1
Godfrey. Derek	Badminton	31.01.1979	2
Goode. Derek	?	12.09.1979	1
Grant. Graham	Medical Adviser	02.03.1959	5
Grace. C.D.	Sailing	27.05.1964	13
Gray. Stan D.	Fullbore Rifle Shooting	05.10.1972	31
Greaves. G.R.H.	Rowing	29.03.1990	1
Green. R.P.	Swimming	20.06.1933	19
Grey. Ted	Hockey Men	27.01.1976	1
Griffiths. A.Wayne	Medical Adviser	27.10.1981	67
Griffiths. Bryn	Cycling	31.03.1949	16
Griffiths. G.A.	Rowing	25.03.1960	1

Griffiths. Kenneth	Athletics Men	22.03.1983	1
Griffiths. Mark	Boxing	23.01.1956	1
Griffiths. William	Lawn Bowling	01.11.1961	1
Gunning. Kenneth	Weightlifting	26.01.1959	1

H

Hall. C.	Power Boat Racing	26.01.1977	1
Hall. F.	Boxing	03.04.1948	1
Hampton. John	Weightlifting	18.01.1949	3
Harries Lynette	Athletics Women	25.11.1969	8
Harries. Kenneth	Athletics Men	30.01.1980	13
Hartland. John	Rowing	02.03.1989	1
Hatto. Frank	Boxing	26.10.1960	2
Hewett. J.	?	24.03.1937	1
Hicks. Ken G	Fencing	18.10.1956	9
Hill. Miss Ann	Athletics Women	27.01.1971	2
Hill. Robert	Clay Pigeon Shooting	26.01.1977	12
Hillman. J.	Fencing	29.10.1952	3
Hockley. Norman	Sailing	26.01.1965	18
Hodge. Eric	Cycling	15.07.1981	4
Holbrook. S.J.	Judo	09.03.1999	1
Hole. Gerry	Weightlifting	22.01.1968	2
Holland. Steven.	Judo	20.03.1985	1
Holmes. John A.	Rifle Shootingl	21.03.1994	5
Holvey. Susan	Netball	06.06.1996	14
Hooper. Berenice	Swimming	29.01.1951	97
Hooper. Wilfred	Swimming	15.12.1954	38
Hope. Michael J.	Fencing	26.01.1986	1
Hopkins. Edward	Athletics	18.10.1956	83
Hopkins. L	Clay Pigeon Shooting	28.01.1981	5
Hosgood. John B.	Hockey	26.01.1966	1
Howell. Cyril M.	Athletics	24.03.1937	197
Howell. Fred	Cycling	08.12.1958	229
Howell. Phillip E.	Clay Target Shooting	29.03.1990	1
Hughes. Dyfrig	Lawn Bowling Men	19.03.1992	1
Hughes E. M.	Athletics	17.02.1937	1
Hunt E.	?	25.04.1934	5
Huxtable.Graham	Swimming	27.01.1976	5
Hybart. Maureen	Badminton	26.01.1977	12

I

Ingledew.Kenneth	Hockey	03.09.1954	56

Ireland. A. Frank   Athletics Men   25.03.1986   13

J

James E.	?	04.05.1937	7
James. Kenneth L.	Swimming	05.03.1984	1
James. Margaret J.	Swimming	30.01.1980	6
James. Robert	Swimming	25.03.1986	2
Jenkins. Dorothy	Archery	31.01.1979	1
Jenkins. Emlyn	Weightlifting	11.03.1955	24
Jenkins. J. Powell	Hockey	04.10.1954	4
Jenkins. N.	Rowing	01.06.1987	2
Jenkins. Arthur	Weightlifting	22.03.1983	8
John. E. Delfrig	Weightlifting	27.01.1972	19
John. Myrddin	Weightlifting	25.01.1960	169
John. Sheila M.	Clerk	04.01.1984	1
John. Sue	Gymnastics	19.03.1998	3
John. Glyn	Bowling	29.01.1975	1
Johns. F.L.	Athletics	17.02.1937	4
Johnson. Rose B.	Athletics Women	28.01.1981	10
Johnson. T.	Table Tennis	16.07.1985	2
Joignant. Peter	Sports Council	15.05.1974	3
Jones. Anthony	Gymnastics	19.03.1992	1
Jones. Alban H.	Weightlifting	26.10.1960	1
Jones. Arthur S.	Weightlifting	01.06.1987	3
Jones. E.R.	Cycling	24.06.1934	13
Jones. I. Rhys	Hockey Men	29.011975	1
Jones. John G.	Weightlifting	25.03.1954	1
Jones. L. Roy	Athletics	30.01.1967	6
Jones. Michael	Archery	20.03.1997	1
Jones. Philip	Cycling	29.03.1990	9
Jones. Raymond E	Weightlifting	26.01.1966	93
Jones. Ron	Sports Council	07.09.1984	6
Jones. Vivian	Gymnastics	31.01.1979	1
Jones. Wyndham H.	Rowing	23.01.1956	138
Jones. Wyndham W.	Bowling	18.10.1956	9
Jones-Prichard. John	Swimming	31.01.1979	120

K

Kannie. P.A.	Clay Pigeon Shooting	05.03.1984	1
Keitch. Rita	Gymnastics	31.01.1979	110
Kelly. T. Eddie	Weightlifting	23.01.1956	10
Kendall. Miss D.	Trampoline	27.01.1970	1

472

| Kerslake. M. | Fencing | 07.12.1953 | 1 |
| Knock. A.H. | Boxing | 15.12.1938 | 14 |

L

Lade. Colin R.	Swimming	28.03.1996	1
Lamb. Mrs Gwen	Lawn Bowling Women	19.03.1992	7
Lawson. Robert	Fencing	29.01.1975	17
Levenson.Maurice	Cycling	29.03.1996	3
Lewis. Gwyn	?	09.09.1937	8
Lewis. John E.	Swimming	29.03.1990	4
Lewis. Morgan E.	Bowling Men	25.03.1987	4
Lewis. Meirion	Appeal	07.07.1971	3
Lewis. R.	Cay Target Shooting	19.03.1992	1
Lewis. Tom V.	Rifle Shooting	29.01.1964	1
Lewis. W. Peter	Sports Council	18.09.1974	3
Liddiard. M.	Athletics Women	27.01.1971	5
Lightfoot. W.	Sailing	29.01.1975	1
Lingard. Gwyneth	Gymnastics	31.01.1962	8
Lisle. Irene M.	Athletics	30.01.1967	46
Lister. John	Athletics Men	27.01.1971	2
Llewellyn. Harry.	Gymnastics	15.12.1954	19
Llewellyn. John P.	Boxing	26.10.1960	14
Llewellyn. W. E.	Gymnastics	28.01.1969	1
Llewellyn.Philip J.	Clay Pigeon Shooting	22.03.1983	2
Lloyd. Kenneth	Medical Adviser	25.09.1963	43
Lloyd-Jones. J.M.	Fencing	30.01.1967	5
Looker. A.T.	?	15.12.1938	3
Lucas. J.	Rowing	27.01.1976	1
Lucas. Ted R.	Fencing	04.10.1954	16
Luke. J.	Rowing	20.10.1965	1

M

Mansel-Edwards. Ann	Archery	27.01.1970	8
Mansel-Edwards.Digby	Archery	25.01.1960	89
Maidment.Walter	Gymnastics	31.03.1948	66
Margerison. M.	Badminton	08.01.1974	1
Mars. D.	Badminton	27.03.1985	1
Matthews. Ivor	Boxing	19.07.1933	21
Mayers. Eugene	Archery	19.03.1993	1
Mayers. Susie	Archery	19.03.1992	1
McCombe.Yvonne	Fencing	27.01.1971	10
Mealing.Christine.	Fencing	29.01.1975	1

Melen. J. Edward	Judo	21.03.1994	3
Melvin.Norma M.	Fencing	02.04.1980	3
Monk.C.Anthony	Smallbore Rifle Shooting	30.01.1980	33
Monk. Diane G.	Smallbore Rifle Shooting	28.01.1981	4
Morgan. Evan	Lawn Bowling	27.01.1971	2
Morgan. Nan	Lawn Bowling Women	19.03.1993	6
Morley. H.	Shooting W.T.G	27.01.1976	3
Morris. T. David	Swimming	01.06.1987	56
Morris. W.	Lawn Bowling	24.04.1958	1
Morrow. Sheila	Hockey Women	01.10.1980	16
Mort. David	Fencing	26.01.1972	2
Mort. Yvonne	Fencing	31.01.1979	1
Moss. Alan J.	Badminton	22.03.1983	2
Mudd. Doris	Lawn Bowling Women	23.02.1982	1
Mulrenan Blarney	Fencing	18.10.1956	9
Mumford. J. S.	Clay Target Shooting	25.03.1987	3
Munt. B. John	Pistol Shooting	11.10.1993	12

N

Neale. Reginald G.	Gymnastics	25.01.1960	26
Nelson. R.	Wrestling	30.01.1961	1
Newham. Charles.	1958 Games	11.03.1955	7
Nicholas. Victor	Fullbore Rifle Shooting	23.02.1982	3
Nicholson. A.H.	Boxing	15.12.1938	4
Nilson. Tony	Archery	29.03.1990	1
Noote. P.F.	Swimming	25.03.1938	2

O

Oakes. C. Harold	Fencing	25.05.1954	5
Oberholzer. H.A.	?	14.02.1934	1
O'Donnel. Eddie.	Athletics	19.07.1933	27
Osborn. Margaret	Lawn Bowling Women	28.01.1981	46
Osborne. John	Clay Target Shooting	29.03.1990	12
Osborne. Tom	Lawn Bowling Men	25.03.1986	1
Owen. David	Boxing	31.01.1962	1
Owen. John	Smallbore Rifle Shooting	26.01.1972	1
Owen. J. Barrie	Athletics	30.01.1967	2
Owen. D.Glyn	London	13.05.1959	5
Owen. William	Cycling	20.03.1995	1

P

Packer. Harry	Athletics	20.06.1933	2
Padfield. Maurice	Appeal	13.12.1990	7
Pallot. Neil C.	Hockey Men	27.01.1970	3
Palmer. M. G.	Rowing	26.01.1972	2
Panter. Phillip	Press	26.01.1972	1
Parfitt. Vernon J.	Rugby	31.01.1962	23
Parker. Linda	Lawn Bowling Women	22.03.1983	41
Parkes. Muriel	Athletics Women	10.12.1975	1
Paterson. P. Jeff	Legal Adviser	11.04.1979	36
Peach. T. Harry	Lawn Bowling	20.06.1933	28
Pearce. Alfred D.	Fencing	06.06.1978	2
Pelopida. Peter	Clay Pigeon Shooting	27.03.1985	1
Percival. Geoffrey	Hockey	04.10.1954	23
Perks. D. Steve	Athletics	20.03.1997	2
Perrins. John R.	Judo	07.09.1984	66
Perrins. Valerie	Judo	29.03.1990	1
Perry. John T	Swimming	22.03.1983	6
Perry. Lorna	Fencing	26.01.1977	5
Phelps. W.C.S.	Smallbore Rifle Shooting	30.01.1980	1
Phelps. W.E. (Bill)	Smallbore Rifle Shooting	30.01.1980	59
Phillips. Clive	Press	26.01.1966	5
Phillips. D.W.			
Powell	Medical Adviser	02.05.1955	5
Phillips. Gordon	Weightlifting	23.02.1982	10
Phillips. Ken	Archery	09.03.1999	1
Phillips. W.	Pistol Shooting	29.03.1990	1
Phillips. W.J.	Swimming	15.12.1938	5
Pierce. A.D.	Fencing	29.03.1990	1
Pine. S. Gordon	Badminton	30.01.1967	84
Pinney. Randall.	Weightlifting	26.01.1959	1
Pomeroy. Margaret	Lawn Bowling Women	31.01.1979	1
Pooley. W.R.	?	04.05.1937	9
Pond. J .	?	25.04.1934	1
Powell. Margaret	Lawn Bowling Women	02.07.1980	1
Poynton. William	Fencing	08.12.1958	3
Prater. Edward H.	CCPR	03.03.1948	46
Price. Margaret A.	Lawn Bowling Women	29.03.1990	1
Pryor. John	Rifle Shooting	22.09.1964	13
Pugh. Richard G.	Legal Adviser	20.04.1993	19

R

Radford. Alan	Athletics	27.01.1970	1
Ramsden. Norman	Badminton	31.01.1973	1
Rees. Chris	Badminton	16.12.1999	1
Rees. Tommy	Appeal	29.01.1975	63
Rees. Philip	Gymnastics	29.03.1990	1
Rees. Philip	Swimming	28.03.1996	1
Rees. Russell	HMI	28.09.1951	28
Regut. R.	Wrestling	02.03.1959	1
Reynolds. Jackie	Fencing	29.10.1952	69
Reynolds. Glyn S.	Fencing	03.03.1948	5
Reynolds. T.	Boxing	22.03.1983	10
Richards. Betty	Lawn Bowling Women	22.03.1983	1
Richards. H.K.	Basketball	27.06.1955	1
Roberts. Alan	Swimming	19.03.1998	2
Roberts. Glyn	Lawn Bowling Men	02.04.1980	28
Roberts. Ieuan	Archery	20.03.1995	3
Roberts. John M.	Tenpin Bowling	19.09.1996	1
Roberts. John P.	Hockey Men	09.05.1973	14
Roberts. Mariane	Badminton	30.01.1967	3
Robins. Graham	Swimming	29.03.1990	3
Robinson. Don	Athletics Men	30.01.1980	1
Robinson. H.V.W.	Athletics	26.01.1966	1
Roblin. Norma	Hockey Women	27.01.1970	4
Ronway. R.	Clay Pigeon Shooting	26.01.1977	1
Roper. Alun F.	Cross Country	16.07.1985	8
Roper. Avril	Netball	09.03.1999	1
Rose. Dennis A.	Swimming	07.10.1988	2
Rosser. Gary	Swimming	10.12.1998	3
Rowlands. Clive	Weightlifting	31.01.1973	2
Rowlands. D.	Sailing	27.01.1970	2
Rowlands. Helen	Hockey Women	22.03.1983	1
Ruscoe. Arthur R.	Lawn Bowling Men	22.01.1953	7
Ryan. Michael	Fencing	31.01.1962	1
Ryan. John	Rugby	03.12.1996	4

S

Salmon. Arthur H.	Swimming	20.07.1949	81
Sanders. C.F.	Observer	20.06.1933	1
Saunders. David	Badminton	29.02.1996	1
Saunders. Harry	Cycling	04.12.1954	23

Savegar.Gertrude	Lawn Bowling Women	02.07.1980	1
Scourfield. B.	Pistol Shooting	20.03.1985	3
Seal. R.M.E.	Sailing	27.05.1964	1
Seaman. Ron	Badminton	10.06.1963	18
Selley. Diane	Squash	27.02.1995	18
Sheridan. W.J.A.	?	08.09.1938	1
Sheryn. J.H.	Cycling	14.02.1933	2
Short. Gary H.	Athletics	25.03.1988	1
Sims. Peter A.	Smallbore Rifle Shooting	21.03.1994	1
Slatter. J.	Athletics	30.01.1963	1
Slaughter. Alan	Gymnastics	23.02.1982	1
Smith. Barry	Cycling	22.03.1983	1
Smith. Frank C.	Boxing	03.07.1961	2
Smith. Paul J.	Athletics	25.03.1988	1
Snow. Reg C.G.	Athletics Men	10.12.1975	5
Spackman. Phyllis	Gymnastics	26.01.1977	1
Spathaky. Ernest	Boxing	02.11.1953	4
Speck. Terry	Rifle Shooting	17.01.1979	59
Stammers.Malcolm	Public Relations	04.07.1994	26
Stephens.E.Charles	Lawn Bowling Men	22.03.1983	1
Stewart. J.	?	08.09.1938	1
Stockwool. H.	Rifle Shooting	26.10.1960	3
Styles. E.T.	Athletics	14.02.1934	4
Sulman. Stanley	Cycling	19.03.1992	1
Swales. Mansel P.	Weightlifting	31.08.1953	1
Swarbrick Ernest	Swimming	17.02.1937	15
Swansea. John	Rifle Shooting	25.01.1960	4

T

Tame. Harold G.	Boxing	26.01.1966	1
Taylor. Augustus	Swimming	19.04.1948	54
Taylor. G.	1958 Games	26.03.1958	1
Taylor. T.	Wrestling	24.04.1958	13
Thrift-Lee. Arthur	Basketball	15.12.1954	11
Thomas. Bryn	Appeal	19.06.1991	1
Thomas. Gomer	Fencing	03.03.1948	18
Thomas. Lyndon	Appeal	13.12.1990	3
Thomas. Meyrick	Rowing	27.06.1955	2
Thomas. Ray	Athletics	08.12.1958	2
Thomas. Raye	Athletics	30.01.1963	1
Thomas. Reginald	Boxing	01.08.1958	1
Thomas. Vaughan	Swimming	29.01.1975	1

Thomas. Vernon	Boxing	30.01.1967	11
Thompson. Agnes	Lawn Bowling Women	22.02.1978	3
Thompson. J.	Lawn Bowling Men	31.01.1979	2
Toms. Trevor	Lawn Bowling	27.01.1971	6
Turner. D. Robert	Fencing	29.01.1964	68

V

Vanstone. William	Rifle Shooting	10.06.1981	3
Vater. Colin	Lawn Bowling Men	01.10.1980	3
Veysey. Ray F.	Lawn Bowling Men	25.03.1987	5

W

Walters. J.A.	Archery	07.12.1953	2
Warfield. Mervyn	Hockey Men	26.01.1972	1
Waring. George	Smallbore Rifle Shooting	23.02.1982	1
Warrington. H.	?	14.02.1934	1
Waterfield. G.	Boxing	28.01.1969	3
Watkins. Gwen	Lawn Bowling Women	19.03.1993	1
Watkins. Jack B.	Boxing	29.01.1975	11
Webb. Graham	Athletics Men	25.03.1988	1
Welch. Dennis	Weightlifting	25.03.1986	1
Wharton. A.	Cycling	25.03.1987	1
Whiteman. Dennis	Archery	25.11.1969	16
Whitford. A. Jack	?	14.02.1934	4
Whyte. Norma	Fencing	27.01.1970	1
Williams. Arthur	Athletics	25.01.1960	20
Williams. Alan H.	Lawn Bowling Men	15.01.1986	51
Williams. Averil	Athletics Women	12.01.1977	115
Williams. Bryn	Appeal	11.06.1985	8
Williams. Dave J.	Athletics Men	07.10.1988	19
Williams. D.G.	Trampoline	27.01.1970	1
Williams. E.	Boxing	03.03.1948	2
Williams. Glen G.	Smallbore Rifle Shooting	25.09.1963	53
Williams. Gordon	Weightlifting	26.01.1972	9
Williams. Jack	Athletics	29.01.1951	101
Williams. John	Weightlifting	27.01.1971	1
Williams. J.Clive	Athletics Men	31.01.1979	1
Williams. Dr. J.P.R	Medical Adviser	13.06.1979	2
Williams. Lyndon	Badminton	29.03.1990	2
Williams. D. Meurin	Weightlifting	26.01.1977	4
Williams. Nancy	Lawn Bowling Women	01.10.1980	3

Williams. S. John	Cycling	31.01.1962	6
Williams. S. J.	Trampoline	09.09.1969	2
Williams. S. O.	Rowing	24.04.1963	1
Williams. T. Peter	Weightlifting	15.01.1986	57
Wilson. Reg	Lawn Bowling Men	27.03.1985	1
Winchcombe. J.	Boxing	27.01.1971	1
Withers. Muriel R.	Badminton	27.01.1970	1
Wood. John A.	Boxing	20.06.1933	15
Worman. J.	Shooting WTC	22.01.1968	1
Wright. D.	Badminton	09.03.1999	1
Wright. Maurice.	Appeal	16.12.1993	31
Wright. Vernon	Cycling	08.12.1958	32
Wyatt. Jean	Hockey Women	28.02.1985	7

Y

| Young. John | Rugby | 06.06.1986 | 1 |
| Yeoman. Tom | Bowling | 26.10.1960 | 1 |

Those who Have Attended One Hundred and Over Meetings.

(Final Attendance At 31 December 1999)

Howell. Fred	229
Howell. Cyril M.	197
John. Myrddin	169
Jones. Wyndham H.	138
Allen. Raymond	110
Keitch. Rita	110
Williams. Jack D.B.	101

INDEX 5

World Population

There are numerous reasons why it is impossible to provide exact population numbers at a given time, but I am confident that the following are fairly adequate for the purpose of this book. (**See Wikipedia**)

* Commonwealth Countries.

** Includes Wales, Northern Ireland, England and Scotland

*** Also noted under the United Kingdom

LIST	COUNTRY	POPULATION	
1	China	1,349,585,838	
2	India	1,220,800,359	*
3	United States of America	316,668,367	
4	Indonesia	251,160,124	

LIST	COUNTRY	POPULATION	
5	Brasil	201,009,622	
6	Pakistan	193,238,868	*
7	Nigeria	174,507,539	*
8	Bangladesh	163,654,860	*
9	Russia	142,500,482	
10	Japan	127,253,075	
11	Mexico	113,724,226	
12	Philippines	101,833,938	
13	Ethiopa	90,873,390	
14	Vietnam	90,549,390	
15	Egypt	82,079,636	
16	Germany	81,471,834	
17	Turkey	78,785,548	
18	Iran	77,891,220	

LIST	COUNTRY	POPULATION	
19	Congo Democratic Republic	71,712,867	
20	Thailand	66,720,153	
21	France	65,922,727	
22	United Kingdom	63,277,244	**
23	Italy	61,016,804	
24	Myanmar	53,999,804	
25	South Africa	49,004,031	*
26	South Korea	48,754,657	
27	Spain	46,754,784	
28	Ukraine	45,134,707	
29	Colombia	44,725,543	
30	Tanzania	42,746,020	*
31	Argentine	41,769,726	
32	Kenya	41,070,934	*

LIST	COUNTRY	POPULATION	
33	Poland	38,441,588	
34	Sudan	36,787,012	
35	Algeria	34,994,937	
36	Uganda	34,612,250	*
37	Canada	34,030,589	*
38	Morocco	32,475,521	
39	Iraq	30,399,572	
40	Afghanistan	29,835,392	
41	Nepal	29,391,883	
42	Peru	29,248,943	
43	Malaysia	28,728,607	*
44	Uzbekistan	28,128,600	
45	Venezuela	27,635,743	
46	Saudi Arabia	26,131,703	

LIST	COUNTRY	POPULATION	
47	Ghana	24,791,073	*
48	North Korea	24,457,492	
49	Yemen	24,133,492	
50	Taiwan, Republic of China	23,071,779	
51	Mozambique	22,948,858	*
52	Syria	22,517,750	
53	Madagascar	21,926,221	
54	Romania	21,904,551	
55	Australia	21,770,878	*
56	Ivory Coast	21,504,162	
57	Sri Lanka	21,283,913	*
58	Cameroon	19,711,291	*
59	Holland	17,132,729	
60	Chile	16,888,760	

LIST	COUNTRY	POPULATION	
61	Burkina Faso	16,751,455	
62	Niger	16,468,886	
63	Malawi	15,879,252	*
64	Kazakhstan	15,522,373	
65	Ecuador	15,007,343	
66	Cambodia	14,701,717	
67	Mali	14,159,905	
68	Zambia	13,881,336	*
69	Guatemala	13,824,463	
70	Angola	13,338,541	
71	Senegal	12,643,799	
72	Zimbabwe	12,084,304	*
73	Rwanda	11,370,425	
74	Cuba	11,087,330	

LIST	COUNTRY	POPULATION	
75	Portugal	10,760,305	
76	Greece	10,760,136	
77	Chad	10,758,945	
78	Tunisia	10,629,186	
79	Guinea	10,601,009	
80	Belgium	10,431,477	
81	Burundi	10,216,190	
82	Czech Republic	10,190,213	
83	Bolivia	10,118,683	
84	Hungary	9,976,062	
85	Dominican Republic	9,956,648	
86	Somalia	9,925,640	
87	Haiti	9,719,932	
88	Belarus	9,577,552	

LIST	COUNTRY	POPULATION	
89	Benin	9,325,032	
90	Sweden	9,088,728	
91	Azerbaijan	8,372,373	
92	South Sudan	8,260,490	
93	Argentina	8,217,280	
94	Honduras	8,143,564	
95	Switzerland	7,639,961	
96	Tajikistan	7,627,200	
97	Israel	7,473,052	
98	Serbia	7,310,555	
99	Bulgaria	7,093,635	
100	Togo	6,771,993	
101	Libya	6,597,960	
102	Jordan	6,508,271	

LIST	COUNTRY	POPULATION	
103	Laos	6,477,211	
104	Paraguay	6,459,058	
105	Papua New Guinea	6,187,591	
106	El Salvador	6,071,774	
107	Eritrea	5,939,484	
108	Nicaragua	5,666,301	
109	Kyrgyzstan	5,587,443	
110	Denmark	5,529,888	
111	Slovakia	5,477,038	
112	Sierra Leone	5,363,669	
113	Finland	5,259,250	
114	United Arab Emirates	5,148,664	
115	Turkmenistan	4,997,503	
116	Central African Republic	4,950,027	

LIST	COUNTRY	POPULATION	
117	Singapore	4,740,737	*
118	Norway	4,691,849	
119	Republic of Ireland	4,670,976	
120	Bosnia Herzegovia	4,622,163	
121	Georgia	4,595,874	
122	Costa Rica	4,576,562	
123	Croatia	4,483,804	
124	Moldova	4,314,377	
125	New Zealand	4,290,347	*
126	Republic of Congo	4,243,929	
127	Libya	4,143,101	
128	Liberia	3,786,764	
129	Lithuania	3,535,547	
130	Panama	3,460,462	

LIST	COUNTRY	POPULATION	
131	Uruguay	3,308,535	
132	Mauritania	3,281,634	
133	Mongolia	3,133,318	
134	Oman	3,027,959	
135	WALES	3,063,456	***
135	Albania	2,994,667	
136	Armenia	2,967,975	
137	Jamaica	2,868,380	*
138	Kuwait	2,595,628	
139	Latvia	2,204,708	
140	Namibia	2,147,585	*
141	Macedonia	2,077,328	
142	Botswana	2,065,398	*
143	Slovenia	2,000,092	

LIST	COUNTRY	POPULATION	
144	Lesotho	1,924,886	*
145	Kosovo	1,825,632	
146	Gambia	1,797,860	*
147	Guinea-Bissau	1,596,677	
148	Gabon	1,576,665	
149	Swaziland	1,370,424	
150	Mauritius	1,303,717	*
151	Estonia	1,282,963	
152	Trinidad & Tobago	1,227,505	*
153	Bahrain	1,214,705	
154	East Timor	1,177,834	
155	Cyprus	1,120,489	*
156	Fiji	883,125	*
157	Qatar	848,016	

LIST	COUNTRY	POPULATION	
158	Comoros	794,683	
159	Djibouti	757,074	
160	Guyana	744,768	*
161	Bhutan	708,427	
162	Equatorial Guinea	668,225	
163	Montenegro	661,807	
164	Solomon Islands	571,890	*
165	Cape Verde	516,100	
166	Luxembourg	503,302	
167	Surinam	491,989	
168	Malta	408,333	*
169	Brunei	401,890	
170	The Maldives	394,999	*
171	Belize	321,115	*

LIST	COUNTRY	POPULATION	
172	Bahamas	313,312	*
173	Iceland	311,058	
174	Barbados	286,705	*
175	Vanuatu	224,564	*
176	Samoa	193,161	*
177	São Tomé & Principe	179,506	
178	Saint Lucia	161,557	*
179	Grenada	108,419	*
180	Federal States of Micronesia	106,836	
181	Tonga	105,916	*
182	Saint Vincent & Grenadines	103,869	*
183	Kiribati	100,743	*
184	Seychelles	89,188	*

LIST	COUNTRY	POPULATION	
185	Antigua and Barbuda	87,884	*
186	Andorra	84,825	
187	Dominica	72,969	*
188	Marshall Islands	67,182	
189	St. Kitts a Nevis	50,314	*
	Liechtenstein	35,236	
191	San Marino	31,817	
192	Monaco	30,539	
193	Palau	20,956	
194	Tuvalu	10,554	*
195	Nauru	9,322	*
196	Vatican City	832	

Index 6

The Queen's Message at the Opening Ceremony 1958

"By a cruel stroke of fate I have been prevented from visiting North and South Wales and seeing something of the British Empire and Commonwealth Games. I regret particularly not being with you in Cardiff today for the closing ceremonies of this great meeting of Commonwealth athletes.

I am glad to say that I have been able to watch many of the competitions on television, and I was especially impressed by the atmosphere of good-natured sportsmanship which attended all the events.

The Games have been an undoubted success from every point of view and I would like to congratulate all the many people who have worked so hard to perfect the arrangements.

I would also like to congratulate the medal winners on their remarkable achievements, and to all competitors I send my very best wishes, You have given a wonderful demonstration of the strength of those links of friendship which bind us all together in the Commonwealth.

I want to take this opportunity of speaking to all Welsh people, not only in this arena but wherever they may be.

The British Empire and Commonwealth Games in the capital, together with all the activities of the Festival of Wales, have made this a memorable year for the Principality.

I have, therefore, decided to mark it further by an act which will, I hope, give as much pleasure to all Welshmen as it does to me.

I intend to create my son Charles Prince of Wales today. When he is grown up I will present him to you at Caernarvon.

And now I proclaim the Sixth British Empire and Commonwealth Games of 1958 at Cardiff to be concluded: and in accordance with tradition, I call upon the youth of the Commonwealth to assemble in four years' time in Perth, Western Australia, there to celebrate the Seventh British Empire and Commonwealth Games.

May they display cheerfulness and concord, so that the spirit of our family of nations may be carried on with ever greater eagerness, courage and honour for the good of humanity and the peace of the world."

INDEX 7

Letter From David Dixon, Secretary Commonwealth Games Federation

WITHERS
▲SOLICITORS

20 ESSEX STREET LONDON WC2R 3AL
TELEPHONE 01-836 8400   FAX 01-240 2278
TELEX 24213 WITHER G   DX 160 LONDON/CHANCERY LANE

DMD/jc

28th March 1990

Myrddin John
Commonwealth Games Council for Wales

Dear Myrddin

I am glad to confirm my thanks to you for the action you took over the weightlifting problems in Auckland.

The Federation imposed certain procedures on the CGAs of the competitors involved and you, for Wales, and those concerned for India, carried out those procedures correctly and to the satisfaction of the Federation.

With all good wishes.

Yours ever

▲ WITHERS IS REGULATED BY THE LAW SOCIETY IN THE CONDUCT OF INVESTMENT BUSINESS

BTJ STEVENS   DM DIXON   EDA RAM   CE DOUGHTY   PW DURRANCE   AJ THOMPSON   SC COOKE   N HALLAM   AP MAITLAND HUDSON   AEH GERRY
RJM PAUL   YJ BRUCE-SMITH   ELODIE MJ STANLEY   DEM JANNEY   JJ EASTWOOD   MJ ROSS   THERESA J GRANT PETERKIN   DIANA C PARKER   ANNABEL L BRENTON
HCM PAGE   DAWN WM GOODMAN   I JOHNSON   MJ SOUL   JP ARNOLD   TJ TAYLOR   CONSULTANTS: SIR ARTHUR COLLINS KCVO   JW ROOME

PARIS OFFICE 15 RUE DE MARIGNAN 75008 PARIS   TELEPHONE 49.53.06.66   FAX 49.53.05.76   TELEX WAYLAND 640057P   AP MAITLAND HUDSON   JJ EASTWOOD   HCM PAGE
IN ASSOCIATION WITH CABINET DANIEL AZEMA (FRENCH LAWYERS) AND MICHAEL SOUL AND ASSOCIATES   REPRESENTED IN MADRID   BARCELONA   MALAGA   MARBELLA   PALMA DE MALLORCA

Index 8

Letter From John Powell, Chairman Sports Council for Wales

The National Sports Centre
for Wales,
Sophia Gardens,
Cardiff. CF1 9SW
Telephone: 0222 397571

Chairman/Cadeirydd: John H. Powell MC.
Director/Cyfarwyddwr: Linford Tatham

Canolfan Chwaraeon
Cymru,
Gerddi Sophia.
Caerdydd. CF1 9SW
Teleffôn: 0222 397571

Our Ref.
SCW1 (86)

Your Ref.
--

Date
5 August 1986

Dear Myrddin,

Congratulations as General Team Manager on an
excellent Commonwealth Games.

First of all I thought the turn-out and sheer presence
of the Team on the Opening Ceremony was easily the best
of all of the competing countries. I thought the number
of medals that we won reflected the greatest credit on
all those who had worked so hard with the athletes to
achieve success.

Secondly, I thought the organisation at the Village was
very good and the office made everybody feel very welcome
indeed. I think your staff worked extremely hard and it
was very nice to see some old faces there again from
Brisbane.

Lastly, congratulations on your appointment to the
Federation. I think this is a very great feather in
your cap.

I look forward to hearing your report to the Council on
how you consider the various aspects of the Games and
any other improvements that were noticeable to you.

Well done Myrddin.

Yours sincerely,

John Powell

Chairman

Myrddin John, Esq., MBE
Hon General Secretary/Team Manager,
Commonwealth Games Council for Wales,
Pennant,
Blaenau,
Ammanford, Dyfed

499

WESTERN MAIL 🦅

WESTERN MAIL & ECHO LTD., THOMSON HOUSE,
HAVELOCK STREET, CARDIFF, CF1 1WR. TELEPHONE CARDIFF (0222) 33022
Registered Office. Registered Number 49646 England.

6 August, 1986

Dear Myrddin,

Just a quick note to thank you once again for all your help during the Commonwealth Games. It was not merely confined to the splendid two weeks spent in Edinburgh itself, but also in the build up to the great event.

You can rightly take great credit, not only in the fantastic performances of your team, but also from the large amount of press coverage their efforts gained. For both David Facey and myself your honest, easy going style of management made our job easier and all the more enjoyable.

The achievements of the team speak for themselves. Boycott or no boycott, 23 medals is an amazing haul. More than that, the performances of those who didn't win medals were equally commendable.

Your team at the 13th Commonwealth Games helped raise the standard and reputation of Welsh sport immeasureably. Let us hope the Edinburgh experience is only the starting point of a great revival and that in Auckland in four years time the success continues.

With Cardiff bidding for the 1994 Games I am sure there will be plenty of interesting stories developing. Please keep us well informed as we would like to help in any way to bring the Games back to Wales.

Yours sincerely,

Robert Cole

Myrddin John Esq., MBE.,
Pennant,
Blaenau,
AMMANFORD, Dyfed.

Index 10
Letter From Mark Robinson, M.P.

Y SWYDDFA GYMREIG
GWYDYR HOUSE
WHITEHALL LONDON SW1A 2ER
Tel. 01-233 3000 (Switsfwrdd)
01-233 7172 (Llinell Union)

Oddi wrth yr Is-Ysgrifennydd Senneddol

WELSH OFFICE
GWYDYR HOUSE
WHITEHALL LONDON SW1A 2ER
Tel. 01-233 3000 (Switchboard)
01-233 7172 (Direct Line)

From The Parliamentary Under-Secretary

19 August 1986

Dear Mr. John,

The Secretary of State and I wish to congratulate the Welsh team on their
achievements in the Commonwealth Games in Edinburgh. It was heart-warming
to hear of the growing list of medal-winners day by day and to see Wales
placed fifth in the final table with an unprecedented total of twenty-three
medals.

I am writing individually to the gold medal winners but would be grateful
if you could pass on our congratulations to the whole team for an outstanding
performance.

My visit to the Games was most enjoyable and I was grateful for the time you
were able to spend with me. It was a particular thrill to see three gold
medals in the making (bowls) or won (Kirsty Wade).

With best wishes,

Yours sincerely,

MARK ROBINSON

Myrddin John Esq MBE
Pennant
Blaenau
AMMANFORD
Dyfed

Index 11
Letter From Cerith Williams, B.B.C.

Y GORFFORAETH DDARLLEDU BRYDEINIG
CANOLFAN Y BBC
LLANDAF, CAERDYDD CF5 2YQ
TELEPHONE: 0222 572888
FAX: 0222 552973

BRITISH BROADCASTING CORPORATION
BROADCASTING HOUSE
LLANDAFF, CARDIFF CF5 2YQ

Medi 13, 1994

Annwyl Myrddin,

Dim ond gair i ddiolch am eich holl cyd-weithrediad yn ystod
Gemau'r Gymanwlad mis Awst yn Victoria.

O ran teledu, roedd y rhaglenni uchafbwyntiau bob bore ar S4C
yn llwyddiant mawr, ac o'r herwydd mae'r angen am sylw manwl i
hynt a helynt tim Cymru yn y dyfodol yn amlwg.

Ga'i hefyd fanteisio ar y cyfle i estyn diolch i Malcolm
Stammers am ei barodrwydd (a'i amynedd) wrth drefnu
cyfweliadau, sesiynnau ymarfer ac unrhyw geisiadau anarferol
eraill y gofynwyd amdanynt yn ystod y pythefnos. Heb os,
hwyluswyd ein gwaith ni o ganlyniad.

Unwaith eto, mawr ddiolch am bopeth - braint oedd cael y cyfle
i adlewyrchu ymgyrch lwyddiannus arall gan y Cymry yng
Nghemau'r Gymanwlad.

Yr eiddoch yn gywir,

(Cerith Williams)
(Cynhyrchydd, Adran Chwaraeon)

Index 12
Letter From Brenda Owen, Mother of a Competitor.

7th September, 1994

Mr. Myrddin John M.B.E.
Pennant
Blaenau
Ammanford
Dyfed SA18 3BZ

Dear Mr. John,

I should like to thank you very much for arranging my accommodation in Victoria for the Commonwealth Games, especially when you did it at such short notice, when I am sure you were extremely busy.

The people where I stayed were very friendly, and apart from Alun breaking his collar bone I enjoyed my stay very much.

I appreciate all the work yourself and your committee put into organising the Welsh Team for the Commonwealth Games.

Yours sincerely,

Brenda

Brenda Owen

INDEX 13
Letter From Linda Parker, M.B.E.

WELSH WOMEN'S BOWLING ASSOCIATION
Affiliated to the Commonwealth Games Council for Wales

Hon Treasurer:
Mrs Gwen Lamb

Hon Secretary:
Miss Linda Parker MBE

President:

Mrs. Barbara Hunt, Port Talbot.
3rd September, 2002.

Mr. Myrddin John, MBE.,
Chief Executive,
Commonwealth Games Council for Wales,
Pennant, Blaenau,
Ammanford, Dyfed. SA18 3BZ

Dear Myrddin,

I don't know how to start to thank all the Headquarters Staff for all their kindness and efficiency at The Games. Everything was just splendid and they were – certainly as far as Wales was concerned – the 'Friendly Games'.

To everyone who worked so hard to see that we had everything we needed, a big 'thank you'. A very big 'thank you' too to Dr. Wayne for his superb leadership; to Chef de Mission, John, for all his kindness and, as I have said, to everyone in Headquarters. To all the medical staff and physiotherapists, too, weren't they just super. I felt that we were extremely lucky in having such dedicated people looking after us.

Many congratulations, too, on all our clothing. Although the parade uniform arrived late it was superb and we had many compliments. At the bowling green, too, they loved our track suit and tops and many told us that Wales was the smartest team there and, believe me, we felt good in it!

We all know that a great deal of work was put in to make everything so perfect and I can assure you it was much appreciated by our team. Many, many thanks once more to everyone connected with Manchester 2002. You must all have felt very proud of your work as we were certainly proud of what you did for us. Special thanks to you too Myrddin; what a great workload it was for you but with such splendid results you must have been very, very pleased. Many, many congratulations!

Kindest regards,

Yours sincerely,

Linda Parker, Team Manageress Ladies' Bowls.

INDEX 14

The Lecture by The Right Reverend Ethelbert Talbot, Bishop of Central Pennsylvania at the Conference of Bishops in St. Paul's Cathedral.

"We have just been contemplating the great Olympic Games. What does it mean? It means that young men of robust physical life have come from all parts of the world. It does mean, I think, as someone has said, that this era of internationalism as seen in the Stadium, has an element of danger. Of course, it is very true, as he says, that each athlete strives not only for the sake of sport, but for the sake of his country. Thus a new rivalry is invented.

If England be beaten on their river, or America outdistanced on the racing path or that America has lost the strength which she once possessed. Well, what of it? The only safety after all lies in the lesson of the real Olympia – that the Games are better than the prize. St. Paul tells us how insignificant is the prize. Our prize is not corruptible, but incorruptible, and though only one may wear the laurel wreath, all may share the equal joy of the contest.

All encouragement therefore, be given to the exhilarating – I might also say soul - saving interest that comes in active and fair and clean athletic sports".

In his lecture at the Grafton Galleries, on the 4th June, Pierre de Coubertin interpreted the philosophy behind Ethelbert Talbot's lecture -

"L'important dans la vie ce n'est point le triomphe mais le combat. L'essential ce n'est pas d'avoir vain cu mais de s'être bien batu."

(The important thing in life is not the triumph but the struggle. The essential thing is not to have won but to have fought well.")

INDEX 15. Names and pages

Arthur. Alex, 213

Arthur. Jamie, 389, 455

Arthur. Lindsay, 240

Arthur. Peter J, 293, 302, 378, 391, 393, 454

Asati. Charles, 104, 126

Ashcroft. Chris, 365

Ashcroft. Christina, 232

Ashton. Anthony F.(Tony, 298

Ashurst. Andrew, 116

Ashworth. Robyn, 360

Aspin. David A, 245

Asselin. Roland, 170

Atherton. Andrew, 189

Atkinson. H, 163

Atkinson. Leigh, 317, 322, 342

Aubin. Jack, 196

Audain. Anne, 132

Awome. Julius, 219

Ayinla. Fatai, 218

Ayling. Geoffrey, 234

Ayres. Andrew, 351, 371

Backley. Steve, 120

Badger. Stephen, 197

Baharin. Nurul Hudda, 231

Baildon. Andrew, 192, 193, 195

Bailey. Donovan, 124

Bailey. Geoffrey, 288, 466

Bailey. George, 111

Baird. Donald, 116

Baird. W., 466

Bairstow. Angela, 145, 147

Baker. Geoffrey Noel, 125

Baker. Simon, 113

Baldwin. Dave, 164

Ball. Geoffrey, 362

Banahan. David, 466

Banning. Phil, 358, 466

Gunnell. Sally Jane, 143

Gwilt. Peter, 323

Hack. Roderick
Douglas, 241

Hacker. David, 366

Hackett. Grant, 201

Hackney. Roger, 320,
327, 338, 375, 391,
457

Hadjiandreou. Marius,
115

Haining. Peter, 222

Haisley. Ernest, 115

Haist. Jane, 136

Halberg. Murray G.,
107

Hale. Ian Maxwell, 238

Hale. Victoria, 351, 371

Haley. Patrick, 122

Hall. F., 471

Hall. Leonard A., 215

Hallam. Chris, 348

Hallam. Ian, 152, 153

Hallam. Tracey, 149

Haller. David, 371

Halliday. Jim, 174, 176

Halstead. Eleanor, 139

Hamer. Clare, 351

Hamer. Ian, 338, 375,
394, 457

Hames. Jagan, 121

Hamil. Gerard, 214

Hamilton. Jane F., 303

Hamilton. Norman, 196

Hampson. Thomas, 105

Handley. Ann, 368

Hansen. Ashia, 135

Harby. A.J., 224

Harby. Kathryn, 220

Hardiman. Marius, 364

Harding. Aileen, 279,
378, 394, 399, 457

Hardwick. Harold, 29

Hare. William, 236

Harman. Kenneth, 238,
241

Harper. Brian, 219

Smith. Tricia, 229

Smith. W. George, 198

Smith. William, 215

Smyth. Michael, 344

Snell. Peter G., 105, 106

Snow. Reg, 307, 313, 320, 477

Sobrian. Jules, 236

Solly. Jonathan, 108

Somerville. John, 164

Sorensen. Wayne, 235, 240

Southby. David, 191

Souza. George A., 164

Sowry. Justine, 190

Spackman. Phyllis, 477

Spathaky. Ernest, 477

Speck. Terry, 319, 335, 344, 477

Spence. Malcolm Clive, 126

Spence. Melville, 126

Spracklen. Michael, 221

Sprot. Robert, 160

Squire. Peter, 342

St. Jean. Pierre, 176

Staden. Piet Van, 214

Staite. Neil, 222

Stanton. Christine, 135

Starre. Kate, 190

Statt. Anne, 147

Steed. Trent Joseph, 200

Steen. David, 117

Steer. Irene, 440

Stellios. Bill, 176

Stephens. C.L.V., 289

Stephens. Charles, 321

Stephens. Gail F., 304

Stephenson. Christian, 359

Stevens. Marion, 160

Stevens. Raymond, 191

Stewart. Errol, 123

Stewart. Gale, 240

Ingram Content Group UK Ltd.
Milton Keynes UK
UKHW020015160323
418608UK00007B/13